Can't Pay? Won't Pay!, Elizabeth, The Open Couple, An Ordinary Day

Dario Fo is Italy's leading contem̲̲̲̲̲̲̲̲̲̲̲former/playwright, renowned throughout the world for his daz̲̲̲̲

Can't Pay? Won't Pay!: 'The set̲̲̲̲̲̲̲̲̲̲̲̲̲̲̲̲̲̲̲̲̲̲̲̲̲̲̲̲̲̲ desperately familiar. This, howe̲̲̲̲̲̲̲̲̲̲̲̲̲̲̲̲̲̲̲̲̲̲̲̲̲̲̲̲̲̲ wears a broad smile and procee̲̲*es*

Elizabeth: 'It portrays our last Tudor̲̲̲̲̲̲̲̲̲̲̲̲̲̲̲̲̲̲̲̲̲̲̲̲̲ rollicking vein . . . A triumph for Gillian Hanna as translator̲̲̲̲

Martin Hoyle, *Financial Times*

The Open Couple and *An Ordinary Day*, written with Franca Rame, deal wittily with the fate of women in a society in which both the social system in which they live and its dominant ideology are shaped by men.

Dario Fo was born in 1926 in Lombardy. He began working in the theatre in 1951 as a comic and mime. Together with Franca Rame, he was highly successful as actor, director and writer of satirical comedies for the conventional theatre. In the sixties they abandoned it; Fo began to write for a wider audience in factories and workers' clubs and produced work which was not only an important political intervention in Italy but has been internationally acclaimed. In 1970 Fo and Rame founded the theatrical collective, La Comune, in Milan. His work – and the work of Franca Rame – has been performed in England with great success: *Can't Pay? Won't Pay!* (Half Moon Theatre and Criterion Theatre, London, 1981); *Accidental Death of an Anarchist* (Half Moon Theatre and Wyndham's Theatre, London, 1980); *Female Parts* by Franca Rame (National Theatre, London, 1981); *Mistero Buffo* (Riverside Theatre, London, 1983); *Trumpets and Raspberries* (Palace Theatre, Watford; Phoenix Theatre, London, 1984); *Archangels Don't Play Pinball* (Bristol Old Vic, 1986); *Elizabeth* (Half Moon Theatre, London, 1986); *An Ordinary Day* (Borderline Theatre Company, Scotland, touring, 1988) and *The Pope and the Witch* (West Yorkshire Playhouse, Leeds, 1991; Comedy Theatre, London, 1992). *An Ordinary Day* has also been translated by Ed Emery as *A Day Like Any Other*.

DARIO FO

Plays: 2

Can't Pay? Won't Pay!
translated by Lino Pertile
adapted by Bill Colvill and Robert Walker

Elizabeth: Almost by Chance a Woman
translated by Gillian Hanna

The Open Couple
written with Franca Rame
translated by Stuart Hood

An Ordinary Day
written with Franca Rame
translated by Joe Farrell

with an introduction by series editor
Stuart Hood

and an introduction by Franca Rame

Methuen Drama

METHUEN CONTEMPORARY DRAMATISTS

This collection first published in Great Britain in 1994 by Methuen Drama

Reissued in this series in 1997

Random House UK Limited
20 Vauxhall Bridge Road, London SW1V 2SA

Random House Australia (Pty) Limited
20 Alfred Street, Milsons Point, Sydney, New South Wales 2061, Australia

Random House New Zealand Limited
18 Poland Road, Glenfield, Auckland 10, New Zealand

Random House South Africa (Pty) Limited
Endulini, 5a Jubilee Road, Parktown 2193, South Africa

Random House UK Limited Reg. No. 954009

Can't Pay? Won't Pay! first published in this translation in 1978 by
Pluto Press Ltd. This revised edition first published in 1987 by
Methuen London Ltd. Translation copyright © 1978 Robert Walker
Original Italian title *Non si paga! Non si paga!*
Elizabeth: Almost by Chance a Woman first published in this
translation in 1987 by Methuen London Ltd, translation copyright
© 1987 by Gillian Hanna
Original Italian title *Quasi per caso una donna*
The Open Couple first published in this translation in 1990 by Methuen
Drama, translation copyright © 1985, 1990 Stuart Hood
Original Italian title *Coppia aperta, quasi spalancata*
An Ordinary Day first published in this translation in 1990 by Methuen
Drama, translation copyright © 1990 Joe Farrell
Original Italian title *Un giornata, qualumque*

This collection copyright © 1994 Methuen Drama
Introduction copyright © 1994 Stuart Hood

The authors and translators have asserted their moral rights

A CIP catalogue record for this book is available from the British Library

ISBN 0-413-68020-7

Introduction by Franca Rame translated by Lino Pertile from *Le
Commedie di Dario Fo*, pp. v–xv, Einaudi (Turin, 1975)

Printed and bound in Great Britain by Cox & Wyman Ltd Reading, Berkshire

Contents

Chronology

1926   Born in the province of Varese, North Italy. Attends art school in Milan and studies architecture at the Politecnico.

1952-54   Writes and performs monologues for radio which transfer to the theatre. Takes part in satirical revues and meets with censorship.

1957-59   Produces classical farces working with Franca Rame, his wife and close collaborator. They include *One Was Nude and One Wore Tails* and *The Virtuous Burglar*.

1959-67   Writes and produces a series of comedies for the bourgeois theatre, including *Archangels Don't Play Pinball*. He has difficulty because of his criticism of bourgeois society.

In 1962 Fo is asked to produce the popular TV programme *Canzonissima*, which is heavily censored because of its satirical content. Fo and Rame refuse to accept the cuts.

In 1966 he produces and works on *Ci Ragiono e Canto*, which draws on popular and folk songs.

1968-70   Together with Franca Rame sets up the Nuova Scena company, which breaks with the bourgeois theatre and works through the cultural institutions of the Italian Communist Party. It is to this period that *Mistero Buffo* belongs.

1970-74   Fo and Rame break with the Communist Party, which they consider too reformist, and set up the theatrical collective La Comune. In the 1970-71 season they put on *Accidental Death of an Anarchist* and *Can't Pay? Won't Pay!*

1977   Franca Rame and Fo publish *All Home, Bed and Church*, a volume of monologues for female voices.

1983   *The Open Couple* by Rame and Fo looks at the place
        of women in society.

1984   *Elizabeth: Almost by Chance a Woman*, set at the
        court of the ageing Elizabeth I.

1986   *An Ordinary Day* and a new edition of *The Open
        Couple* are published under the title *Female Parts*, by
        Rame and Fo.

1989   *The Pope and the Witch* looks at the problems of
        drugs and contraception. *Twenty-five Monologues for
        a Woman* (English title *A Woman Alone and Other
        Plays*) assembles texts by Rame and Dario Fo on the
        theme of woman's fate in society.

1990   *Zitti! Stiamo Precipitando* looks at Aids.

1991   Franca Rame's *Parliamo di Donne*, and Fo's *Johan
        Padan a la Descoverta de le Americhe*, a worm's eye
        view of the 'discovery' of America.

1992   Franca Rame's monologue *The Thieves' Ball* (a
        reworking of *Seventh: Steal A Little Less*) deals with
        the Italian political scene.

1993   Fo and Rame tour Italy with a new comedy *The
        Country in the Dustbin*, which looks at bribery and
        corruption in Italian society.

Introduction

Dario Fo is at once extremely traditional and extremely
modern. He is traditional in that his theatrical roots lie in the
Renaissance commedia dell'arte with its cast of stereotypical
comic characters – the boastful soldier, the lecherous old man,
the cunning servant and the star-crossed lovers. Further back,
he draws on the tradition of the *giullari*, the travelling
performers of the Middle Ages. They invented the figure of
Zanni, the slapstick clown, whose name is the Venetian dialect
version of Giovanni and who is the prototype of our 'zany'. Fo
is a descendant of Zanni. What all these figures have in
common is a healthy disrespect for authority. Further back
still, Fo traces his theatrical lineage to the Latin farces of
Plautus and Terence and to even more primitive performances.
All this is part of his tradition. Where Fo is modern is in the
way he uses techniques evolved centuries ago to hold up to
ridicule figures in society today – in particular, naturally, in
Italian society which, as recent events have shown, is rich in
corruption and in the abusive use of power.

Fo grew up in Northern Italy in a society of lakeside
fishermen and smugglers who were also great storytellers.
From an early age he was fascinated by spoken narrative, by
language and in particular by dialect, which continues to
flourish in many parts of Italy. The skills in storytelling learned
as a boy he put to good use early in his career by writing
monologues in dialect for radio – work he would later adapt for
the theatre, which he reached by way of art school and stage
design. One of his many gifts is that he is a talented artist who
illustrates the Italian texts of his work with pen and
watercolour drawings. In the fifties – along with his extremely
talented wife, Franca Rame – he became the equivalent in
Italian theatre of a successful West End actor; but the couple
abandoned this career to search for a new audience that was
not composed of middle-class playgoers. By the sixties they had
found that audience and were playing to huge crowds in new

venues: circus tents, parking lots at factories or the cultural centres of the Italian Communist Party. They and their company became part of the radical political movements of the day. But their connection with the Communist Party was of short duration for the Communists were inflexible in terms of sexual and other politics and unable to understand or approve of that disrespect for established authorities, which large numbers of people – especially the young – felt in those days and to which Fo gave expression.

The most famous work from this period is *Mistero Buffo* (1969). Based on medieval and later texts and the traditions of the *giullari*, it reflects Fo's subversive reading of scripture, which is certainly anti-clerical but on another level reflects the view that the Christian tradition is capable of being interpreted in a radical, life-affirming way – the same view as inspired the radical priests working in the *favelas* of South America. Thus in the episode from *Mistero Buffo* which portrays the Marriage at Cana, 'We find,' in Fo's words, 'Christ coming to earth as a god and seeking to give mankind back their spring,' that is to say their dignity: a Dionysiac figure in short. What characterises Fo's retellings of Bible stories is the fact that the narrator or chief character in the sketches is frequently a disadvantaged spectator of events – like the blind man who, along with his lame mate with his trolley, sees Jesus pass on the way to Calvary and flees from the danger of being 'miracled' by a glance from him. For if they are made whole they will be robbed of their only livelihood. But Fo's anger is reserved for the Pope in all his magnificent vestments who spurns Jesus as a poor and worthless creature. It is not surprising therefore that Fo had problems with the Church but not with the Italian public. In the course of two and half years, as Fo toured Italy, *Mistero Buffo* attracted a global audience which Fo puts at more than a million spectators – 25,000 on one evening alone in Milan and 14,000 in Turin.

The seventies was a murky period in Italian history. It was marked on the one hand by efforts from the Right with the connivance of the security services and the army, along with dark forces in a famous Masonic lodge, to pursue 'a strategy of tension', aiming thereby to destabilise the state in a way that would justify a coup d'état. The result was a series of bombings that killed a number of innocent people. The guilty persons in the view of the authorities and the press were 'anarchists'. One such explosion in a bank in Piazza Fontana, Milan, in December 1969 killed sixteen people and wounded eighty-eight. The authorities laid the blame on 'anarchists', one of whom, Giuseppe Pinelli, 'fell' from a fourth-floor window in the police headquarters where he was being interrogated. One of Fo's most famous farces, *Accidental Death of an Anarchist*, was his bitterly ironic reaction to this event – a political intervention using the weapon of laughter. When, many years later, there was a proposal to remove the plaque commemorating Pinelli's death, his reaction typically was to go to Milan and restage the piece.

This was a period of political hysteria in the Italian media, among the public and in political circles; a time when it was dangerous to challenge the prevailing mood. The perils of the course he and Franca Rame embarked on in this highly volatile situation are demonstrated by his arrest by the authorities for disrespect to the American president and – a much graver matter – her kidnapping by Fascists for her courageous support of movements on the Left that included women, workers and the parents and relatives of political prisoners. Franca Rame has explained their stance in these terms:

> In order to feel at one with our political commitments it was no longer enough to consider ourselves democratic, left-wing artists full of sympathy for the working class and the exploited . . . The lesson came to us directly from the extraordinary struggles of the working people, from the young people's fight against authoritarianism and injustice in the schools and from their struggle for a new culture and relationship with the exploited classes . . . We had to place ourselves entirely at the service of the exploited and become their minstrels.

The movement of the sixties and seventies developed outside the framework of the established political parties and invented its own tactics. They took many forms, from the policy of armed struggle, kidnapping and political murder, adopted by the terrorists of the Red Brigades, to civil disobedience of various kinds. Widespread discontent among young people – schoolchildren, students and workers – found aggressive expression in dress and social behaviour, in squatting, drug-taking, dropping out of the educational system. On another less violent but politically effective level there was the policy of *autoriduzione*. It was developed by workers who of their own accord limited their working hours and output. The tactic was taken up and applied in different ways and contexts by young manual and white-collar workers and students, who refused, for instance, to pay the prices demanded by cinemas or by the organisers of pop concerts. It was also applied in shops and supermarkets where the protesters carried out acts of expropriation by refusing to pay for goods. The established parties of the Left found this development difficult to deal with. The Communist Party, which was aiming at respectability, reacted to developments, which it could not control, with puritanical disapproval. It seems probable in retrospect that the inability of the Communists to harness the energies behind these unfamiliar political manifestations caused them to lose contact with a section of their natural constituency – the young workers – and so to miss a political opportunity.

Autoriduzione inspired *Can't Pay? Won't Pay!* (1974) – a title which found an echo in the anti-poll tax protests in Britain. The first few lines set the scene: working-class women have rebelled against the rise in the cost of living by taking goods without payment from the stores. The plot concerns their efforts to conceal their bold decision from their menfolk and from the police. It is noticeable that the husband of one of them is strongly opposed to these activities and it is no mere coincidence that he is a Communist shop steward. Fo's admirable comic invention creates a situation involving the women, who attempt to cover up their activities, their men, who are suspected by the police who in their turn – as often in Fo – are blundering figures of fun. The dénouement involves characters appearing and disappearing out of windows and doors – the kind of farcical business of which Fo is a master and which is no less effective for being highly traditional.

Fo's reaction to the hysteria and hypocrisy of the Italian press and the political figures of both Right and Left in this and the following years was to use the weapon of laughter which he strongly believes opens people's minds to receive ideas they might otherwise reject. In *Trumpets and Raspberries* he exploits one of his favourite devices which is part of the stock-in-trade of the commedia dell'arte – the confusion of identities. Agnelli, the boss of Fiat, who is injured in what appears to be a terrorist attack, is mistaken for a Fiat shop steward and suspected of being himself a terrorist. In the end the 'terrorist' is let off because under interrogation by the police he demonstrates that he knows the truth behind the façade of Italian politics and is too dangerous to hold.

In the original performance in January 1981, Fo played both the workman and the industrialist, the latter being so swathed in bandages and connected to pulleys that he is little more than a human puppet (a situation that recurs in Fo's work). This is farce with a cutting-edge. In the original Italian production there were sharp comments on prominent politicians of the day, their hypocrisy and 'the stench of corpses' (to use Fo's words) that accompanied it. Today we read and see the play in the light of the accusations of corruption and links with the Mafia which the Italian judiciary has levelled at prominent political figures. It still stands up as splendid comic writing and a comment on power and its abuse.

At the end of one performance the political temperature was raised several degrees when three women, all relatives of political prisoners, came on stage and read the text of a complaint about conditions in the maximum security gaols where the prisoners were held and on whose behalf Franca Rame had sent an appeal to Amnesty International. The ensuing press campaign was astonishing and unrestrained. The row over what was inaccurately described in some papers as a demonstration in favour of the Red Brigades spread to Parliament and the Senate where there were calls for the censorship of parts of the play.

Fo's work came to be strongly marked by the thinking of the women's movement – witness the strong women in *Can't Pay? Won't Pay!* This development undoubtedly owes much to Franca Rame who has progressively established herself as a political figure (more active in this sense than her husband) and a powerful feminist voice. She has produced a number of one-woman monologues in collaboration with Fo, to be found in the collection *All Home, Bed and Church*. In the case of *An Ordinary Day* the collaboration took a different form, for here the episode with the burglars was originally a piece written by Franca Rame based on a break-in to her sister's flat. It is a text which, as she says, Dario 'stole'. Her collaboration took a different form again in *The Open Couple*, where the original idea and text is by Fo but the text *as performed* has been shaped by Franca Rame who plays the principal character. In the course of performances to audiences all over Italy she has made hundreds – if not thousands – of changes in the prompt copy which is a palimpsest incorporating references to current events, new pieces of dialogue, textual alterations.

Franca Rame is perhaps best described as an actor-manager. She travels from city to city with her own team of actors and technicians. After the curtain comes down the team is likely to meet over a meal and discuss the evening's performance; it is a process in which her interventions range from the technicalities of lighting or sound to the nuances of acting and presentation. So it is no wonder that she has also evolved the text in a dialogue with the public to the point where it is very difficult for an editor to determine which is the definitive version. This view of the text as something open to alteration, without closure, is in line with a tradition familiar in the popular theatre and to the travelling troupes like the family into which Franca Rame was born. It goes back to the commedia dell'arte in which the plot was merely an outline around which the actors improvised and in which they inserted their *lazzi*, their comic routines, and their reactions to the audience of the day.

Both *The Open Couple* and *An Ordinary Day* deal with the fate of women in a society in which both the social system in which they live and its ideology are shaped by men. From their earliest days, Franca Rame argues, women are brought up to accept as natural certain social phenomena – that marriage, for instance, is an institution into which a woman is expected to enter for life but the man not necessarily so, that an ageing woman must resign herself to her fate but the man (especially if he is 'a great man') may leave her for a much younger partner, that she must endure loneliness, be misunderstood and considered mad when she cries for help in unacceptable ways.

Elizabeth: Almost by Chance a Woman has as its theme how in a world where she is a rare exception, a woman of strength and beauty, endowed with a passionate nature, must face and conquer fears – fears at the loss of sexual power and fears of death. It is nevertheless a comedy, the main characters being Queen Elizabeth of England, the Virgin Queen of the history books, and Dame Grosslady, a bawdy dealer in quack medicines. These are obviously roles created to fit the talents of Franca Rame as the love-torn queen, whose paranoia reads conspiracies into Shakespeare's plays, and Dario Fo in a transvestite part as Grosslady, the licensed jester who has an ability to see through to the truth of things, not granted even to queens. Both are demanding parts: the queen's passion, fears and nightmares come to a climax at the end of the play in a monologue which is as taxing as an operatic aria; Dame Grosslady comments on life, on sex, on power and on *Hamlet* in the extraordinary jargon Fo created in *Mistero Buffo* for his clowns – a mixture of North Italian dialects and archaisms. In the present English version Gillian Hanna has created a brilliantly effective equivalent out of elements from a variety of sources: Elizabethan slang (drawn from Nashe, the contemporary chronicler of the Elizabethan underworld), Italian, Cockney rhyming slang, spoonerisms, puns and regional expressions from Scotland, Ireland, Norfolk, Yorkshire and elsewhere, together with words drawn from a dictionary of eighteenth-century slang. Different cultures would no doubt produce different versions of Grosslady's part – we could imagine one in the language of rap. This edition therefore includes in an Appendix Gillian Hanna's plain-language text of that role on which other actors or producers might want to work.

Elizabeth is not in an obvious sense political although Italian audiences would quickly pick up political references. One is to the so-called 'repenters' – members of organisations like the Red Brigades or the Mafia who have 'repented' in prison and turned into super-grasses. (There are obvious parallels in Northern Ireland.) There is the business of rival secret services, penetrating each other and plotting risings: a clear reference to the tangled web of conspiracies involving the Italian security services in the seventies. Yet another is the way the central authorities turn a deaf ear to appeals for help from hostages on the grounds that any dealings with terrorists must be a sign of weakness. This relates to the fate of the Christian Democrat politician, Aldo Moro, kidnapped by the Red Brigades in 1978, whose death-sentence was sealed by his own colleagues in the name of firm government.

There is behind the plot of Fo's play a certain historical substance in that Elizabeth's lover – but what did that mean precisely? – the Earl of Essex, did conspire against her and was duly executed. Shakespeare was a member of Essex's circle; indeed some scholars have seen in Hamlet a reflection of Essex's indecisive character. But as Fo disarmingly says, historical authenticity is not his aim: he is more interested in the terrible nature of the power wielded by persons who can send others to their deaths.

Since the heady days of the sixties and seventies Dario Fo has faced the problem that confronts many people on the Left – how to express their feelings about the great social changes in European society, the shifting of the political parameters, the confusions about goals, about ends and means. Like her husband, Franca Rame has found political intervention difficult in a period which she defines as one of indifference, cynicism and alienation; one in which the grand social causes have been replaced by other issues – green issues, issues affecting deprived children, children with Down's syndrome, issues like those of drugs and Aids, which are indeed political and of almost universal application. She has in the wake of the crisis in the Italian Communist Party emerged as a supporter of the Rifondazione Comunista (Communist Renewal) which advocates a broad alliance with other radical forces of the Left. When the prominent Christian Democrat politician, Andreotti, was accused of corruption he publicly accused her of instigating a telephone campaign against him. One of her recent highly effective interventions has been a long monologue called *The Thieves' Ball* (it is a reworking of an older piece *Seventh: Steal A Little Less*) delivered against a backcloth which is a montage of photographs of Italian politicians. Naming names – for libel is not the threat in Italy that it is in Britain – she simply tells stories about them with admirable wit. Italian audiences listen to her with excitement, recognition and bursts of laughter.

That Fo has turned to the same themes as those advocated by his wife is demonstrated in *The Pope and the Witch*. Here he takes as his target social attitudes to the drugs problem and the prejudices inherent in certain perceptions of Aids, always using to discuss these most controversial topics the skills he has learned from the past and continues to apply in his work, whether as performer, writer or director. It is a measure of his reputation as the latter that he was invited – the first foreigner to be so honoured – to direct a production of Molière's *Malade Imaginaire* at the Comédie Française.

But Fo is also a controversial figure. Not everybody accepts his interpretation of the medieval texts on which much of his work is founded. There are those who find that he devalues the role of the director in favour of the performer. It is possible for a recent volume on the Italian theatre by an important Italian publisher to contain no reference to his work. There are those who reject his attempt to create a popular culture drawing on old traditions as a counter to the culture of consumerism and the mass media. There are others who dispute his version of the history of Italian theatre.

There seemed to be a moment in the eighties when Fo lacked political targets at which to aim his shafts. That is no longer the case. In the autumn of 1993 he began to tour Italy with a new comedy *The Country in the Dustbin* (*Il Paese nella pantumiera*) of which he and Franca Rame are joint authors.

The main character is a magistrate, played by Fo, with Franca Rame playing a policewoman. The magistrate is 'certainly not exemplary but someone who serves us as the starting point for a *pochade* which tells the tale of Tangentopoli' – Tangentopoli being the name universally used in Italy to describe the system of pay-offs (*tangenti*) which has been gradually brought to light and which has involved leading figures in most of the main Italian political parties. The plot has all the complications of farce involving the secret services, politicians, spies and men of power. Names are named. 'We have always named names,' Fo has said. 'But this time rather than dealing with the politicians we have involved the whole country, the present moment, what must be done to pull us out of this slough.' Their aim is to propose tactics to answer the skilful manoeuvres of men of power who aim to put off the moment of judgement and wish to see everything swept under the carpet. In the realm of politics Franca Rame and Fo launched an appeal to have members of parliament under investigation for bribery suspended – it gathered over 300,000 signatures – their hope being that it might become a motion to be put before the Italian parliament.

Once more the Fos had entered the political arena armed with the weapon of laughter.

Stuart Hood, 1993

Introduction

by Franca Rame

There are many people who seem to think – perhaps because it is easier and more exciting – that our transition (I mean Dario's and mine) from the traditional theatre to that in which we now work, occurred suddenly, almost overnight, as a consequence of a sort of mystical crisis, as though we had been overcome by the 1968 wave of students' protest and workers' struggles. As if one fine morning we woke up saying: 'That's enough, let's wrap ourselves up in the red flag, let's have our own cultural revolution!'

In fact our true turning point, the point that really mattered, we took at the very beginning of our journey, twenty-two years ago, when with Paventi, Durano and Lecoq we staged for the first time *The Finger in the Eye*. Those were the days of Scelba and his 'subculture', of Pacelli (the pope) with his civic committees, the days of total censorship. Police superintendents, ministers, bishops and cops understood it immediately: we were 'a company of communists' and we were making 'red propaganda'. Every night there would be an inspector in the auditorium checking our words one by one against the script and the Ministry for Entertainment would obstruct our touring arrangements, while the most reactionary theatre-owners would refuse us their buildings and the bishops would ask the police to tear our programmes from the walls of their cities.

The Finger in the Eye was underlined everywhere we went, among the shows 'advised against' in the parish bulletins. This hounding of 'the communist enemy of civilisation and of Holy Mary' went on for many years with all our shows. However, the workers, the students and the progressive bourgeoisie were supporting us, thereby allowing us to move on and make ourselves known, despite the lack of any prizes.

On more than one occasion we were almost prevented from

performing our plays. The opening of *He Had Two Guns*, a play about the collusion between fascism and the bourgeoisie, and between political power and organised crime, was halted by the extremely severe interference of censorship which literally butchered our script. We decided to take no notice of the cuts and get on with the play. There was a trial of strength between us and the Milan prefecture which threatened us with immediate arrest, but in the end the Ministry, worried about a possible scandal, lifted the cuts. The script of the *Archangels* was taken away from us because of the many unauthorised jokes we had added to it during the performance. For the same show we collected 'reports' to the police superintendent of every single town we visited. I was reported for making a remark against the army in a play about Columbus. While running the same *Columbus* we were assaulted by fascists outside the Valle Theatre in Rome, just at a moment when, by a strange coincidence, the police had disappeared. Dario was even challenged to a duel by an artillery officer, for having slighted the honour of the Italian army, and, crazy as he is, he even accepted the challenge on condition that the duel should be fought barefoot as a Thai boxing match, of which he boasted being regional champion. The artillery officer was never seen again. However, there weren't just funny incidents. Though we were operating inside the 'official' theatre, we were beset by endless troubles and difficulties. The reactionaries and the conservatives could not swallow the kind of 'satirical violence' present in our scripts. Dozens of critics accused us of debasing the stage by introducing politics at every step and they went on proposing the usual, worn out model of 'art for art's sake'.

Our theatre was becoming increasingly provocative, leaving no room for purely 'digestive' entertainment. The reactionaries were getting furious. On more than one occasion there were brawls among the audience, provoked by the fascists in the stalls. The Chief of Siena police had Dario taken in by two 'carabinieri' at the end of a show, because he had offended a foreign head of state (Johnson). Whatever the criticism of our work, it must be recognised that our theatre was alive – we spoke of 'facts' which people needed to hear about. For this reason and for the direct language we used, ours was a popular theatre.

Audiences increased at every performance. From 1964 to 1968 our box-office takings were always the highest among the major companies in Italy and we were among those who charged the lowest prices. Yet it was just at the end of the 1968 season (a true record in terms of takings) that we arrived at the decision to leave the traditional structures of the official theatre. We had realised that, despite the hostility of a few, obtuse reactionaries, the high bourgeoisie reacted to our 'spankings' almost with pleasure. Masochists? No, without realising it, we were helping their digestion. Our 'whipping' boosted their blood circulation, like some good birching after a refreshing sauna. In other words we had become the minstrels of a fat and intelligent bourgeoisie. This bourgeoisie did not mind our criticism, no matter how pitiless it had become through our use of satire and grotesque technique, but only so long as the exposure of their 'vices' occurred exclusively within the structures they controlled.

An example of this rationale was offered by our participation in a TV programme, *Canzonissima*. A few months earlier we had done a show, *Who's Seen Him?*, for the second TV channel which had only recently become operative and was still the privilege of the well-to-do. On that occasion we had been allowed to do a socio-political satire of rather unusual violence, at least by TV standards. Everything went well, without great hitches. Indeed the reviews were totally favourable and we were 'warmly' applauded by the 'selected' audience. However, when we tried to say the same sort of things before an audience of over 20 million people and in the most popular programme of the year (which *Canzonissima* certainly was), the heavens fell. The same newspapers that had applauded our earlier show now unleashed a lynching campaign. 'It is infamous,' they would say, 'to feed such wickedness, worthy of the basest political propaganda, to an audience as uneducated and easily swayed as the great mass of TV viewers.' Consequently the TV governors, urged by civic committees and by the most

backward centres of authority, imposed cuts and vetoes of
unimaginable severity. Our scripts were being massacred. It
was a return to Scelba's censorship. We were forced to
abandon the programme and faced four law suits. For eighteen
years now we haven't set foot in the TV studios. Thirteen years
of 'banishment' and 200 million lire in damages, plus 26 million
to pay. Authority does not forgive those who do not respect
the rules of *its* game.

It's the usual story. The great kings, the potentates who
understand such things, have always paid fools to recite before
a public of highly-educated courtiers, their rigmaroles of
satirical humours and even of irreverent allusions to their
masters' power and injustices. The courtiers could exclaim in
amazement: 'What a democratic king! He has the moral
strength to laugh at himself!' But we well know that, if the
fools had been impudent enough to leave the court and sing
the same satires in the town squares, before the peasants, the
workers and the exploited, the king and his sycophants would
pay them back in a different currency. You are allowed to
mock authority, but if you do it from the outside, it will burn
you. This is what we had understood. In order to feel at one
with our political commitment, it was no longer enough to
consider ourselves as democratic, left-wing artists full of
sympathy for the working class and, in general, for the
exploited. Sympathy was no longer sufficient. The lesson came
to us directly from the extraordinary struggles of the working
people, from the new impulse that young people were giving in
the schools to the fight against authoritarianism and social
injustice and for the creation of a new culture and a new
relationship with the exploited classes. No longer could we act
as intellectuals, sitting comfortably within and above our own
privileges, deigning in our goodness to deal with the
predicament of the exploited. We had to place ourselves
entirely at the service of the exploited, become their minstrels.
Which meant going to work within the structures provided by
the working class. That is why we immediately thought of the
workers' clubs.

The workers' social clubs (*case del popolo*) in Italy represent a peculiar and very widespread phenomenon. They were set up by workers and peasants at the turn of the century, when the first socialist cells began to appear. The fronts of these first buildings used to bear the following inscription: 'If you want to give to the poor, give five coppers, two for bread and three for culture', and culture does not only mean being able to read and write, but also to express one's own creativity on the basis of one's own world-view.

However, by working in these places, we realised that the original need to study and produce culture together, which inspired workers and peasants to build their own clubs, had been completely dissipated. The clubs had become nothing more than shops, selling more or less alcoholic drinks, or dance halls or billiard rooms. I'm not saying that drinking, dancing and playing cards or billiards is unimportant. The trouble is that nothing more went on there. There were almost no discussions. Some documentary films or little shows were put on, but only as a recreational activity. The working class parties had failed to follow up the needs for creative expression that had been manifested so powerfully among workers and peasants. This failure was based on their persuasion that it is useless to stimulate the development of a proletarian culture, since this does not and cannot exist. 'Only one culture exists' – is what those 'who know' say – 'and it is above all classes. Culture is one, as one is the moon or the sun that shine equally for all those who want and can take advantage of them.'

Naturally we soon found ourselves fighting against this unity of classes theory. In the arguments that followed we often quoted the example of the Chinese revolution, where the Party had shown a very different faith in the creativity of the masses and in their ability and willingness to build a different language and a different philosophy of human relationships and social life. Above all we pointed to the great, truly revolutionary determination of the Chinese leaders to urge the intellectuals towards active political participation beyond any personal artistic interest. The intellectuals were asked to commit themselves totally to class struggle, with the aim of studying the culture of peasants and workers and learning about their

needs in order to transform them *together* into artistic
expression. These ideas drove the Party bureaucrats furious.
They would cling to the usual cliché that 'we must move on
gradually, starting from the lowest levels, avoiding any flight
forward'. They also evinced a certain mistrust of the workers'
intelligence and ability not only to express but also to invent a
particular cultural world of their own. In fact the workers'
clubs' audiences not only listened but actively participated in
our debates and our work.

Now, as I read the proofs of those early plays, I remember
our first show at the Sant' Egidio club in the suburbs of
Cesena. We had decided to go there for our main rehearsals
four or five days before the opening. We were assembling the
scaffolding for the stage with the help of the lads in the
organisation (ARCI) and a few workers and students.
However, the club members went on playing cards at the other
end of the hall, looking at us now and again, but with
diffidence. Clearly for them we were a group of intellectuals,
mildly affected perhaps by the populist bug, stopping over for a
few days to refresh our spirit among the proletariat and then
away again to where we had come from. What took them by
surprise was actually seeing us working, working with our own
hands, lifting boxes, carrying steel tubes, fixing nuts and bolts,
setting up the stage lights. What? Actors, both male and
female, slogging away? Incredible!

In the meantime a rather serious problem had arisen: voices
reverberated too much in the hall. We wouldn't perform in
those conditions. We had to first arrange some cables
underneath the ceiling and to hang a few acoustic panels. We
decided to use egg-boxes, the kind made of cardboard. But it
was necessary first to tie them together with string, a job which
I took on myself together with two other women comrades. We
started stringing the boxes together with the help of some
upholstering needles, but it wasn't at all easy. After swearing
for a couple of hours trying to get the needles through the
cardboard, we noticed that the comrades from the club had
interrupted their games and were looking at us, following our
work with interest but in complete silence. After a while an old

comrade muttered, as though talking to himself: 'One would want a much longer needle for that job.' Then, silence again for a few more minutes. Then someone else said: 'I could easily make one with a bicycle spoke.' 'Go!' they all said. In a moment the comrade was back with ten very long needles. Then everybody started to help us to get the string through the boxes and hang them, climbing on step-ladders, like jugglers, cracking jokes, laughing as though it were a big game. A few hours later there were so many people in the hall that we could hardly move. Even the most stubborn billiard players had come to help us and some women too, who had just come to get their husbands back home.

The ice was broken and their diffidence entirely overcome. We had won their sympathy by showing that we too could work and sweat. In the late afternoon, after work, they would come to help us and when we started rehearsing, they would sit at the opposite end of the hall looking at us very quietly. The old men would silence the young ones, who burst out laughing at our jokes: 'You mustn't disturb,' they would say. Then little by little they all loosened up. At the end of our rehearsals we would ask for their views, whether they had any criticism to make. At first they wouldn't unbutton, saying that they knew nothing about theatre, but later they became less shy and began to make critical remarks and give us some advice too, which invariably was as unassuming as it was pertinent and to the point. When we finally got to the opening night, the show didn't just belong to 'The New Stage': it was our show in the sense that it belonged to all of us in that hall, who had built it together. Later on, when we moved to other clubs in the vicinity, those comrades followed us and introduced the show to the local comrades. They went out hanging posters and were always the first to speak in the debates. They supported us, we were their team.

In that first year we performed in more than 80 workers' clubs, indoor bowling alleys, occupied factories, suburban cinemas and even in some theatres. We performed before 200,000 and more spectators, of whom 70 per cent had never before seen a play. The debates that followed our shows were

always lively, going on till very late at night. Everyone spoke –
women, boys, grown-ups and old people. They all talked about
their experiences – the Resistance and their struggles – and
they told us what we could put on the stage in future: their
history.

We drew new themes and plots from those debates, and we
found above all a new, direct language without rhetoric or
sophistication. For this reason we were accused of populism,
but populists are those who parachute down to the people from
high above, not those who are up to their necks inside the
world of the people and who do their utmost to learn about the
struggles of everyday men and women. And by living with the
people we have also been able to verify for ourselves the great
truth expressed by Brecht when he said: 'The people can say
deep and complex things with great simplicity; the populists
who descend from above to write for the people say with great
simplicity hollow and banal things.'

However, the debates, the polemics and especially the shows
that resulted from them, began to annoy the clubs' managers,
not to mention those of ARCI, the organisation within which
we all were operating. We held on for a while, but in the end
were forced to give up. The tension was causing real rows and
all sorts of outbursts against us, in oral and written form – in
polemical articles in the *Unità* and the Party's cultural journals.
Sometimes we reacted without much dialectical sense, in a
confused and fanciful manner. We had very little experience of
political subtleties nor did we know how to be restrained and
accommodating. Nevertheless today, if we look back
objectively, while recognising how sectarian we sometimes
were and admitting our mistakes, we must say that we could do
nothing else. Had we stayed within those structures, we
wouldn't have made a single step forward, we would have been
ensnared by a thousand compromises.

The separation with ARCI didn't come easily. There was a
further division within us too. More than half the company
chose to continue working within the ARCI structures and kept
calling themselves 'The New Stage'. We called our group 'The
Commune'. We had come through a great crisis, but it had

been a crisis towards growth and clarity. Basically there had
always been a conflict in the company between two
fundamentally different ways of looking at our roles as actors.
What were we, militants at the complete service of the working
class or, more simply, left-wing artists? The dilemma kept
emerging. The latter point of view meant accepting more or
less correct compromises, veering towards opportunism,
renouncing any vigour not only in respect of our own criteria,
but also of our collective and individual behaviour both inside
and outside the activity of the group. Moreover, there was
among ourselves a sort of self-defeating democraticism that was
the first cause of arguments, conflicts and division. Dario and I,
while trying to avoid acting as managers, made the opposite
mistake. We didn't provide any direction at all for the group.
What is worse, we allowed some ambitious individuals who
were after 'power', to organise political factions to the point of
endangering our autonomy. Therefore, two years ago, at the
time of the last break-up, Dario and I found ourselves with
only four other comrades, completely alone and bereft of
everything – the lorry, the vans, the electrical equipment,
including our personal stage equipment – we had put together
during twenty years' work and which, on leaving the official
theatre, we brought to the company.

   Whether those comrades were correct in bringing about the
split can perhaps best be judged from the fact that in less than
one year their productions have achieved only indescribable
failures. They have been cutting each other's throats, they have
broken up again, wasted money, sold or abandoned all the
equipment. And now they have broken up for good, they don't
exist any more. This disaster does not give us any pleasure at
all. It only makes us very sad, as we realise how many
comrades, with the ability and the quality of good actors, how
many who could have continued working for our common aim,
can have been so easily undone by the deleterious ideology
which time and again emerges like a tumour inside every
company: individualism, the struggle for personal power and
all the evils that go with it. But we learned one thing, that this
mistake can be fought and overcome only if we tie ourselves

even more closely to the working class and their struggles, if
we let the workers direct our activity and put ourselves entirely
at their disposal and service with the utmost confidence. It is
because of this principle that the mood inside our group has
entirely changed: there is no more tension, no more personal
arguing.

Well, despite all the problems, rows, conflicts and splits, the
positive thing is the result of these seven years' work – the
millions of people who have seen our plays, our intervention
with purpose-written scripts in occupied factories and cities
where political trials were being held (as was the case with
Accidental Death of an Anarchist, performed in Milan during
the Calabresi–*Lotta Continua* trial; or with *Bang Bang, Who's
There? Police!*, performed in Rome for the Valpreda trial; or
our interventions on behalf of Giovanni Marius in Salerno and
Vallo della Lucania, in Pescara during the trial of fifty
prisoners who had rebelled in the city's jail in Mestre to help
the Marghera workers; and many other shows in other cities,
when the total takings went to support the striking workers of
Padua, Bergamo, Asti, Varese, Turin and for a long period,
Milan; or the sale of 10,000 glasses from an occupied Milanese
factory carried out at the Palazzetto dello Sport of Bologna,
which was an incredible event, every comrade, every spectator
carrying a glass in his hands.)

The fact that Dario, despite so many internal and external
worries (trials, assaults, arrests, attempts on his life), managed
to write and produce something like three scripts every year
(not to mention all the emergency sketches) seems amazing
even to me, though I have personally lived through all these
ordeals.

At this point I should say something about Dario's craft as a
writer, or, I should say, as a maker of scripts for the stage.
Why a maker rather than writer? Because, when he writes,
Dario needs to think out and build a stage or, preferably, a
sequence of scenic spaces and planes on which the dramatic
action can take place. It is also a question of theatrical
construction rather than simple writing because his theatre is
not based on characters, but on *situations*. The characters

become masks, i.e. emblematic pretexts at the service of a
situation. The stage moves on by virtue of an action, just as the
actor moves by virtue of his gestures and his words. Even the
stage props therefore become part of an action. This demands
great open-mindedness at the level of stage management.
Therefore Dario can allow himself to bring on to the stage
puppets and marionettes, masks and mannikins, actors with
natural or painted faces. And all this he joins together from the
inside with the songs, the jokes, the coarse shouting, the use of
noisy instruments, the pauses, the exasperated rhythm –
though never overdone, because his style is rigorous even when
everything seems haphazard and accidental. Only superficial
people can in fact think that Dario's theatre is 'handmade'. On
the contrary, it is all reasoned out in advance, written,
rehearsed, rewritten and rehearsed again and always in a
practical relationship to and with the audience. It must be
remembered that Dario studied as an architect and that,
besides being an actor and a writer, he is also a choreographer.
He always sees the stage (and he insists on this) as 'plan,
elevation, foreshortening and perspective'. Personally, coming
from a family of actors, I've seen, since I was a child, all kinds
of shows being prepared and written, but I have always been
struck by Dario's method. He has a constant inventiveness and
is always lively and young, never banal and obvious. His scripts
are always technically perfect, never boring or tiresome. What
amazes me most of all is that when he writes, he always keeps
the structure of his text entirely open, he doesn't build in
advance a complete framework. He invents dialogue based on
a paradoxical or a real situation and goes on from there by
virtue of some kind of natural, geometric logic, inventing
conflicts that find their solutions in one gag after another in
correspondence with a parallel political theme, a political
theme which must be clear and didactic. You are moved and
you laugh, but above all you are made to think, realise and
develop your understanding of everyday events that had before
escaped your attention.

This is what I think of Dario Fo as playwright. Many others
have talked about Dario as writer-director-actor. I can add

something about Dario's behaviour as an actor on the stage.
He is always alert, ready to catch the mood of an audience with
inimitable timing. For the comrades who work with him he is a
comrade up until the end of every show. He regrets his success
when it compromises that of other actors and he does his
utmost to make sure that each one achieves adequate personal
satisfaction. If a comrade misses a burst of laughter, he goes on
working at it and isn't satisfied until the colleague gets it back.

About Dario the man and partner I am reluctant to say
anything, except that his honesty and his inner beauty can be
seen better on his face as he grows older. He is getting more
gentle, nice and calm, humble, generous and patient. I don't
know anybody with so much patience, especially with those
who pester him, and God knows how many of them we have
met in these years. Moreover, he is generous and stubborn.
Nothing depresses him, I've never heard him say 'let's give up'.
Even the hardest ordeals, such as my kidnapping by the
fascists, or the 1972 split, he has overcome by reasoning with
his usual strength, confident that he would make it, trusting the
support and the respect of the comrades who have followed us
by the thousands. What would you say? Do you think that I am
quite 'crazy' about Dario? That I admire him a lot? Too much?
Well, I say that yes, I admire him, but even more, I respect
him. I was so lucky to meet him! If I hadn't already done it, I'd
marry him now.

Franca Rame

Can't Pay?
Won't Pay!

translated by Lino Pertile
adapted by Bill Colvill *and*
Robert Walker

This adaptation of *Can't Pay? Won't Pay!* was commissioned by Omega Stage and first presented at the Criterion Theatre, London on 15 July 1981. The cast was as follows:

ANTONIA	Nick Bartlett
MARGHERITA	Karen Dury
GIOVANNI	Alfred Molina
SERGEANT/INSPECTOR/ OLD MAN/UNDERTAKER	Sylvestre McCoy
LUIGI	Christopher Ryan

On 19 April 1982 the cast changed as follows:

ANTONIA	Paolo Dionisotti
MARGHERITA	Lizzie Queen
GIOVANNI	Christopher Ryan
SERGEANT/INSPECTOR/ OLD MAN/UNDERTAKER	Nick Edmett
LUIGI	Michael Burlington

Adapted & directed by Robert Walker
Designed by Geoff Rose

Produced by Ian B. Albery for Omega Stage Limited, Albery Theatre, St Martin's Lane, London WC2.

The first two scenes of Act 2 may be transposed at the director's discretion.

We Can't Pay? We Won't Pay! was first produced at the Half Moon Theatre on 22 May 1978. The cast was as follows:

ANTONIA	Frances de la Tour
MARGHERITA	Patti Love
GIOVANNI	Christopher Malcolm
SERGEANT/INSPECTOR/ OLD MAN/UNDERTAKER	Matthew Robertson
LUIGI	Denis Lawson

Directed by Robert Walker
Designed by Mary Lawton, Lolly Hahn (students of the Central School of Art and Design)

ACT ONE

The living room and kitchen area of an old, worn second-floor flat in a tenement block. It is clean and neat.

The door bangs open and ANTONIA staggers in breathless and burdened with four or five plastic bags overflowing with food. MARGHERITA follows, likewise breathless and even more heavily burdened with shopping.

ANTONIA: Blimey, home at last. My feet are killing me. I'll never get use to those stairs. Thank goodness I met you Margherita.

MARGHERITA: Christ, Antonia, what happened? Where did you get all this stuff? Won the pools have you?

ANTONIA: That's right.

MARGHERITA: Come off it.

ANTONIA: No, tell a lie. I got it all with Green Shield stamps.

MARGHERITA: Pull the other one.

ANTONIA: All right I'll come clean. I swopped it for a two-for-the-price-of-one off-peak return to Florence. It came with the coupon with the cornflakes.

MARGHERITA: What, Brekki Wheat?

ANTONIA: No. After Germ.

MARGHERITA: Get away.

ANTONIA: All right, seeing as you're my best friend, and you keep it to yourself, I've got a rich lover.

MARGHERITA: That's it. I'm off.

ANTONIA: Where are you going?

MARGHERITA: Home.

ANTONIA: Come on then. Shut the door. I was only kidding.

MARGHERITA: Is this going to be one of your stories?

ANTONIA: Margherita how could you. This is not a story. This is an epic.

MARGHERITA: Right, out with it then.

ANTONIA: You're not going to believe this. I went to the supermarket as usual and there were a load of women making an almighty row about the prices going up again.

MARGHERITA: What's new?

ANTONIA: Well, quite. I mean, spaghetti, sugar, bread, cheese, macaroni.

MARGHERITA: Never mind meat and butter.

ANTONIA: Where was I?

MARGHERITA: Anchovies.

ANTONIA: No, I wasn't. Oh yes, anyway, everyone shouting the odds about the price of things, and the manager's trying to be reasonable and calm everyone down.

MARGHERITA: How'd he do that?

ANTONIA: Shouting his brains out and snatching bog rolls out of people's baskets.

MARGHERITA: O, very calming. Very reasonable.

ANTONIA: Well, quite. 'It's not my fault,' he kept saying. 'It's head office. They decide the increases. They're dictated by market forces.' 'We're the market forces.' 'It's free enterprise,' he says, 'competition.' 'Competition?' I says. 'Competition? Can we enter?' So everyone starts, don't they? 'Competition?' 'Where's my entry form?' Then this big woman starts. You know her, Mrs Manzi.

MARGHERITA: Mrs Manzi?

ANTONIA: Yeah you know. Big woman. Wears a big hat. Spanner in her hand-bag.

MARGHERITA: Ah Mrs Manzi.

ANTONIA: Well she says 'We've had enough. From now on we decide the prices. We'll only pay a fair price and no more. And you don't like it we'll nick the stuff.'

MARGHERITA: Ooooer.

ANTONIA: 'Hang on,' I said, 'hang on Mrs Manzi.' 'Nick? Nick?' I say. 'Leave it out, we'll liberate the stuff.' 'You're mad the lot of you,' says the manager, going red as a beetroot.

MARGHERITA: Did you get some?

ANTONIA: No, they looked a bit raddled. By now he's surrounded by women, so he starts to push. Well, that was it! A woman falls down. Then Mrs Manzi yells, 'Coward, attacking a pregnant woman, if she loses her baby, we know who's to blame.' Then I start, don't I? 'Murderer, pervert, paediatrician!'

MARGHERITA: I wish I'd been there. What happened then?

ANTONIA: What do you think? He copulated immediately, We all paid exactly what we wanted. Some people went over the top, of course. Insisted on taking all their stuff on credit.

MARGHERITA: What's wrong with that? I always shop on tick.

ANTONIA: Without leaving your address? 'No, we're not giving you an address, you'll only give it to the police,' they said. 'Isn't business based on trust?' they said. 'Well, you'll have to trust us. Ta Ta.' Just then someone shouted 'Police!' Panic stations; and everyone made for the door.

MARGHERITA: Oh my good Lord!

ANTONIA: Lucky, it was a false alarm.

MARGHERITA: Thank God for that.

ANTONIA: Some workers from the factory opposite told us not to worry about the police. 'It's your right to pay your own price. It's like a strike.' They said. 'In fact, it's better than a strike. Instead of the workers losing out this time the bosses lose out.'

MARGHERITA: What happened then?

ANTONIA: By now everyone is chanting 'Can't pay, won't pay. Can't pay, won't pay'. Doing a rhumba y'know up and down the supermarket and the manager's lying around somewhere and so we scarpered. I came out, head held high, my chest stuck out like a peacock. Everyone's still chanting 'Can't pay. Won't pay!' all up and down the street. It was like a carnival.

MARGHERITA: Sod it, and I wasn't there.

ANTONIA: Then the police arrived.

MARGHERITA: Thank God, I wasn't there!

ANTONIA: We just stood there rooted to the spot. Not moving a muscle. The cops came running up, and of course couldn't make out what was going on. They're looking for a riot and all they could see was a bunch of housewives loaded down with shopping. For a minute we just stood there. Face to face. High Noon. Nobody knew what to do. Then I said, 'At last you're here. There's a load of robbers in there. Frightened the life out of us. They've highjacked the supermarket.' Then we really scarpered.

MARGHERITA: Marvellous. Must have been like the storming of the Bastille or the Winter Palace in Leningrad, and I could have got Luigi his kippers.

ANTONIA: It was a marvellous feeling. Not because we got away with something, but because we were all in it together. Men and women doing something against the bosses.

MARGHERITA: They'll be so bleeding scared. Now they'll put the prices down tomorrow.

ANTONIA: Started already, I shouldn't wonder.

MARGHERITA: Yea well. Never mind all that. What are you going to tell Giovanni? He won't like it one little bit.

ANTONIA: I'll think up a story.

MARGHERITA: Like what?

ANTONIA: You think he'd swallow the off-peak return to Florence?

MARGHERITA: Not a chance.

ANTONIA: Green Shield stamps?

MARGHERITA: Come off it.

ANTONIA: You're right. That's the trouble with Giovanni.

MARGHERITA: What?

ANTONIA: He respects the law. Trouble is I've already spent the money he gave me. I haven't a bean to pay the gas and electric. Mind you, I'm not worried about the rent.

MARGHERITA: Why not?

ANTONIA: I haven't paid it for five months.

MARGHERITA: Same here.

ANTONIA: Ooh, naughty.

MARGHERITA: Oh, I wish I'd been with you. At least I'd have something for my old man's tea.

ANTONIA: You can have some of this. I can't hide it all anyway.

MARGHERITA: Ooer. I couldn't.

ANTONIA: Ah go on. Do us a favour.

MARGHERITA: Oo no. Luigi'd know, where could I put it? And there's Mama and Papa and Auntie Clara.

ANTONIA: Stop clucking. When you can, pay me. When you've got the money, you can give me for what I've paid for and no more and the rest you can have free.

MARGHERITA: Eh?

ANTONIA: Half of this I've half paid for fully, the other half is half free. Oh forget it. Just take it.

MARGHERITA: You're forgetting my husband. He's as bad as yours. He'll half kill me if I tell him it's only half paid for.

ANTONIA: My old man'll just nag me to death. 'That's it, cover my name in mud, I've always paid my way, I can hold

my head up anywhere, poor, but honest blah blah blah,'
until he rabbits me to death. (*Pulls a tin from the nearest
bag*) Hello! Dog food?!

MARGHERITA: You haven't got a dog.

ANTONIA: I know I haven't got a dog. Supermeat! What's
Supermeat? I must have grabbed it in all the confusion.
(*Another packet*) Look at this. Millet for birds.

MARGHERITA: Let's have a look.

ANTONIA: It's just as well I didn't pay for this lot otherwise
we'd have to live on frozen rabbits' heads. (*Third packet*)

MARGHERITA: You what? Rabbits' heads?

ANTONIA: Here you are. 'Enrich your poultry's diet with best
frozen rabbits' heads.' At least they're the best. 'Two
hundred lira.'

MARGHERITA: And you want me to take this muck for my
Luigi?

ANTONIA: You've got a point. Look I'll take this stuff and
you have the rest.

MARGHERITA: What if the police search the house?

ANTONIA: There's ten thousand families in this area. Most of
them were at the supermarket today. It'd take the police for
ever to search us all. Sssshhh. Sod it, it's him. He's home.
Take this lot under your coat . . . That's it, so it's not
sticking out.

*She starts to stash the shopping under the couch, running
between the couch and the kitchen table.* MARGHERITA, *in
panic, hovers between, clutching the millet and getting in the
way.* ANTONIA *hangs one bag round* MARGHERITA's
neck and buttons her coat.

I thought you were helping me. Dozy cow. Button your coat.
That's it . . . Help me put my share under the sofa. No,
forget it. This stuff in the cupboard, you put that in the sink.
Hurry up! Now get going. Act natural.

Enter GIOVANNI, *who freezes when he sees* MARGHERITA's *coat billowing like a bell tent.*

MARGHERITA: Oh Giovanni! Hello. How are you? Well, Antonia, must be going. Be seeing you.

ANTONIA: Mind how you go, Margherita. Give my love to Luigi.

MARGHERITA: Bye. Tra la la. (*Exits*)

ANTONIA: Tra la la. She can be such a gossip. I haven't the time to chit chat about drinking coffee all day. Have you heard about thingy . . . What's wrong with you? And why are you late?

GIOVANNI: Did you notice that?

ANTONIA: What?

GIOVANNI: Margherita.

ANTONIA: Yes, that's Margherita.

GIOVANNI: No, I mean, did you notice her . . . (*He gestures*)

ANTONIA: Oh that. Yes, that's her belly. Don't worry. She's married.

GIOVANNI: You mean she's pregnant?

ANTONIA: Yes. Miraculous.

GIOVANNI: No. It's a miracle. I mean last Sunday she was this size and suddenly she's out here somewhere.

ANTONIA: Last Sunday is what it is, last Sunday. More things happen in a week. Anyway, since when have you understood anything about women's plumbing?

GIOVANNI: Look, I'm not stupid –

ANTONIA: No?

GIOVANNI: Luigi didn't say anything about this and he tells me everything.

ANTONIA: Everything?

GIOVANNI: About his wife and, you know –

ANTONIA: And?

GIOVANNI: And, well, blimey, we work on the same line. What are you supposed to talk about?

ANTONIA: Maybe Luigi wants to keep some things secret.

GIOVANNI: Secret? What does he want to keep it a secret for? Anyone would want to tell everybody if they were expecting.

ANTONIA: Well, perhaps he doesn't know yet. He could hardly tell you if he didn't know.

GIOVANNI: Doesn't know? Doesn't know?

ANTONIA: Perhaps she doesn't want to tell him yet.

GIOVANNI: Who would she not want to tell yet?

ANTONIA: Him! Luigi! He was always on at her. 'It's too early, we're too young, there's the economic crisis.' And if they found out at work she was pregnant she'd get the sack. So he got her to take the pill.

GIOVANNI: But if she took the pill, how did she get pregnant?

ANTONIA: Maybe it didn't work in her case.

GIOVANNI: Well, she can't help that, that's not her fault. Why not tell Luigi?

ANTONIA: Perhaps the pill didn't work because she didn't take it and if you don't take it, you know, it won't work.

GIOVANNI: Look, hold on –

ANTONIA: You know very well that Margherita is a good Catholic, I'm sure I don't know why. And if the Pope says it's a sin to take the pill, then it's a sin to take the pill and that's that as far as she's concerned.

GIOVANNI: Have you gone bananas? The pill that doesn't work? The Pope and her with a nine-month-old baby? And a husband who doesn't even notice?

ANTONIA: How could he notice it and her all bandaged up like that?

GIOVANNI: Bandaged up?

ANTONIA: Yes, such a shame isn't it, poor soul. Wrapped herself up with bandages just because of him. I told her, finally, if you don't undo them bandages you don't know what you'll get.

GIOVANNI: What would you get?

ANTONIA: (*Thinks*) A flat baby. Undo those bandages at once, I told her, and stop worrying about your job. Life's too important for that. Well, I couldn't leave her like that, now, could I? I was right to say that, wasn't I, Giovanni? Was I right?

GIOVANNI: Sure you were.

ANTONIA: Have I been good?

GIOVANNI: Yes yes. So what did she do?

ANTONIA: Well, she did as I told her and off came the bandages and out came the belly. Pouf! Like a barrage balloon. Then I told her if her husband makes a fuss, tell him to come over here and see Giovanni and he'll see him off. Giovanni, I was right to do that, wasn't I?

GIOVANNI: Very good. Well done.

ANTONIA: Have I been good?

GIOVANNI: OK, OK.

ANTONIA: OK, OK? What sort of answer is that? OK, OK! I knew you'd have a go at me. I knew it. So what have I done to annoy his lordship now. Don't tell me, I know, trouble at work.

GIOVANNI: As a matter of fact there was.

ANTONIA: Go on, you had a strike.

GIOVANNI: No. It was the canteen. I went up for my dinner as I always do at dinner time and there was a bunch of louts complaining about the food being so disgusting.

ANTONIA: What a shame. I bet the food was really nice.

GIOVANNI: No, it was disgusting. But what's the point of a mass meeting?

ANTONIA: Mass meeting? I thought you said it was a bunch of louts?

GIOVANNI: It was to start with. Then everybody joined in. And d'you know what they did? Everyone ate their dinner and went off without paying!

ANTONIA: Them too?

GIOVANNI: What do you mean, them too?

ANTONIA: Well, I meant not just the bunch of louts but all the others, too.

GIOVANNI: Even, I might add, the shop stewards.

ANTONIA: Well I never.

GIOVANNI: Yes. Shop stewards are supposed to set an example.

ANTONIA: Well, quite.

GIOVANNI: And that's not all.

ANTONIA: You mean there's more?

GIOVANNI: I left the canteen and went for a walk right past this supermarket.

ANTONIA: You mean the one by your work?

GIOVANNI: And blow me if there weren't hundreds of women –

ANTONIA: Yes?

GIOVANNI: Walking out of the store loaded up with goods.

ANTONIA: Yes?

GIOVANNI: And d'you know what they told me?

ANTONIA: No.

GIOVANNI: They hadn't paid for a thing!

ANTONIA: Well, what a turn out.

GIOVANNI: Did you ever hear such a thing? They left without paying!

ANTONIA: Them too.

GIOVANNI: What d'you mean, them too?

ANTONIA: Well, them, just like the bunch of louts and the mass meeting in the canteen. Them too.

GIOVANNI: And, what's more, they roughed up the manager.

ANTONIA: Which, the supermarket or the canteen?

GIOVANNI: Both.

ANTONIA: I don't know what to say.

GIOVANNI: No wonder. These layabouts, these louts, ultra-left extremists play right into the hands of the ruling class. And they'll start calling us decent responsible working men thieves and scum of the earth.

ANTONIA: But I thought it was all women who did the supermarket?

GIOVANNI: Same thing. How d'you think the men will react when they get home?

ANTONIA: No, tell me, I'm all ears.

GIOVANNI: They'll probably congratulate their wives for nicking all that gear. 'Very well nicked, my dear,' they'll say, and off down the boozer to have a good laugh. Instead of . . . instead of . . .

ANTONIA: Instead of what?

GIOVANNI: Instead of teaching the wife a lesson. That's what I'd do. I'd chuck the lot at her head, then I'd make her eat everything without opening a can, the key and all and then I'd give her a good talking to.

ANTONIA: You would, would you?

GIOVANNI: Certainly I would. So don't get any fancy ideas, because if I found so much as a tin of anchovies in the cupboard that hadn't been paid for or that had been nicked I'd –

ANTONIA: Don't tell me, I know. Key and all.

GIOVANNI: No, worse. I'd leave, I'd pack and leave and never come back. No, I'd kill you first and after apply for a divorce.

ANTONIA: Now look, if you feel that strongly about it you can pack and leave right now. Divorce or no divorce. How can you suggest such a thing! Me! I'd let you starve to death rather than make you eat stolen food. I'd let you starve to death first.

GIOVANNI: Right! I'd rather starve than eat stolen food. Which reminds me, I never got any dinner. With all the fuss at the canteen I couldn't risk eating anything in case I got it free. What's for tea?

He sits at the kitchen table. ANTONIA *nervously selects a can at random and puts it in front of him.*

ANTONIA: Here you are.

GIOVANNI: What's that?

ANTONIA: It's good.

GIOVANNI: I know it's good, but what is it?

ANTONIA: Supermeat.

GIOVANNI: Supermeat?

ANTONIA: Supermeat for dogs.

GIOVANNI: What?

ANTONIA: It's very good.

GIOVANNI: It may be, for dogs!

ANTONIA: Nourishing, full of protein, prolongs active life. It says so. There wasn't anything else. And it's cheap.

GIOVANNI: You're joking.

ANTONIA: Who's joking? Ever tried shopping lately? You any idea of the prices nowadays? Everything's double what it was a few months ago. If they stock it. They're hoarding everything, it's the black market all over again. It's worse than wartime.

GIOVANNI: Don't overdo it. Worse than wartime! Anyway, I'm not having that. I'm not a dog yet! Give us a drink of milk then.

ANTONIA: There's no milk.

GIOVANNI: What do you mean, no milk?

ANTONIA: Apparently. Milk's gone up again, so this morning when the milkman came round, a whole bunch of louts – including CP friends of yours –

GIOVANNI: Not our branch.

ANTONIA: – jumped on the float and started giving out the milk at one hundred lira a litre.

GIOVANNI: Did you get some?

ANTONIA: What? Me? Buy half stolen milk? And would you have drunk it?

GIOVANNI: No, you're right.

ANTONIA: Good, then don't drink it.

GIOVANNI: I can't, can I?

ANTONIA: That's what I'm saying.

GIOVANNI: Isn't there anything else?

ANTONIA: Yes. I'll make soup.

GIOVANNI: Sounds good. What kind?

ANTONIA *selects a packet at random and puts it in front of him.*

ANTONIA: Millet.

GIOVANNI: Millet? What millet?

ANTONIA: Millet for canaries.

GIOVANNI: Millet for canaries?!

ANTONIA: Yes. Good for you. Great for diabetes.

GIOVANNI: I haven't got diabetes.

ANTONIA: Stops you getting it. Builds up a barrier. Anyway it costs half as much as rice. Which you don't like anyway.

GIOVANNI: Millet! First you try and turn me into a dog. Now into a canary.

ANTONIA: Well Gloria – you know the fourth floor – she makes it every day for her old man. She swears by it. The

secret is in the flavour. Luckily I've got the rabbits' heads
and if you give them a good boiling –

GIOVANNI: Rabbits' heads!

ANTONIA: Of course rabbits' heads! Blimey, if you don't
know that! Millet soup is made with rabbits' heads. Only the
heads, mind you, not the bodies, and they're frozen. That's
so they won't rot. Don't tell me you're against frozen food
now?

GIOVANNI: That's it. Goodbye. (*He starts to go*)

ANTONIA: Where are you going?

GIOVANNI: Where d'you think? The caff.

ANTONIA: What about money?

GIOVANNI: Oh yes. Give me some money.

ANTONIA: What money?

GIOVANNI: What do you mean, what money? You're not
going to tell me you've run out already?

ANTONIA: Have you forgotten tomorrow we have to pay the
gas, electric and rent? Or do you want to be evicted as well
as cut off?

GIOVANNI: Course not.

ANTONIA: Well then, the caff is out. But don't worry, I'll see
to it.

GIOVANNI: Where are you going?

ANTONIA: To Margherita's. She's been shopping. I'll borrow
from her.

GIOVANNI: But no rabbits' heads, please.

ANTONIA: Don't worry. I'll bring you the paws next time.
Bring you luck.

GIOVANNI: That's it. Have a good laugh! Go on. Blimey, I'm
starving. (*He picks up the tin*) 'Supermeat for dogs.
Homogenised, tasty.' Wonder what it tastes like? Hello,
she's lost the key, as usual. Wait a minute. Screwtop. (*He*

opens the tin) Doesn't smell too bad. Bit like pickled jam with a soupçon of truffled kidneys, laced with cod liver oil. A dog'd be a madman to eat this crap. Think I'll have a drop of lemon on top against the cholera. (*Police sirens*) What's all that? (*He calls out the window to neighbour opposite*) Aldo, what's going on? . . . Which supermarket? . . . No, my wife wasn't there! She's dead against these riots, even bought me rabbits' heads to prove it . . . No, she wasn't out at all today. She had to undo a friend's belly . . . Not like that! No, she made her undo the bandages . . . It's her husband, Luigi, he doesn't want her to get pregnant. But she listened to the Pope and so the pill didn't work and she swelled up overnight . . . You don't understand? Thick burk . . . Hello, they're really storming all over the place. Well, if they come here they'll get what for. This is just intimidation, sheer provocation!

SERGEANT *appears in window at rear, clinging to swaying drainpipe.*

SERGEANT: Oi!

GIOVANNI, *back to window, shoots arms up.*

GIOVANNI: O my good God. I'll get shot in the back resisting arrest.

SERGEANT *sways across window again.*

SERGEANT: Oi!

GIOVANNI: All right, all right. I'll come quietly.

SERGEANT *sways back into view.*

SERGEANT: Oi. You. Desist. (*He hooks a foot over window sill*)

GIOVANNI: Desist? Desist? I am desisting, aren't I? What more can I desist?

SERGEANT: Does this flat belong to you?

GIOVANNI: Yes.

SERGEANT: I order you to assist me.

GIOVANNI: Oh yeah? How? Beat myself up? Punch myself in the nuts?

SERGEANT: Help!

GIOVANNI: Stop mucking about.

SERGEANT: Help!

GIOVANNI: What a sense of humour. (*Now GIOVANNI turns round and sees policeman clinging to drainpipe with foot in saucepan on window sill*) I don't believe it. What are you playing at?

SERGEANT: Help! EEEEK!

GIOVANNI: (*Out front*) Now that's the law all over. Popping round to do you over they can't come in the door like everyone else. No: door's not good enough for the like of them. Oh no. Tell you what, there was this copper who wanted to get a new pair of boots – this'll kill you –

SERGEANT: No. It'll kill me. HELP!

GIOVANNI: Don't interrupt. Oh sorry.

SERGEANT: Get me out of this.

GIOVANNI: What's wrong with the door?

SERGEANT: Get me out of this.

GIOVANNI: What are you doing out there?

SERGEANT: It's a search.

GIOVANNI: Oh yeah? Find anything?

SERGEANT: We're searching your flat.

GIOVANNI: Oh yeah? Got a warrant?

SERGEANT: IF YOU DON'T GET ME –

GIOVANNI: All right. All right. Don't get shirty. (*Ad libs*)

SERGEANT *drops onto balcony and comes through french windows. Goes up behind GIOVANNI.*

GIOVANNI: (*Not realising who he's talking to*) There's a copper hanging out of the window.

SERGEANT: Oh really?

GIOVANNI: He wants to come in.

SERGEANT: Why doesn't he use the door?

GIOVANNI: (*Realising*) What do you want?

SERGEANT: It's a search.

GIOVANNI: Where's your warrant?

SERGEANT: Here's the warrant.

GIOVANNI: What for?

SERGEANT: What for? What for? Thousands of liras' worth of goods were looted from the supermarket today. And he asks me what for?

GIOVANNI: And you dare to come through my window without a shred of evidence? That's character assassination.

SERGEANT: Call it what you like.

GIOVANNI: I will.

SERGEANT: Suit yourself. Nothing to do with me. I follow my orders. That's all.

GIOVANNI: I see. I see. All right. All right then, do your worst.

SERGEANT: Right, I will.

GIOVANNI: But I warn you, this is intimidation, provocation and what's worse . . . it's not very nice. Oh yes. You keep us in a state of subjugation and starvation, then you come round here to take the piss. Look at what I've got to eat. Supermeat for dogs.

SERGEANT: I beg your pardon?

GIOVANNI: Yes, you see. Go on, have a look. Have a sniff of that. And you know why I have to endure this shite? Because real food costs a fortune. Yeah. And look at this. Rabbits' heads. Get your laughing gear around that.

SERGEANT: All right, all right. You've made your point.

SERGEANT *looks carefully round the room, then lifting the flap to his tunic pocket, he lifts two inches of* The Little Red

Book *out for an instant, then swiftly stuffs it down again.*
GIOVANNI *starts.*

GIOVANNI: What's that?

SERGEANT: All reactionaries are paper tigers.

GIOVANNI: Well knock me sideways with a feather! Sergeant,
if I didn't know better I'd say that was a little red book.

SERGEANT: (*Looks round flat*) Not a word. (*Slips pack of
cards to* GIOVANNI) That, my old son, is a source of
comfort to me on a cold night.

GIOVANNI *perplexed. Fans out cards.*

SERGEANT: That, sonny jim, represents the high point of
Eastern political thought. If you pardon the phrase.

GIOVANNI: Ace?

SERGEANT: Precisely. I knew you'd cop it. Well what do you
say to that?

GIOVANNI: Four no trumps?

SERGEANT: (*Noticing*) Oh sorry. Wrong box. Listen, you
working classes have got to stop seeing us police as ignorant
twits. You see us as creatures of habit with no brain. 'Here
boy, down boy, sit, sit, seize him!' A guard dog who can't
disagree or have an opinion. 'Heel, heel, lie down, down,
Rover.'

VOICE: (*Outside*) Sergeant!

SERGEANT: Up here, second floor! Next floor, lads.

GIOVANNI: All right, I take your point. Maybe we do see you
as thick as pigshit. Present company excepted. Of course.
After all we all started in the same class. Right? Sons of the
soil as we – as the Communists say.

SERGEANT: Sons of the soil. That's a laugh. Guard dogs for
the ruling class, defending their property, their right to
exploit, their fiddles, kickbacks.

GIOVANNI: Well, blimey, if you think like that, why did you
choose the job?

SERGEANT: Choose, choose? Did you choose to eat this crap, the rabbits' heads and the canary millet?

GIOVANNI: Course not. But there's no choice. There's nothing else.

SERGEANT: Exactly. Exactly. My point precisely. What choice did I have? Emigrate, sweep the streets or join the police. What would you do?

GIOVANNI: Must be terrible. But wait a minute. You've got to have the law, after all.

SERGEANT: Oh yeah? Really? Have you? What if the law's purely for the benefit of the rich? Eh? Eh?

GIOVANNI: Well, then you've got your democratic procedure. Laws can be reformed, you know.

SERGEANT: Oh really? Reform? Reform? Don't make me laugh. We've been hearing that for 30 years. Reforms. No mate. If the people want change they'll have to do it themselves. They'll have to melt the shackles of capitalism and the iron fist of oppression with the boiling blood of Karl Marx. 'Where the broom does not reach, the dust will not vanish of itself.' Know what I mean? Anyway, comrade, I better continue with this search or I'll get shot.

GIOVANNI: You see! Blimey, what a turn up. First you're talking like a raving subversive and next you're getting down to your job of turning over innocent people's homes. You kill me!

SERGEANT: Yeah, well, not today. Look, I'm only human. Obviously, at the moment, at this precise moment I haven't got the commitment and courage and the sheer get-up-and-go. Know what I mean?

GIOVANNI: 'At this moment.' At this moment I know what you mean. You're all left talk. You're all wind, mate. Giving me all this bollocks about having no choice but get into the police and sorry about that, but I can't help it smashing people over the head, but there you go! You should have taken the other road; emigrate or road sweep. Least you'd have your bleeding dignity intact. Know where you'll be tomorrow?

SERGEANT: No.

GIOVANNI: Beating me up on the picket line. That's where you'll be.

SERGEANT: You're so right. So terribly, tragically right.

GIOVANNI: Too right, I'm right.

SERGEANT: But. But. Nevertheless. The police have stood back on occasions, you know. Even dare I say, thrown themselves on the other side.

GIOVANNI: Oh yeah when?

SERGEANT: Venice Water Riots. August the 5th.

GIOVANNI: (*Impressed*) Oh.

SERGEANT: 1723.

GIOVANNI: Oh very relevant. Very topical. I won't hold me breath till it happens again.

SERGEANT: Ah ye of little faith. But remember 'A revolution is not a dinner party nor is it doing embroidery.' 'The wheel of history is turning.' Well I better get underway. Comrade. (*He exits*)

GIOVANNI: And good night! Well, fuck a brick! Whatever next. The died-in-the-wool, raving, steeped-in-Marxism out-and-out red copper! Right in there with the lunatic fascists, psycho bullies and subnormal everyday street coppers. Well that's where the bleeding extremists fetch up, obviously. In the police! And he's got the neck to stand there in front of me, twenty years a member, and criticise the CP! From the left too! Wait a minute! He was trying to get me going. That's it! That sly bastard. He was just trying to provoke me. Get me talking. 'Assault the bastions of Capital! Rebellion in the Police!' And if I fell for it and agreed with him: Wallop! 'Freeze. Red Brigade. You're under arrest.' Yeah, well, this little fish didn't fall for it. Not me. Not interested in the bait, mate. You'll need a better baited hook to catch this fish. Ah well, back to the dog food.

Enter ANTONIA *and* MARGHERITA. MARGHERITA *hides behind the door.*

GIOVANNI: What are you doing?

ANTONIA: Have they been here?

GIOVANNI: Who?

ANTONIA: They're searching every house.

GIOVANNI: Oh yes. I know.

ANTONIA: They've already arrested Mandetti and Fossani. They found stuff in their cisterns.

GIOVANNI: Good. That'll teach them.

ANTONIA: Oh very nice. They also took a load of gear that had been properly paid for. I suppose that's good too?

GIOVANNI: Well, that's what happens when unprincipled louts go grabbing stuff at random. The innocent suffer, too. At least we don't have to worry. They've been here already.

ANTONIA: They've been?

GIOVANNI: Sure.

ANTONIA: Did they find anything?

GIOVANNI: What was there to find?

ANTONIA: Nothing. I mean, you think you've got nothing and it turns out –

GIOVANNI: Turns out what?

ANTONIA: It turns out they've planted stuff on you to frame you. It's not the first time it's happened, you know. As they were searching Rosa's son's room – Rosa on the fifth floor – they planted a gun and a pile of leaflets under his bed.

GIOVANNI: Don't be daft. You think they're coming round here planting packets of cornflakes under our sofa.

ANTONIA: Well, I don't know. Not exactly under the sofa, I wouldn't say. It was just for argument's sake.

GIOVANNI: Come to think of it, you may be right! I better have a look.

ANTONIA: No!

GIOVANNI: Why not?

ANTONIA: Well, it's silly, it's daft. What's the point, mmmm, ummm, see? And keep your dirty mitts off of my cushions. I'll have a look. No. Nothing there. See?

GIOVANNI: Well I better check the cupboards.

ANTONIA *squeals*.

GIOVANNI: What was that?

ANTONIA: Margherita.

GIOVANNI: Margherita? Where?

ANTONIA: Outside. (*A quick look under the sofa*)

GIOVANNI: What did you leave her outside for? What's she doing out there? (*He opens the door*) Margherita, what are you doing there? Are you all right? Come in. What are you crying for?

MARGHERITA: Aoaaaooouuu!

ANTONIA: She's speechless.

GIOVANNI: I can see that.

ANTONIA: It's the shock of the police raid. She was on her own at home, when they came storming all over the kitchen. She was terrified. Then this inspector wanted to inspect her stomach.

GIOVANNI: The bastards. How can they – He wanted to *what*?

ANTONIA: He had this mad idea that she had food, packets of pasta and stuff, stuffed up there and she wasn't pregnant at all. I ask you!

GIOVANNI: Callous swine! How do you feel now?

ANTONIA: She's still speechless. Come on Margherita, sit down for a minute. I had to bring her round here, didn't I? I mean, I couldn't leave her.

GIOVANNI: Course not. Let's get her coat off.

MARGHERITA: No!

GIOVANNI: She's getting better already. She spoke! Just make yourself at home, dear.

ANTONIA: Leave her alone. She doesn't want to take her coat off. She's cold.

GIOVANNI: It's hot in here.

ANTONIA: It's hot for you. It's cold for her. Maybe she's got a temperature?

GIOVANNI: A temperature? Has she got something?

ANTONIA: What do you mean? Has she got something? Course she's got something. She's got a baby! What should she have?

MARGHERITA: Aaah!

GIOVANNI: What's that?

ANTONIA: In fact she's in labour.

GIOVANNI: Already?

ANTONIA: What do you mean already? What do you know? Half an hour ago he didn't even know she was pregnant. Now he's surprised she's in labour.

GIOVANNI: Well, it just seemed a bit quick. You don't think she's premature?

ANTONIA: You don't half go on. What would you know about her being premature or not? Suddenly you're the world's expert and know all about it and, I suppose, much more than we do! Stay there! Now dear, you get under the blankets. And you. Turn round. She's getting undressed.

MARGHERITA: No I'm not!

ANTONIA: Ssshhh. There there. It'll soon be over. Don't cry, we'll get out of this.

MARGHERITA: How?

GIOVANNI: Mmmm?

MARGHERITA: Owoowww.

GIOVANNI: Look, if she's in labour, we'd better get a doctor. Or better still an ambulance.

ANTONIA: Oh you're full of bright ideas you are. We call an ambulance and then drive all round Milan looking for a free bed. You know you have to book months in advance.

GIOVANNI: Why didn't she book then? You get nine months' warning with a pregnancy.

ANTONIA: Typical. Of course, it's down to us. Run the house, do the washing, have the babies, and book the beds. And why didn't Luigi do it?

GIOVANNI: He didn't know, did he? What was he supposed to do? Guess?

ANTONIA: Good excuse: 'He didn't know!' Ooo, that's so typical. You give us the pay packet, 'You'll have to manage on that,' insist on your conjugal rights, God forbid you should go without that, then we get pregnant, surprise, surprise, 'Well, go on the pill,' and not a thought for the poor woman who's a Catholic who has double feature nightmares every night, starring the Pope looming up and warning her: 'You're sinning, you know. You should bear children!'

GIOVANNI: Hang on a minute, never mind the conjugal whatsits and the Pope who, I agree is always trying to break our balls too, you know, in our dreams, never mind all that and the pill and the pay packet. When is she supposed to have got pregnant?

ANTONIA: What's it got to do with you? Prying sod! Then he complains about the Pope.

GIOVANNI: No, I meant, they've only been married five months.

ANTONIA: Why couldn't they have done it before? People do, you know. Or are you a bleeding moralist, worse than the Pope? Have you forgotten?

GIOVANNI: Of course not.

ANTONIA: I have.

GIOVANNI: No. But Luigi told me they only made love after they were married.

MARGHERITA: My Luigi has told you all these things? My God!

ANTONIA: There, you've upset her with your gossip. Fancy people telling all and sundry the intimate details of their life.

GIOVANNI: I'm not all and sundry. I'm his best friend! He asked my advice because I'm more experienced.

ANTONIA: Oh yeah. What at? Don't answer that.

A knock at the door.

ANTONIA: Who is it?

INSPECTOR: Police. Open up.

MARGHERITA: Oh my God, aaaaooouuu.

GIOVANNI: It's all right. We've been done.

Enter INSPECTOR, *who is the same actor as the* SERGEANT, *only he wears a moustache.*

GIOVANNI: Oh good evening. Hello, it's you again.

INSPECTOR: What do you mean, again?

GIOVANNI: Sorry. My mistake. For a minute I thought you were the one who was here before.

INSPECTOR: A likely story.

GIOVANNI: Yes there was. A police sergeant.

INSPECTOR: Well, I'm an inspector in the carabinieri.

GIOVANNI: I can see that, you've got a moustache –

INSPECTOR: Are you being witty at my expense?

GIOVANNI: No, no.

INSPECTOR: Right. We're searching here.

GIOVANNI: I told you. We've been done already.

INSPECTOR: Well, we'll do it again, won't we?

GIOVANNI: Oh I see, you're checking on each other. Then we'll have the customs police, the railway police, the Alpine regiment –

INSPECTOR: That's enough of that! We'll just get on with the job. (*He heads for the sofa*)

ANTONIA: Oh, we all have to get on with that. In our case sweating eight hours a day on the assembly line, like animals, and in your case making sure we behave and – most of all – pay the right price for everything. You don't ever check, for example, that the bosses keep their promises, pay what they've agreed, that they don't kill us with piecework, or by speeding up the line, or screw us with their three-day weeks, that they comply with the safety regulations and pay the proper compensation, that they don't just up the prices, chuck us out in the street or starve us to death!?

INSPECTOR *exits into wardrobe.*

GIOVANNI: That's pitching it a bit strong. Where's he gone? They don't all think like that you know.

ANTONIA: Whose side are you on?

GIOVANNI: Yours, of course, but the previous search party, the sergeant had had a bellyful of being ordered about. 'I'm just a doggy,' he said, 'who can't disobey. Down, boy, lie down, Rover.' So they're not all the same.

INSPECTOR: (*Emerging from cupboard suddenly*) What's all that? Rover? Where does this dog come into it?

GIOVANNI: He doesn't come into it at all. The sergeant said we think all policemen are ignorant twits, you see, servants of the most brutal exploiters, catspaws and watchdogs with no brains –

INSPECTOR: Right. That does it. Handcuff him!

GIOVANNI: What for?

INSPECTOR: For offending and insulting an officer of the law. And causing an affray.

GIOVANNI: What affray? What insults? You've got it wrong. I was merely making the point to my wife that the police aren't all the same and that the previous sergeant, the other one, took the view that *you* were all brainless servants of . . . of . . . of . . .

INSPECTOR: Who's you? Me? The police?

ANTONIA: Yes. No. I dunno. Giovanni.

GIOVANNI: I said, no *he* said, you, meaning them, the other police – the carabinieri.

ANTONIA: No!

GIOVANNI: *Not* the carabinieri. Naturally. Course not. I mean, would he?

INSPECTOR: Well, as his lot probably are brainless servants to the public. And quite right. Let him go. You be careful in future.

GIOVANNI: I will be. Don't worry.

INSPECTOR: Where was I? (*The* INSPECTOR *approaches sofa to finish search*)

ANTONIA: Moan. Go on moan.

MARGHERITA: Aaaoouu.

ANTONIA: Louder.

MARGHERITA: AAAAAOOOOOUUUIII.

INSPECTOR: My God. What's that? What's the matter with her?

ANTONIA: Can't you tell?

INSPECTOR: Not really.

ANTONIA: She's in labour, poor soul.

GIOVANNI: Premature birth. Five months, at least.

ANTONIA: She had a trauma earlier when the police wanted to check out her stomach.

INSPECTOR: Check out her stomach?

GIOVANNI: That's right. To see if she was hiding rice and spaghetti packets up there. I ask you! But of course she's just a working woman without any influence. She's not

Pirelli's wife who could cause a lot of trouble for you. So go ahead. How about an all round strip search –

MARGHERITA: Aaaooouuu!

GIOVANNI: You see? Go on, turn the place over, wreck everything, fingerprint the place, turn everything out, the wife's undies, why not? Turn the whole place upside down. X-ray the place.

INSPECTOR: Oi. Cut it out! This is incitement.

ANTONIA: Yes. Cut it out. You're overdoing it.

MARGHERITA: Aaaoooouuu!

ANTONIA: And don't you overdo it, either.

INSPECTOR: Have you called an ambulance?

GIOVANNI: An ambulance?

INSPECTOR: Well, that's the minimum facility you need to get her to hospital. In any case she might die on you. And if it's premature, she might lose the child.

GIOVANNI: He's right. I told you we should have called an ambulance.

ANTONIA: Yeah, and I told you she hasn't got a bed booked. She'll be driving round every hospital in town. She'll kick the bucket on the road.

Siren.

INSPECTOR: There's the ambulance we called for that woman who felt sick upstairs.

ANTONIA: Not Rosa? From the fifth floor?

INSPECTOR: I don't know. This is a real emergency. Come on, let's carry her down.

ANTONIA: Don't touch her. She's too nervous. She won't go.

MARGHERITA: No, I don't want to go to hospital!

ANTONIA: See, she doesn't want to go.

MARGHERITA: I want my husband.

ANTONIA: She wants her husband.

MARGHERITA: Luigi.

ANTONIA: Her husband, Luigi.

MARGHERITA: Luigi, Luigi.

ANTONIA: You see. She wants her husband. Who wouldn't? And him on nights. We can't take the responsibility without her husband's consent.

GIOVANNI: Now that's true. We can't.

INSPECTOR: Who can't. Will you take the responsibility when she dies on you?

ANTONIA: Why? What difference does it make at the hospital?

INSPECTOR: It'd be negligence. Their responsibility. You could sue.

GIOVANNI: But it's premature.

MARGHERITA: Yes, yes, I'm premature. Aaaaoooui!

ANTONIA: And with the jolting of the ambulance, she'll give birth. It can't survive in the back of an ambulance.

INSPECTOR: You've clearly no notion of the advances of modern medicine. You must have heard of oxygen tents.

GIOVANNI: What's a five-month premature baby going to do with an oxygen tent? Camp?

INSPECTOR: In extreme cases, they can even transplant them.

GIOVANNI and **ANTONIA:** Transplants?!

INSPECTOR: Yes. Easy as pie. They perform a caesarian operation . . .

MARGHERITA: Aaaaaoooouuu!

ANTONIA: Now look what you've done.

INSPECTOR: . . . and transfer the whole shebang, baby, placenta, the lot to another woman who's had another caesarian.

GIOVANNI: Another mother?

INSPECTOR: Exactly. Then they sew everyone up and Bob's your uncle. Five months later out it pops safe and sound and fit as a fiddle, yelling fit to bust.

ANTONIA: Sounds very dodgy to me.

GIOVANNI: A baby born twice. A child of two mothers.

MARGHERITA: No! I don't want to! Aaaaoooouuuu!

ANTONIA: She's right, poor girl. I'd never give my baby for another woman to deliver.

MARGHERITA: No I don't want to. Ugh. No, no.

ANTONIA: See? She doesn't want to. We can't cart her off if she doesn't want to go.

INSPECTOR: I can. On the grounds of diminished responsibility due to extreme pain. Never let it be said the carabinieri are unhelpful or turn their back on suffering.

ANTONIA: I protest. This is out and out violence. First they frisk us, then they wreck the place, then they handcuff us, now they want to load us on to ambulances without a by-your-leave. If they won't let us live as we want, at least let us die where we choose.

INSPECTOR: No. You can't die where you choose.

GIOVANNI: I knew there'd be a law against it.

INSPECTOR: Watch yourself.

ANTONIA: Leave off. Giovanni, it's no good, let's get her down.

INSPECTOR: I'll get the stretcher.

ANTONIA: No she'll walk. She's got enough troubles. You can walk, can't you?

MARGHERITA: (*Getting up*) Yes, yes. (*Lying down quick*) No, no. It's slipping.

ANTONIA: Damn it. Would you mind getting out a minute. My friend is a little bit naked and I've got to dress her.

INSPECTOR: Right. All out.

The men exit.

ANTONIA: Quick, pull up your bags! Typical, isn't it? You need a cop they're nowhere in sight. Then when you don't want them they're swarming all over the place. It's the same with the ambulance. I dunno.

MARGHERITA: I'm scared stiff. I knew it was going to end like this. What's going to happen when I get to the hospital and they find out I'm pregnant with shopping?

ANTONIA: Nothing'll happen. We're not going to the hospital.

MARGHERITA: You're right. We're going to prison.

ANTONIA: Oh stop whining. Pessimist. When we get into the ambulance we'll talk to the driver. They're good blokes. They'll help us.

MARGHERITA: And if they don't. If they drive straight round to the nearest nick?

ANTONIA: Oh, cut it out. They won't. They wouldn't dare.

MARGHERITA: It's slipping. Another bag. It's coming out.

ANTONIA: Hang on to it! Ooo, you're such a pain.

MARGHERITA: Don't shove! You'll bust something. (*They freeze*) Oh! You've bust something.

Olives shower down from a split bag.

ANTONIA: What?

MARGHERITA: A bag of olives has split and it's leaking all over me.

ANTONIA: You are a nuisance!

Re-enter men.

GIOVANNI: What's going on, now?

MARGHERITA: It's coming out, it's all coming out!

GIOVANNI: The baby's coming already. Don't panic. Inspector, quick, help me carry her!

INSPECTOR: (*Behind him*) I'm here.

GIOVANNI: Oh.

INSPECTOR: Stand aside, you haven't got the training.

ANTONIA: Now keep her horizontal, for God's sake.

GIOVANNI: Might it come shooting out?

INSPECTOR: She's dripping.

ANTONIA: Yes, she's broken water.

GIOVANNI: Is that good?

INSPECTOR: It means she's near her time! Hurry.

ANTONIA: All right, calm down. Gently with her.

MARGHERITA: Very gently! It's coming – Oooo it's coming!

ANTONIA: Hang on. Wrap her in this blanket. (*Wraps her in blanket*) Gently, Inspector, please.

GIOVANNI: I'll get my coat and come too.

ANTONIA: No. You stay here. This is women's business. You mop the floor.

GIOVANNI: Right. Right. I'll mop the floor. Don't worry about a thing. (*They've gone*) What a bleeding riot! Poor old Luigi'll get back knackered from the night shift and find himself a dad. He'll have a heart attack. When he finds out his child's been transplanted to another woman, he'll have a counter-attack. I'll have to break it to him gently. A really roundabout way. I'll start with the Pope. That's roundabout enough. (*Mopping*) Blimey, all this water. (*He's now crawling on all fours, mopping up the floor with the rag*) Blimey, all this water! But, what a strange smell, like vinegar . . . yeah, sort of brine, that's it. I'll be damned, I didn't know that before being born we spent nine months in brine?! Hello? . . . what's this now? An olive? Olives and brine? I can't believe it! No, I must be crazy. Olives don't come into it! Oh, look, there, another one! Two olives? If it wasn't for their rather uncertain origin, I'd eat them . . . I'm so hungry! I almost feel like making myself some millet soup. It might even be good. I'll stick in two stock-cubes . . . a head of onion . . . (*He opens the fridge*) What's my welding equipment doing here? I've told her not to use it to light the gas. (*He lights gas with it*)

LUIGI: Can I come in? Anybody home?

GIOVANNI: Hello, Luigi. Why aren't you at work?

LUIGI: (*Gasps*) This'll kill you.

GIOVANNI: There's a Cuban?

LUIGI: (*Gasps*) This'll kill you!!

GIOVANNI: A Cuban wants to kill me?!!

LUIGI: Something's happened. We all got to the factory gates this morning . . . This'll kill you – tell you in a minute . . . first, you seen the wife? I've been home, doors wide open, nobody there.

GIOVANNI: Ah. That's because she was here.

LUIGI: Oh good.

GIOVANNI: But she's popped out with Antonia. Ten minutes ago.

LUIGI: Oh. Where to? And what to do?

GIOVANNI: You know. Women's things.

LUIGI: What women's things?

GIOVANNI: You know. Women's business. None of our business.

LUIGI: What do you mean it's none of our business? It's some of my business.

GIOVANNI: Oh it is, is it? Suddenly, all of a sudden. Then how come you never booked a bed when you should have?

LUIGI: Booked a bed? What for?

GIOVANNI: What for? What for? Dear oh dear oh me. That's it. That's men all over. We give them the pay packet, 'You'll have to manage on that,' insist on the conjugal rights, get pregnant, 'Take the pill,' and nightmares, if you're a Catholic, featuring the Pope. Then it's the nappies and the nurseries . . .

LUIGI: Er. Giovanni. What are you talking about?

GIOVANNI: I'm saying we exploit them as surely as we are exploited by our boss!

LUIGI: Oh, that's what you're saying? But what has this to do with Margherita being out, leaving the door wide open, without so much as a little note and disappearing just like that?

GIOVANNI: Why should she leave a note when she expects you to be at work until breakfast time? Tell me that? And why aren't you at work?

LUIGI: The train was held up.

GIOVANNI: Broken down!

LUIGI: No. We held it up.

GIOVANNI: I know there's always breakdowns on that – You what?

LUIGI: Well, they put the season tickets up by thirty per cent!

GIOVANNI: How can you stop a train?

LUIGI: It's easy. You just pull the alarm. There's me, Tonino, Marco, we got down on to the tracks and held up all the other trains. You should have been there. Middle of nowhere.

GIOVANNI: What other trains?

LUIGI: All of them. Even the inter-city and the Paris Express. (*Eats olive*)

GIOVANNI: Oh, brilliant. Why couldn't I have thought of that? Ticket prices go up, so the entire European railway network has to be disrupted. Marvellous! Don't you realise these wild-man guerrilla tactics disrupting industry play right into the hands of the reactionaries?

LUIGI: Quite right. That's what I told the others. Totally senseless. Not worth trying to reduce the fares. We've got to abolish them completely.

GIOVANNI: No fares at all!?

LUIGI: Just what I said. The firm ought to pay. And they ought to pay us from the time we leave home. We're not sight-seeing when we're getting to work, we're getting to work.

GIOVANNI: What are you babbling about? I know. You've been talking to a lot of maniac provocateurs, infiltrators and police agents.

LUIGI: What, Tonino? Marco? Police agents? No. I thought them up myself. It wasn't difficult, you know. What is quite clear is that it's no good working people waiting for the government to do something, the union's intervention and a good word from your party. We have to stop expecting a white paper from the government and a strongly worded declaration of intent from the union every time we want to turn round and have a piss! If we don't do things for ourselves, then no one will.

GIOVANNI: You haven't been talking to a copper without a moustache?

LUIGI: You what?

GIOVANNI: That extremist copper that goes round trying to incite supermarket riots.

LUIGI: Never heard of him. (*Tasting dog food*) Here. Nice this. What is it?

GIOVANNI: Have you been eating that?

LUIGI: Yes, it's not bad. Sorry. Were you saving it?

GIOVANNI: You had it without lemon?

LUIGI: Should I put some lemon on it?

GIOVANNI: I don't know. Are you sure it tastes all right?

LUIGI: Yeah. Lovely.

GIOVANNI: Let me taste.

LUIGI: All right, innit?

GIOVANNI: Not bad. Want to start on this one? (*Passing other tin*)

LUIGI: Certainly. What is it?

GIOVANNI: A sort of pâté for rich cats and dogs.

LUIGI: Pâté for cats and dogs! Are you barmy?

GIOVANNI: No. A gourmet. Here. Taste this. (*Puts soup saucepan on the table*)

LUIGI: What is it?

GIOVANNI: Speciality of mine: millet soup garnished with frozen rabbits' heads.

LUIGI: Frozen?

GIOVANNI: That's so they won't rot. Speciality de la maison.

LUIGI: The millet's a bit underdone.

GIOVANNI: That's the secret of the recipe. Underdone millet, medium-done rabbits' heads. Oi. Who's gone and eaten that olive?

LUIGI: What olive? Oh, that olive. Shouldn't I have?

GIOVANNI: No, you shouldn't have. It was your wife's olive. Blimey, he even nicks the food from his baby's mouth.

LUIGI: My wife's olive. The baby's mouth. Here. What are you talking about?

GIOVANNI: Don't you know nothing? You heard of natural childbirth, the rhythm method? You have heard of biology?

LUIGI: No. Not a lot.

GIOVANNI: When you're born, there's all this brine sort of stuff, dribbling about, see? Wait a minute. I'll start from the beginning. Right. Take it step by step. Now there's Pope Paul, right, nagging all the women and scaring the pants off them with pregnancy –

LUIGI: The Pope's pregnant?

GIOVANNI: Not him. Your wife. I'm talking about your wife.

LUIGI: Has my wife been seeing the Pope?

GIOVANNI: I see, pretend you don't know.

LUIGI: No, I don't know! What's all this about the Pope?

GIOVANNI: You know what the Pope says in your wife's dreams?

LUIGI: I've no idea.

GIOVANNI: 'Don't take the pill,' my son.

LUIGI: But she doesn't take the pill.

GIOVANNI: So you *do* know.

LUIGI: Know what?

GIOVANNI: She doesn't take the pill.

LUIGI: I just told you.

GIOVANNI: Who's told you?

LUIGI: Nobody's told me. I know already. No point in the pill. She can't have kids, something wrong with the waterworks.

GIOVANNI: Nothing at all wrong with her waterworks, mate. I've just had to mop it all up.

LUIGI: You've mopped up my wife's waterworks?!

GIOVANNI: Well, not exactly water, more like brine. And a few olives. You've just eaten one.

LUIGI: You've lost me. Can we go back to the Pope?

GIOVANNI: No thanks. Look, Margherita had herself all bandaged up and Antonia made her undo it and, wallop, out it popped.

LUIGI: My Margherita?

GIOVANNI: Now they've gone off to hospital in an ambulance as she was about to give birth in here.

LUIGI: Here?

GIOVANNI: No there. (*Pointing to couch*)

LUIGI: Don't piss about. Where's my wife?

GIOVANNI: Told you, in hospital.

LUIGI: Which hospital?

GIOVANNI: Who knows. If you had booked it, we'd know, wouldn't we? As it is the poor little bleeder will probably be born in the ambulance on the way there with all them olives.

LUIGI: Will you leave the olives out of this! Tell me which hospital she's gone to.

GIOVANNI: It's the gynaecological clinic.

LUIGI: Do you mean the baby clinic?

GIOVANNI: Where they transplant the premature baby from one belly to another.

LUIGI: Transplants?

GIOVANNI: Yeah?

LUIGI: Baby transplants??

GIOVANNI: Oh. You've heard of it.

LUIGI: No.

GIOVANNI: That's it. It's obvious you're totally ignorant of modern techniques of premature delivery.

LUIGI: Yes, I am.

GIOVANNI: They get a baby tent, blow it up, like, with oxygen, then they put the mothers under . . . No, it's the fathers . . . No, I mean the kid, then they take the other mother after she's had her caesarian, fully automatic . . .

LUIGI: Cut it out will you!

GIOVANNI: Exactly what they do!!

LUIGI: I don't give a monkey's about no baby tent, transplant or fully automatic caesarian. I want to know where this gynaecology place is. Where's the phone book?

GIOVANNI: I haven't got one.

LUIGI: Why not?

GIOVANNI: No phone.

LUIGI: I'm going down the bar. They've got one.

GIOVANNI: Hold it. Niguarda! Niguarda clinic!

LUIGI: Niguarda. Blimey, that's the other side of town. Why have they taken her that far?

GIOVANNI: I told you. It's where they've developed this special technique. The transplant. They get the other woman. The first one prepared to take the child off the donor, a friend perhaps, and they take her into the hospital – some dozy old cow who's loony enough to contemplate the idea in the first place. Anyway they get this woman – My wife! She's so stupid she'll say yes straight away. Come on we've got to make this phone call. Luigi, I'm sorry to say this, but I can't give my permission.

LUIGI: Who's asking?

GIOVANNI: But I'm the next of kin.

LUIGI: Not to me you ain't.

GIOVANNI: I am the husband.

LUIGI: No, no, no. You're the husband to the second mother. I'm the husband to the first mother.

GIOVANNI: But the transplanted mother is mine!

LUIGI: I don't give a monkey's. I'm giving my permission and that's that.

GIOVANNI: Are you sure?

LUIGI: No.

GIOVANNI: I tell you if you go ahead with this, I'll pack her off to live with you.

LUIGI: She already does.

GIOVANNI: *My wife*, I mean. You can keep her. If she's going to feed your kid, you can keep me too.

LUIGI: Why you too?

GIOVANNI: I'm the other father, ain't I?

LUIGI: Yeah, but I'm the first father.

GIOVANNI: Yeah, but I'm the first other other father.

They exit ad libbing.

ACT TWO

ANTONIA: (*Off*) Giovanni? Giovanni? Can I borrow your spanner? (*Enters*) Thank God. He's not in. Blimey, look at the time, we've been gone for more than four hours. Come on Margherita, come in. He must have already gone to work, he can't even have had a kip yet poor old sod. Y'know Ma . . . (*Opens door*) You dozy cow.

MARGHERITA: Is he in?

ANTONIA: No he's not. Come in.

MARGHERITA: It's all your fault. You never listen to me. Look at the mess we're in.

ANTONIA: Oh, stop whining. Blimey what a pain. We haven't been caught out yet. The ambulance men were great.

MARGHERITA: Yes, they were.

ANTONIA: And you were worried about it! You've got to trust people. Who's nicked the butter? (*Looking in fridge*) Oh, here it is. I'll make some soup. Hello, what's this? (*Tastes*) Oh, Giovanni. He's made some soup. Ohh. Can your Luigi look after himself when you're not around? Mmmm nice aroma. Oh millet! Very experimental. Wonder what else he's put in it . . . Rabbits' heads!!! You can't even tell a lie without him swallowing it. I'll make some proper soup. You should hear the fuss when I put something in front of him.

Well, I'll show him. Rabbits' heads with raspberry yoghurt. Rabbits' heads with custard. Rabbits' heads with chicken liver and brown sauce. It'll be curried rabbits' heads from now on. Here, you've gone all green, Margherita.

MARGHERITA: Listen, if you're only making the soup for me, don't bother.

ANTONIA: Oh go on.

MARGHERITA: I'm not hungry suddenly. My stomach is all knotted up.

ANTONIA: This'll unknot it for you. You shouldn't be so nervous. Most people are decent underneath. Not everybody, of course. But people like us. Working people having a job making ends meet. People like that are on our side, as long as you show them you won't let the bosses kick you in the teeth, that you're prepared to fight for your rights, and don't wait for St Peter to leave his pearly gates and come down and do it all for you. I remember when I worked at the biscuit factory. What a bloody job. But it was a living. Then suddenly the owners decided to 'rationalise' the place, as they call it, because profits were down. In fact, they were only kicking us out because they were planning to close it completely. So we occupied the place. Three hundred of us. Then we started to run the place, we formed a co-operative. Especially the union leaders. 'It's a losing battle, brothers,' they told us. But do you know what? All of us put every penny we could spare into the factory. Some people put their savings in and one bloke even sold his flat. All of us pawned silver and stuff that we never saw again. Sheets and blankets even. That's how we got our first bag of flour. We went round the shops ourselves with the biscuits and sold them at the factory gates. Plenty of people bought biscuits they didn't need, just to help us out. And to show solidarity. Then when things got bad for us, thousands of workers collected money for us. I'll never forget when they brought the money in. We were all kneading the dough as usual and they put the money on the table. All wrapped up in a big dishcloth – a great big pile, and all the women started to cry like rain into the dough. Nobody moved and nobody spoke. We just went on mixing tears and dough for biscuits. What are you crying for now?

MARGHERITA: It's the story . . .

ANTONIA: Well what about it?

MARGHERITA: It's so moving. I'm dripping everywhere.

ANTONIA: Yeah, well, before we all get drowned, just you have a think about what I'm saying. It's not just a fairy story, you know. It ain't got a happy ending.

MARGHERITA: What happened?

ANTONIA: The CP moved in, didn't they? 'You can't last out,' they said. So they persuaded us to negotiate with the management. That was the end of it. Two months later the factory closed down. Another 300 jobs up the spout. The fights I had with Giovanni about that. I nearly left him. Reformist git. Anyway, enough of all that. What are you doing?

MARGHERITA: Unloading. (*She is taking the shopping off*)

ANTONIA: Not here. We'll stash the stuff in Dad's allotment shed. It's only round the corner. The gear'll be safe there. I'll make myself a big belly, too. In two or three trips we'll be done.

MARGHERITA: No. No. No, no, no, no. I'm dead tired and I'm not going on. I'm leaving the lot here. I don't want any of it.

ANTONIA: You dozy cow.

MARGHERITA: I see, I'm a dozy cow, am I? Well, you with all your bright ideas can work out what I'm going to tell my old man when he discovers that I'm not pregnant after all.

ANTONIA: That's simple. We'll tell him you had a phantom pregnancy.

MARGHERITA: What's that?

ANTONIA: Happens all the time. A woman thinks she's pregnant, her belly swells up and then, when the baby's about to come out, she just gives birth to a lot of wind.

MARGHERITA: That's not very nice. How could that happen to me?

ANTONIA: Simple. Because of the Pope keeping coming into your dreams and telling you: 'Havea da child, my childa.' And you made a child, only it was a lot of hot air. Like the Pope.

MARGHERITA: Antonia! How can you drag the Pope into this business?

ANTONIA: Well, he's always dragging us into his business, isn't he? Do this, do that, all you wops keep off my grass. Why can't women be priests? You could be a good priest Margherita. You're a good listener.

MARGHERITA: Do you think so?

ANTONIA: Right, I'm ready. I'll be back in ten minutes. Keep an eye on the soup.

MARGHERITA: Why can't we forget the belly business and take the shopping bags over in one trip?

ANTONIA: And what will you do when the law stops you? Now watch the gas and if it goes out light it with that thing.

MARGHERITA: What's that?

ANTONIA: It's Giovanni's welder. Light it like this. (ANTONIA *shows her*)

MARGHERITA: Doesn't it get red hot?

ANTONIA: No. It's not iron. It's some stuff called antimony and it gets really hot without ever glowing. So don't touch it. Now let's see if the coast's clear.

They go to the window.

MARGHERITA: That's Maria.

ANTONIA: From the third floor.

MARGHERITA: She's pregnant, too.

ANTONIA: The men'll be at it soon.

MARGHERITA: What, pregnant?!

ANTONIA: No hunchbacks. Right. I'm off. Don't forget this. (*Starts for the door*)

MARGHERITA: I've changed my mind. I'm coming with you. (*Loads up*)

ANTONIA: Good. You've been thinking about my biscuit factory.

MARGHERITA: Yes. But I'm willing to co-operate.

ANTONIA: You know, all this out here reminds me of my baby.

MARGHERITA: Your baby?

ANTONIA: Nearly a man now. Couldn't wait to get out and get a job. He got out all right, but he's still waiting for a job.

MARGHERITA: What's a job? I've forgotten what it was when you could get one.

ANTONIA: Yeah, mind you, they won't break his spirit. He'll just get cross. If they get on the wrong side of him they'll know what for. Right! Are you ready?

Both exit.

The street. LUIGI enters, walking determinedly, followed by the exhausted GIOVANNI.

GIOVANNI: Luigi, I'm knackered. (*He sits*) If they say on the phone that your wife isn't at their hospital, do we have to check it out? Don't you trust them?

LUIGI: Would you? With baby transplants?

GIOVANNI: Now you mention it, no. But my feet are killing me.

LUIGI looks skyward.

LUIGI: Oh no.

GIOVANNI: What?

LUIGI: Rain.

GIOVANNI: Shit.

LUIGI: Bloody government.

GIOVANNI: Look, let's give up. I'm getting off to work. I've lost time already.

LUIGI: (*Remembering*) Oh yeah. I wanted to tell you something about that. About the firm.

GIOVANNI: (*Loud crash*) What's that? Hold it. Wait a minute. Look at that!

LUIGI: Jesus. What a mess.

GIOVANNI: It's a juggernaut.

LUIGI: Must have skidded and jack-knifed.

GIOVANNI: Someone better watch all them sacks or someone's liable to nick them.

Enter SERGEANT *from right.*

SERGEANT: All right. Keep calm. Don't panic. Stand back. It's all right. No one's hurt. Don't panic. (*Exit left*)

LUIGI: Who's panicking?

GIOVANNI: Hello. Keep meeting, him and me.

LUIGI: Know him?

GIOVANNI: Good mates. I can't work him out. He's either a Maoist or an agent provocateur . . .

LUIGI: Agent provocateur. Definitely.

GIOVANNI: Just what I said.

Enter SERGEANT.

SERGEANT: Stand back, there. That's dangerous stuff. It could blow any time.

GIOVANNI: That won't blow. That's caustic soda. That's what it says on the lorry.

SERGEANT: Yes. Well. That's what it says on the outside. But appearances can be deceiving.

GIOVANNI: You don't trust anything do you?

SERGEANT: I know you, don't I?

GIOVANNI: Yeah. You was round my house.

SERGEANT: Oh yeah. Anyway, things aren't always what they seem.

GIOVANNI: Blimey, mate. We're talking about clearly labelled International Road Transport. We're talking about Common Market regulations! We're talking about border certificates in triplicate! And I'm talking about something else. When this rain gets into that soda it's going to smoulder into a right smelly old pudding. So someone ought to get that stuff out of the rain.

SERGEANT: You're right. How we going to do that?

LUIGI *taps* GIOVANNI's *shoulder.*

GIOVANNI: Shouldn't be too much of a problem.

LUIGI: Giovanni.

GIOVANNI: Well, let's have a look.

LUIGI: Giovanni.

GIOVANNI: Best thing is form a chain . . .

LUIGI: Giovanni.

GIOVANNI: . . . mobilise those fellows over there, get all the stuff back over there.

SERGEANT: Very good idea. I'll get them going, you man this area. Brilliant idea.(*Goes off left*) Oi! You lot! Give us a hand here.

GIOVANNI: Fuck me and my big ideas.

LUIGI: You'll never listen and never learn, will ya?

SERGEANT *re-enters.*

SERGEANT: (*Organising*) OK, spread out. Pass them along. That's the way!

Sacks are thrown from left to LUIGI *to* GIOVANNI *and off right.*

GIOVANNI: See that? You ask for help and you've got it. You shouldn't be such a pessimist. Look at that. All mucking in.

SERGEANT: I never said people weren't generous.

GIOVANNI: No, but you're still a mistrustful old berk. I had a boss once like you. He couldn't trust anyone except this mangy old dog of his. He loved this dog and he decided to buy him a deaf-aid.

LUIGI: A deaf-aid?

GIOVANNI: That's right.

LUIGI: For a dog?

GIOVANNI: That's right. So he bought this deaf-aid and he strapped the battery to the dog's belly.

LUIGI: So what happened?

GIOVANNI: The first time the dog cocked his leg to have a piss, he pissed on the battery and electrocuted himself to death.

They laugh. SERGEANT *looks puzzled.*

SERGEANT: There's a moral to that story. Can't think what.

LUIGI: Where's the drivers?

GIOVANNI: Gone for help?

SERGEANT: No, done a bunk.

GIOVANNI: Why?

SERGEANT: Let's have a look.

They all poke a finger into the neck of a sack and taste the contents.

SERGEANT: Sugar.

LUIGI: Flour.

GIOVANNI: Rice! Someone's made a mistake with the labelling.

LUIGI: Fancy that.

SERGEANT: Just as I thought. It's containered at the depot and the seals aren't broken till they get there. They're flogging it round Europe. You get better prices in Switzerland. Just a bit of funny book-keeping, a few forged papers and no one's the wiser.

LUIGI: Unless they happen to turn over on the road. They're telling the truth for once when they talk about shortages. They're running it all out of the country. No wonder there's a shortage.

GIOVANNI: Shortage? Shortage? What about the butter mountain? The Beaujolais lake? The Leaning Tower of Pizza? That's not shortage. That's excessage.

SERGEANT: You clearly don't understand the working of your Common Market.

GIOVANNI: I certainly don't. Fill me in, *do*.

SERGEANT: It's to do with the Greek and Portuguese economy.

GIOVANNI: They're not in the Common Market.

SERGEANT: Exactly. But they will be and then you need a strong Deutschmark.

LUIGI: O yeah?

SERGEANT: Course. Your German economy is dependent on the car industry, but hardly anybody can afford them dirty great German Mercedes and BMWs.

LUIGI: So?

SERGEANT: Simple. You pay your French farmer dirty great subsidies to pay for the dirty great German cars.

GIOVANNI: You've lost me.

LUIGI: It's simple. It's like the Irish pigs.

GIOVANNI: Course it is.

LUIGI: They keep driving them backwards and forwards over the border of Northern Ireland picking up Common Market subsidies every time. They call it 'take your pick, every trip'.

SERGEANT: That's it. See? Simple.

LUIGI: Only thing is the British Army get annoyed. Every time the pigs stampede they get trampled underfoot.

SERGEANT: Take this lorry, for instance. You drive all over Europe and every time you cross a border you pick up your subsidies. *And* you save labour costs because you never have to unload it.

GIOVANNI: You'll have to take action.

SERGEANT: Oh, I will! Most definitely.

GIOVANNI: What's the matter now?

SERGEANT: Do you want to know what'll happen from here? I shall write a full report, a model of brevity and procedure, the result of which charges will be laid. A brief item on News at Ten will allude to a brilliant police operation where contraband has been seized and men are sought. Duly alerted by the said item the industrialists will take a quick fortuitous trip over the border. Having laid my evidence before the judge, he will, with a pained expression, because it's a bit like welching on your own kind, sentence them to four months. The industrialists will hear about this whilst sunning themselves on the beaches of St Tropez and will immediately appeal to the President who will commute the sentence to a stiff fine.

GIOVANNI: And that's the end of it?

SERGEANT: By no means. They'll appeal the stiff fine and get off with a stiff talking to.

LUIGI: You what?

SERGEANT: And they get their sugar, rice and flour back. (*Looks off left*) Oi! Where are you going with them bags? (*Exits*)

GIOVANNI: It's criminal, that's what it is.

LUIGI: Mr Gullible. (*Making a decision*) Grab a bag.

GIOVANNI: What for?

LUIGI: We're going to whip a couple.

GIOVANNI: Oh yeah?

LUIGI: Oh yeah!

GIOVANNI: Are you out of your mind? Are you descending to the level of that rabble over there?

LUIGI: That's right. That rabble over there! Blimey, what is all this middle-class shit? You sound like a Social Democrat – all right, not that bad.

GIOVANNI: I don't steal what isn't mine.

LUIGI: Well you're all right, because it is yours. So steal away. Blimey, do I have to spell it out to you? Who produces it? Who sows it? Who reaps it? Who processes it and packs it? Who cooks it and eats it?

GIOVANNI: Luigi. You're looking after Number One. It's a slippery slope you're on. You won't have a principled bone left in your body soon. That's just the excuse they want.

LUIGI: Who?

GIOVANNI: The military? That's who! They only have to call this a breakdown in law and order and they can roll out the troops and the tanks, suspend the constitution, and before you can say fettuccine, we have fascism.

LUIGI: Oh? What do you suggest then?

GIOVANNI: Legal action through the unions.

LUIGI: Oh, terrific.

GIOVANNI: Against the unions are we? All right. All right. Who mobilised the entire workforce at Fiat's to strike in the dinner hour?

LUIGI: Who organised the women today? Not the unions. The women rioted because they can't take any more. See these hands? They want what's theirs. But your union leaders and your precious party tie them behind our backs. And that's when the army take over. Not when you're on the offensive, but when you're being led up the garden. No. What we want's leadership, mate. Oh, by the way, that reminds me, I was going to tell you about the firm.

GIOVANNI: Yes?

LUIGI: What's the union doing about that?

GIOVANNI: Doing about what?

  INSPECTOR *approaches unobserved.*

INSPECTOR: What's going on here?

LUIGI: Do you mind not interrupting?

INSPECTOR: What's going on?

LUIGI: Bugger off. (*Seeing* INSPECTOR) Oh! We're slogging away here for the balance of payments.

GIOVANNI: Blimey, don't he look like the other one?

LUIGI: You're right. The one without the moustache.

INSPECTOR: What you on about?

LUIGI: Forget it.

INSPECTOR: What are you doing holding them bags?

LUIGI: These?

INSPECTOR: I don't see any other type of bags littering the place.

LUIGI: Oh. We're moving them to a safe place.

INSPECTOR: Where did they come from?

LUIGI: Fell off the back of a lorry.

INSPECTOR: I bet.

GIOVANNI: Trying to be helpful, that's all.

INSPECTOR: Yeah. Helping yourself.

GIOVANNI: Ask the sergeant. He said to move them. He asked us to.

INSPECTOR: Which sergeant?

GIOVANNI: Over there.

INSPECTOR *pulls pistol and* LUIGI *and* GIOVANNI *shoot their hands up.*

INSPECTOR: Don't you move a muscle. You'll get shot. (*Off left*)

LUIGI: Now we'll go and get shot.

GIOVANNI: Yeah. The police have a funny habit of accidentally shooting people on purpose.

LUIGI: Bastard.

GIOVANNI: Mind you, he's all right. He's the one who helped your wife into the ambulance with the olives.

LUIGI: Stuff the olives. (*Remembering*) Oh yeah. The firm. I've been trying to tell you. We've been made redundant.

GIOVANNI: We haven't. Nobody told me.

LUIGI: We have. Everyone in the night shift got a dear John from the management. You'll get yours. They're closing down and moving somewhere else.

GIOVANNI: We're supposed to have a full order book.

LUIGI: They're going to move somewhere where the labour is cheaper.

GIOVANNI: Labour doesn't come any cheaper than us!

LUIGI: It does now.

GIOVANNI stands thinking, hands up. Then dropping them suddenly.

GIOVANNI: That's it. I'm finished. Pass me my bag.

LUIGI: You can't do that.

GIOVANNI: Who can't? It's ours, ain't it?

They start to exit right with bags. INSPECTOR enters left.

INSPECTOR: Oi. Freeze!

Pause.

GIOVANNI: Inspector. Catch.

GIOVANNI throws bag high in the air. LUIGI throws a bag to GIOVANNI and grabs another.

LUIGI: Run! – (*Exit pursued by* INSPECTOR)

Another part of town. GIOVANNI cycles on with LUIGI and two sacks on the crossbar.

GIOVANNI: Another hundred yards and we've made it.

LUIGI *falls off.*

Stop mucking about.

LUIGI: I still think you shouldn't have nicked the bike.

GIOVANNI: I haven't nicked it. I told you. I've liberated it.

LUIGI: Liberated? What if it belongs to a poor blind granny?

GIOVANNI: What's a poor blind granny doing on a bike?

LUIGI: Forty miles an hour.

GIOVANNI: Blimey, a police van. Outside my house.

LUIGI: Here, look, those two women. Isn't that your old lady?

GIOVANNI: No. Looks like yours though.

LUIGI: They're going into your block. That one's pregnant.

GIOVANNI: You're right. No look. They're both pregnant.

LUIGI: Oh yes. It can't be them. It must be two others completely.

GIOVANNI: Shit. Look.

LUIGI: What. What?

GIOVANNI: That bleeding copper has been following us. With half the town doing all the nicking why does he have to pick on us?

LUIGI: He knows where you live. That's why. He'll be waiting round your house for when you get there.

GIOVANNI: You're right. All right, we'll go round your house. He won't think of that.

They exit right. After a moment the INSPECTOR *puffs across the stage still carrying his bag. Blackout.*

ANTONIA's *flat.* ANTONIA *and* MARGHERITA *are discovered hanging shopping round their necks and buttoning their coats over it.*

ANTONIA: Come on Margherita. Let's load up. This is the last trip.

MARGHERITA: Thank goodness. Load up. Unload. Load up. Unload. I feel like a lorry.

ANTONIA: Stop moaning.

MARGHERITA: Look, enough salad to last a month.

ANTONIA: Yes, I went a bit mad on the salad. I hope we don't get caught this trip. I'd hate to get frisked with a belly full of celery.

MARGHERITA: You've got a point there.

ANTONIA *at the gas stove.*

ANTONIA: Oh shit. The soup hasn't cooked. They've cut the gas off. It'll be the electricity next. Bloody bastards.

Knock, knock.

Who is it?

INSPECTOR: (*Off*) I've a message from your husband.

ANTONIA: Oh my God, something happened! (*Starts to the door*)

MARGHERITA: Antonia! The salad!

ANTONIA: Stuff it! (*They hastily conceal bags of salad*) Can you wait? I'm only half-naked.

INSPECTOR *enters carrying bag of flour.*

INSPECTOR: Stop. Turn round. Don't touch a thing. Caught red-handed. You can't fool me with those bellies of yours.

ANTONIA: What you on about?

MARGHERITA: Here we go. I knew it. Aaaaoouuu!

INSPECTOR: Madam, congratulations. I'm happy to see you didn't lose your child. (*To* ANTONIA) And to you too, madam. In five hours you've made love, got pregnant and appear to be about in the ninth month of your confinement! It's a miracle.

ANTONIA: You better watch it cos my husband will . . .

INSPECTOR: Will what?

ANTONIA: Be home soon.

INSPECTOR: Right, open up. Let's have it.

ANTONIA: Have what?

INSPECTOR: Persistent little jailbird, aren't we? Don't think I haven't worked out the *modus operandi* with the belly.

There was a point today when I thought that I was going mad. Every single woman – from nymphets of eight to great-grandmothers of eighty-eight – pregnant!

ANTONIA: Well, exactly. There you are. That explains it. Doesn't it. (*Improvising*) Surely you have heard of the Feast of St Eulalia.

INSPECTOR: I can't say I have and what's that to the point?

ANTONIA: Yes. St Eulalia, the patron saint of fertility.

INSPECTOR: St Eulalia? Fertility? What's all this fertility? St Eulalia . . .

ANTONIA: Er.

MARGHERITA: St Eulalia, the woman who was barren until she was sixty and then was miraculously blessed with a child by our Lord.

INSPECTOR: Sixty years old?

ANTONIA: Yes. Her old man was eighty. Not up on our saints are we? Mind you, he did die. To celebrate this miracle the women in this area go about with fake stomachs.

INSPECTOR: What a touching tradition. And the tradition gives you *carte blanche* to loot supermarkets, what's more. Amazing, the power of religion in this day and age. Right, that's enough nefarious twaddle. Open up.

ANTONIA: Oh yes, have the clothes off our backs! That's it! Go ahead! If you lay one finger on our bellies a terrible thing will happen to you.

INSPECTOR: Like what?

ANTONIA: Yes . . .

MARGHERITA: The curse of St Eulalia.

ANTONIA: Yeah, that.

INSPECTOR: What curse?

ANTONIA: The same curse that befell her old man. When he first saw her with child. 'You pregnant? Do us a favour! Show us what you've got under there! And if you *are* pregnant I'll do you in because I can't be the father, that's for certain.' So St Eulalia exposed herself, so to speak, and out poured a cascade of roses.

INSPECTOR: What a lovely little story.

ANTONIA: Wait for it. I haven't finished yet. Soon after a heavy darkness fell on his eyes. 'I can't see,' he shouted, 'I'm going blind.' And then a minute later, 'I am blind!' Then St Eulalia said, 'See what God does to unbelievers.'

INSPECTOR: This gets better and better.

MARGHERITA: Yes, it does.

ANTONIA: Really?

MARGHERITA: Of course!

ANTONIA: Well, all right then. And then there was a third miracle. From out of the masses of roses pops a little child ten months old already. Speaking perfect Italian with a perfect set of teeth. 'Papa,' he says, 'the Lord forgives you.' Then he touches the old man, who was quite surprised, on the head, who falls down dead there and then. But peacefully.

INSPECTOR: You finished? Right, come on, let's see the roses.

ANTONIA: Well that's enough isn't it?

INSPECTOR: Right, come on, let's see the roses.

ANTONIA: So you're a disbeliever?

INSPECTOR: Yes. Very.

ANTONIA: You're not afraid of the curse?

INSPECTOR: What curse? Do me a favour!

ANTONIA: Right you've asked for it. Margherita, we'll expose ourselves together. Do the poem.

MARGHERITA: The poem?

ANTONIA: Yeah, the poem.

MARGHERITA: *The* poem.

ANTONIA: Yes, the exposure poem.

MARGHERITA: Oh, the exposure poem. St Eulalia, pregnant saint,
He that says that there ain't
In your deeds no miracles,
In your words no oracles.
Make his vision dark and thick,
Make the bastard bloody sick.
St Eulalia touch his head,
Make him fall down completely and utterly dead!

ANTONIA: Right, Margherita.

They throw open their coats and reveal string bags bursting with salad.

INSPECTOR: Gor'blimey. What's all that?

ANTONIA: Good Lord. It's salad. Fancy that.

INSPECTOR: It's salad.

ANTONIA: You're right. Lettuce, chicory, celery, carrots, cabbage.

MARGHERITA: I've got cabbage, too. And a teensy bit of parsley.

ANTONIA: So you have. You know that's really difficult to get . . .

INSPECTOR: What's going on? What's all those greens for? Why are they so hid?

ANTONIA: They're not so hid. It's a miracle.

INSPECTOR: Oh yes? The cabbage miracle. Where's the roses?

MARGHERITA: Who can afford roses? They're very expensive.

ANTONIA: In hard times, one makes what miracles one can. With the veg you've got handy. Anyway, miracles aren't illegal, you know.

INSPECTOR: Don't be so sure of it.

ANTONIA: Also, there's no law that says a person can't carry a mixed salad à la carte on their belly.

INSPECTOR: Don't bank on it.

ANTONIA: A few crudities, can't hurt.

INSPECTOR: Don't be filthy. But what does it all mean?

ANTONIA: Mean? Mean? I've told you. To celebrate St Eulalia. We have to carry a belly around for three days on pain of some fearful, terrible . . . pain. You can be struck – *The lights flicker for a moment and die.*

INSPECTOR: It's getting dark.

ANTONIA: Oh really?

INSPECTOR: There's something wrong with your light.

ANTONIA: What light? What's wrong with my light?

INSPECTOR: It's gone out. It's dark.

ANTONIA: No it hasn't. What a funny idea! It's as light as day – oh, I see, you're a comedian. He's having us on.

INSPECTOR: No. No, it's dark.

ANTONIA: I can see perfectly well. Can't we Margherita?

MARGHERITA: Not really, no. (ANTONIA *kicks her*) Yes, yes. Clear as day.

ANTONIA: Yes, we can both see – oh blessed saint he's going blind.

MARGHERITA: Oh no!

INSPECTOR: Look, don't muck about. Switch on the light, please.

ANTONIA: Of course, but it won't help. Look. Off. On. Off. On. See?

INSPECTOR: No! See, see. No I can't see. D'you see?

ANTONIA: Oh my God, the Lord has punished this man.

MARGHERITA: Yes he has.

INSPECTOR: Open the window. Quick.

ANTONIA: It's open already.

MARGHERITA: He can't see it.

ANTONIA: Come and have a look. (*Moves chair in his path*)

MARGHERITA: Over here.

ANTONIA: Mind the chair.

INSPECTOR: Oooooowwwww! My shin!

ANTONIA: He's bumped into the chair. What a tragedy. Mind the broom.

INSPECTOR: What?

ANTONIA: Never mind. (*Hits him with broom*)

MARGHERITA: I'll get you a plaster.

ANTONIA: Mind the drawer.

INSPECTOR: (*Crash*) Thanks.

MARGHERITA: Sorry.

ANTONIA: Here's the window. Here, here's the window sill. Open up. See? Isn't it light outside.

INSPECTOR *peers into the cupboard.*

MARGHERITA: It is. Definitely. There's a lot of light.

INSPECTOR: Oh no. I can't see. What's happening to me? Light a match.

ANTONIA: I'll do better than that. I'll use my husband's blowlamp. There you are. What a bright flame!

ANTONIA *proffers the welder to the* INSPECTOR.

INSPECTOR: I can't see no flame! Let me feel.

ANTONIA: Are you barmy? You'll burn yourself.

INSPECTOR: No. I won't burn myself. OOOOooooWWWWwwww!!!!

ANTONIA: What's up?

INSPECTOR: I burnt myself.

ANTONIA: That comes of unbelieving.

INSPECTOR: Yeeeooow.

ANTONIA: Now do you believe?

INSPECTOR: I'm blind! My eyes!

MARGHERITA: That's what we've been telling you.

INSPECTOR: Let me out, show me the door!

MARGHERITA: Over there. (*Pointing to door*)

ANTONIA: No over here. (*Pointing to wardrobe*) Here it is.

INSPECTOR *bangs head in cupboard as he enters. He reels out clutching his head.*

INSPECTOR: Ouuu! My head . . . the pain . . . I'm dying . . . my head!

MARGHERITA: He's smashed his head I think.

ANTONIA: It's the child, he's touched you.

INSPECTOR: I'll wring his neck. The bleeding little bastard.

ANTONIA: Language, Inspector, language. (INSPECTOR *faints*) Blimey, he's fainted.

MARGHERITA: Are you sure he's not dead?

ANTONIA: No I'm not.

MARGHERITA: Is he breathing?

ANTONIA: He is . . . Not. He's not! My God he's stopped breathing. His heart's stopped too.

MARGHERITA: Antonia. We've killed a policeman.

ANTONIA: Yeah, we overdid it a bit, didn't we. Never mind. What are we going to do?

MARGHERITA: What are we going to do? You did it. Don't ask me. Include me out. Where's my keys? (*Searching her pockets*)

ANTONIA: Great! The solidarity!

MARGHERITA *finds keys on the table.* ANTONIA *unloads her coat and salad meanwhile.*

MARGHERITA: Here they are. Wait a minute. I've got another set in my pocket! These must be my old man's! He been here!

ANTONIA: Don't panic. He'll be back when he realises he's left them.

MARGHERITA: Don't you see? If he's been here he must have seen Giovanni –

ANTONIA: Not surprising. He lives here.

MARGHERITA *rushes out the front door in a panic re-entering immediately.*

MARGHERITA: No! Giovanni will have told him everything. About me being pregnant, and the ambulance and the clinic and the transplant. Everything! What can I say? Oooooahhh! Sod it, I'm not moving out of here. You'll have to tell one of your stories, I can't do them like you can. You'll have to get me out of this mess.

ANTONIA: All right, all right. I'll think of something.

MARGHERITA: What?

ANTONIA: I can't think what. Look at him. Miserable sod. It's all his fault.

MARGHERITA: No it's not, it's all your fault.

ANTONIA: He shouldn't have believed me. He fell for it, you know, dozy bugger. Let's have a look.

MARGHERITA: What you up to now?

ANTONIA: Artificial respiration. What does it look like?

MARGHERITA: You don't do it like that! You have to give him the kiss of life.

ANTONIA: What? Kiss a copper. There are limits. And what if my old man comes in? You kiss if you want.

MARGHERITA: You must be joking. We should have some oxygen for this.

ANTONIA: Of course. Why didn't I think? Quick, help me with Giovanni's welding gear. Look, one is oxygen, the other's hydrogen. We'll stick the nozzle in his gob. (*She has dragged the equipment over to the body*)

MARGHERITA: Are you sure it'll work?

ANTONIA: Of course. I've seen it on the films.

MARGHERITA: Oh well, that's all right then. It must be OK.

ANTONIA: It's working! Look, his chest is going up and d – up and up and up! It'll go down in a second, don't worry.

MARGHERITA: I'm not worried! Who's worried? Is his belly meant to go up and d – up and up and up?

ANTONIA: Oh dear. I think we got it wrong. It's the hydrogen! He's biting on the pipe. I can't get it out of his gob. Help me pull it out! No. Pull! Tell you what, I'll turn it off. No that's the wrong way round. That's it.

MARGHERITA: Done it.

ANTONIA: Blimey, look at the size of him! We've got a pregnant dead copper on our hands now.

Blackout.

Street outside LUIGI's *house.* LUIGI *and* GIOVANNI *are sitting dolefully on their sacks.*

GIOVANNI: Oh wonderful. Aren't we a clever boy. Locked out of your own house with two tons of sugar and half the police forces in the country on our heels!

LUIGI: Don't look at me.

GIOVANNI: What sort of thief loses his door key. Go on, pick the lock.

LUIGI: I have picked the lock.

GIOVANNI: Kick the door down.

LUIGI: I can't. It's got three bolts. On the inside.

GIOVANNI: What for?

LUIGI: My wife is scared shitless of thieves.

GIOVANNI: What's she worried about? *You* can't get in and you live here!

LUIGI: Wait a minute. I've remembered! I left my keys on your kitchen table.

GIOVANNI: We can't go back there!

LUIGI: Why not? Give us your keys. I'll go.

GIOVANNI: That Inspector will be waiting for us.

LUIGI: He'll have got fed up and gone home.

GIOVANNI: Not him. He's a bleeding terrier. They never let go. (*Sound off*) What's that?!

LUIGI: Calm down. Just a neighbour.

GIOVANNI: Hide the sacks!

Mild panic for a moment.

LUIGI: Stand on them.

GIOVANNI: That's it. They won't notice them. Act casual.

Enter UNDERTAKER. *Very grave. Played by the same actor who plays the* SERGEANT *and the* INSPECTOR.

UNDERTAKER: I wonder if you . . . What are you standing on them sacks for?

LUIGI: What sacks?

UNDERTAKER: Those ones. There. On the ground. Underneath your feet.

GIOVANNI: Oh, *those* ones.

LUIGI: We were keeping our feet dry. Rain. See?

UNDERTAKER: Oh. Anyway, do you know a Sergio Prampolini?

LUIGI: Third floor. But he's away in hospital. Very ill. Goodbye.

UNDERTAKER: No he's not there no more.

LUIGI: He must have discharged himself.

UNDERTAKER: Er. Not really.

LUIGI: He must be better. That's good.

UNDERTAKER: No he's dead.

LUIGI: Dead? That's bad. Jesus, that's terrible!

UNDERTAKER: I know, I know, I never get used to it and I've been in the packing business for twenty years.

GIOVANNI: Packing?

UNDERTAKER: Yes, I pack coffins.

GIOVANNI *and* LUIGI *touch wood, touching crotch.*

GIOVANNI: Sorry mate, force of habit.

UNDERTAKER: It's all right. Everybody does it. When I look in the mirror, I do it myself.

LUIGI: Charming.

UNDERTAKER: Twenty years and I'm still not used to death and grief and sorrow, the weeping widows, the distraught children. Dearie me. I mean, if you're any sort of human being you never get used to it. When will the family be back?

LUIGI: What good will they be? They won't want the body will they?

UNDERTAKER: Well, it wasn't at the hospital so the relatives must have it and if they don't have it God knows where it is. No, the problem is what am I going to do with the coffin?

GIOVANNI: Leave it in the hall.

UNDERTAKER: And have kids aerosoling political statements all over it? What do you take me for? Besides, I've got to get it signed for.

GIOVANNI: What about –

LUIGI: We can't help, mate.

UNDERTAKER: You live here don't you?

LUIGI: Who me?

UNDERTAKER: Only you could sign for it, keep it till the family come back and pass it on to them.

LUIGI: I've only a little flat.

UNDERTAKER: It's only a little coffin.

LUIGI: Can't help you, mate, anyway I'm locked out. See.

UNDERTAKER: Oh well. Back to the parlour.

LUIGI: Giovanni. (*Tapping* GIOVANNI's *shoulder*)

GIOVANNI: Er, tell you what, I'll take it off your hands.

LUIGI: Giovanni.

UNDERTAKER: Can I trust you?

GIOVANNI: I live round here.

UNDERTAKER: It's a deal. Right I'll go and get it. (*Exits*)

LUIGI: Giovanni, are you barmy? We've got enough to cope with apart from looking after people's coffins.

GIOVANNI: Luigi, answer me this: how did the Vietcong get their weapons into Saigon?

LUIGI: I'm sorry Magnus. I'll have to pass on that one.

GIOVANNI: In coffins!

LUIGI: Terrific. Thanks for that bit of socialist history. That's not going to help us get rid of the bags . . . Oh!!

GIOVANNI: See?

UNDERTAKER: (*Off*) Ready!

GIOVANNI: I'll be the corpse. You be the widow. You can carry it with the undertaker.

LUIGI: I don't think widows carry coffins very often. They haven't got the legs for it. Neither have I.

GIOVANNI: There's no answer to that.

LUIGI: Tell you what. I'll borrow his hat.

They start to go.

GIOVANNI: Here. Don't he look like the one with the moustache?

LUIGI: No. The one without.

GIOVANNI: Really?

Blackout.

GIOVANNI *and* ANTONIA's *flat.*

ANTONIA *re-arranges bags and buttons coat.* SERGEANT *lies where he fell.*

MARGHERITA: Oh, sod you, Antonia. Here we are with a dead copper on our hands and you're still playing silly buggers with the salad.

ANTONIA: What else can we do? This'll be our last trip anyway and, as for him, if he's dead he's dead and if he's alive he'll wake up soon enough and thank the Lord for getting his sight and health back and for getting pregnant.

MARGHERITA: Very funny.

ANTONIA: Now let's hide him under the sofa.

MARGHERITA: Do we have to touch him?

ANTONIA: No. The cupboard. I've seen it in films.

MARGHERITA: Oh well then. (*They lift him*) Jesus he weighs a ton.

ANTONIA: My God, my back's killing me. Get him upright. That's it. (*They drag him into the wardrobe*) Stick a hanger in his jacket. Now hang him on the bar. There. Shut the door. Let's see if it's raining.

MARGHERITA *goes to window.*

MARGHERITA: Yes. It is raining.

ANTONIA: I'll get my wellies and a brolly.

ANTONIA *exits into bedroom.* LUIGI *enters.*

LUIGI: Anybody home?

MARGHERITA: No.

LUIGI: Eh?

MARGHERITA: Nobody's home.

LUIGI: You're here.

MARGHERITA: I am.

LUIGI: I think so.

MARGHERITA: So I am. (*Laughs*)

LUIGI: What are you laughing at?

MARGHERITA: I'm getting hysterical. Where did you get that hat? Where did you get that hat?

LUIGI: Isn't it a lovely . . . Forget the hat. What about you? I've tramped half of Milan looking for you. Are you all right, love, and the baby, you haven't lost it?

MARGHERITA: Don't worry. Everything's all right.

LUIGI: Are you sure? Tell me everything.

MARGHERITA: Everything?

LUIGI: Of course!

MARGHERITA: Tell you what. Antonia is much better than me at explaining things. I'll go and get her.

LUIGI: All right.

UNDERTAKER: (*Off*) Ready.

MARGHERITA: What was that noise?

LUIGI: What noise?

MARGHERITA: A voice.

LUIGI: A voice? I can explain everything.

MARGHERITA: So can I.

LUIGI: You can?

MARGHERITA: I'll get Antonia. (MARGHERITA *exits to bedroom*)

LUIGI: (*At front door*) OK. Bring it in.

LUIGI *and* UNDERTAKER *bring coffin in.*

MARGHERITA: (*Off*) Antonia! Come out quickly.

GIOVANNI: (*In the coffin*) The women are in!

ANTONIA: Can't I even piss in peace?

LUIGI: She noticed my hat.

UNDERTAKER: I've got four more deliveries to make. Goodbye. I don't know, what a life. Weeping widows, distraught children. All these quick changes . . . (*Exits*)

LUIGI: I preferred him as the Inspector.

GIOVANNI: Yeah. Now, what are we going to tell Antonia?

LUIGI: I know. Lock the bedroom door, we'll stuff the sack under the sofa and stand the coffin in the cupboard.

GIOVANNI: Good idea.

MARGHERITA: (*Off*) Antonia, I have to talk to you.

ANTONIA: (*Off*) Sod it! It's all slipping out.

LUIGI *pushes sacks under couch.*

GIOVANNI: Push them well out of sight.

LUIGI: Christ, I didn't think we had this much.

GIOVANNI: It's the yoga effect.

LUIGI: Course it is.

GIOVANNI: When you look at things upside down.

LUIGI: What are you on about?

GIOVANNI: When Indians have nothing to eat they stand on their heads and imagine as much food as they can eat.

LUIGI: Does it help?

GIOVANNI: No. They're still starving.

They stash the coffin in the wardrobe.

LUIGI: 'Scuse me, mate. (*Stops*) Funny that.

GIOVANNI: What's that?

LUIGI: It works.

GIOVANNI: What does?

LUIGI: That yoga effect. First the food doubles in quantity. Then I get this silly notion that there's an Inspector in the cupboard. Silly old me.

MARGHERITA: (*Off*) Antonia, that's it. I'm going in. Don't blame me if I let it all out.

GIOVANNI: Quick, unlock the bedroom door.

LUIGI *unlocks the door. The men run to the sofa and sit casually. Enter* MARGHERITA.

Margherita! How are you! You look well. Is the baby well?

MARGHERITA: Good question. Ah –

ANTONIA: (*Enters*) What the bloody hell is – Oh. Giovanni! You're back!

GIOVANNI: Yes. I'm back.

LUIGI: Ha. He's back. See. It's Giovanni.

ANTONIA: And Luigi.

LUIGI: Yes. Me. Luigi.

ANTONIA: Hello Luigi.

LUIGI: Hello Antonia.

ANTONIA: How nice.

MARGHERITA: I'm here too.

GIOVANNI: You've had it!

ANTONIA: Have I?

GIOVANNI: The transplant.

LUIGI: The transplant.

MARGHERITA: The transplant.

ANTONIA: But only a little bit.

GIOVANNI: Which bit?

ANTONIA: Well. It wasn't big, you know.

GIOVANNI: I knew it. She's such an idiot. She's only gone and done a caesarian!

ANTONIA: Only a little one.

GIOVANNI: How little?

ANTONIA: Little enough to work.

GIOVANNI: You see?!

LUIGI: And what about you, dear?

MARGHERITA: Ah. Yes. I don't know. Antonia?

LUIGI: What you asking her for? Don't you know?

ANTONIA: How could she, poor little pet. She was under the anaesthetic.

GIOVANNI: Weren't you under the anaesthetic?

ANTONIA: What is this? Some kind of third degree?

Cupboard door swings open. GIOVANNI *leans on it.*

And why are you leaning on that door?

GIOVANNI: What door?

LUIGI: Yes, what door?

ANTONIA: He's leaning against the door. The cupboard door.

MARGHERITA: *Our* cupboard door?

ANTONIA: You are leaning.

GIOVANNI: (*Moving away*) No I'm not.

ANTONIA: I saw you leaning.

GIOVANNI: Post-natal shock Luigi.

Both cupboard doors open. GIOVANNI *and* ANTONIA *lean.*

ANTONIA: What was that?

LUIGI: What was what?

Sink cupboard door opens. MARGHERITA *leans.*

LUIGI: What was that?

Front door opens. LUIGI *leans.*

ANTONIA: You're leaning now.

LUIGI: What me? Ha Ha Ha.

There follows a mad panic-stricken circus of doors and windows flying open, ending with the collapse of the cuckoo clock in a cloud of feathers.

GIOVANNI: Never mind who's leaning. Who's had the caesarian? Who's had the transplant?

LUIGI: And who's had the baby?

ANTONIA: Cowards! Not a blessed thought for us. We get up from our sick-beds to be with our husbands in this time of crisis and that's the thanks we get! What should I have done, Giovanni? She was in trouble – about to lose her baby – so I helped her out, didn't I? Don't you always say we should help each other? Luigi, tell him.

LUIGI: (*Lost for words*) I'm speechless. Margherita –

MARGHERITA: Antonia – You tell him.

ANTONIA: I'm going to cry.

GIOVANNI: No. (*Moves to comfort her*)

ANTONIA: I'm all right.

GIOVANNI: You look beautiful with that belly. It takes me back.

ANTONIA: I'm going to cry again.

MARGHERITA: Me too.

LUIGI: Is it moving? Can I feel?

MARGHERITA: No Luigi!

LUIGI: It's my baby.

MARGHERITA: But it's her belly!

LUIGI: But we're relatives now.

GIOVANNI: That's right!

MARGHERITA: I don't come into this, I suppose? I'm rubbish. A nothing. (*Cries*)

ANTONIA: How can you treat her like this? Cheer her up. I've got to go out.

GIOVANNI: Are you out of your mind? With all this weather? You'll freeze. Think of the child! Lie down.

Enter OLD MAN, *played by the same actor, of course.*

OLD MAN: Can I come in?

GIOVANNI: Dad! Come in.

ANTONIA: Hello, Dad.

GIOVANNI: These are my friends. Margherita. Luigi. This is my father.

LUIGI *and* **MARGHERITA:** How do you do?

LUIGI: Giovanni, did you know your dad looks like –

GIOVANNI: Don't say it. I know. Without a moustache.

OLD MAN: (*To* MARGHERITA) Antonia how young you're looking.

GIOVANNI: Dad. That's Antonia on the sofa.

OLD MAN: Is she sick? Are you sick?

GIOVANNI: No. She's expecting.

OLD MAN: Who?

GIOVANNI: A child.

OLD MAN: Why? Where's he gone to? Oh you're back already. (*To* LUIGI) Hello, lad. You shouldn't keep your mother waiting. He's a big lad, ain't he? Oh I've got a letter for you. Sent to me by mistake.

GIOVANNI: Who from?

OLD MAN: The bleeding owner of this block. He says you haven't paid the rent for four months. Here's another letter from the gas, they want their money and so do the electric.

GIOVANNI: What!? Give me those! What is this!? They can take a run, I've always paid my way, haven't I, Antonia?

ANTONIA: Oh yes. Oh yes. We've always paid our way, Dad. I can't understand it for the life of me.

GIOVANNI: They've got it wrong! Definitely. Here, turn the light on, Luigi.

MARGHERITA: Oh no.

LUIGI: On, off, on, off.

GIOVANNI: What's wrong here? Funny. Funny. (*Stops and looks at* ANTONIA) Antonia, we have paid those bills . . . Antonia, tell me we've paid!

ANTONIA: Look at him. Screaming at a pregnant woman. Carry on like that and I'll have this baby premature. Then we'll start all over again with the transplants.

MARGHERITA, LUIGI *and* **OLD MAN:** Oh no.

LUIGI: Don't do that. Don't let's start –

GIOVANNI: All right. I'll speak softer. Just answer me.

ANTONIA: What was the question?

GIOVANNI: Have we paid the gas and the rent and the electric?

ANTONIA: Oh that question. It's come back to me.

GIOVANNI: Well?

ANTONIA: No.

GIOVANNI: (*Shouting*) You old cow.

LUIGI, MARGHERITA *and* **OLD MAN:** (*Pointing to their stomachs in warning*) SSsssshhhhh!

GIOVANNI: What have I been working all my life for? Tell me that? Eh? (*Shouting*) Have I been working so I just get cut off –

MARGHERITA, LUIGI *and* **OLD MAN:** SSsssshhhhh!

GIOVANNI: Sorry. Sorry. Sorry. The baby. Of course. Margherita has paid, Margherita has, haven't you, Margherita? Paid.

LUIGI: Of course she has. Haven't you, Margherita? Tell him.

MARGHERITA: Oh dear. As it happens, I haven't.

LUIGI: (*Shouting*) What!

GIOVANNI, MARGHERITA and **OLD MAN:** SSssssshhhhh!

ANTONIA: Well, now you know. Margherita and me and the other wives on this floor, and on the other floors in the block, and the flats opposite, and come to that all the wives and women in this area are just a bunch of old slags. Instead of paying our gas bills we've been buying jewellery and taking day trips to Rome to buy the latest Paris creations –

GIOVANNI: But why didn't you ask for more money?

ANTONIA: You didn't have any more to ask for. What was the point? Would you have stolen to pay the gas?

GIOVANNI: Never! But why didn't you tell me?

ANTONIA: Why didn't you ask? (*Starts to cry*)

OLD MAN: Aaah. There there. Everything will turn out for the best.

GIOVANNI: Who says?

OLD MAN: I says.

ALL: SSssssshhhhh!

OLD MAN: Now lay off your wife for a minute.

ANTONIA: Yeah. (*Sob*) Lay off.

OLD MAN: Anyway, there's always a silver lining. I've brought back all that stuff of yours. So even if you don't have a roof over your head at least you can eat.

LUIGI: What's he on about?

MARGHERITA: Haven't the faintest.

OLD MAN: Yes. You know. All that food and stuff you forgot about in my shed. Well, I've brought it back. Here, I'll bring it in. (*Fetches stuff in from outside the door*)

GIOVANNI: Dad, you've got it wrong. It's not ours. Antonia. Is it?

ANTONIA: Don't look at me.

OLD MAN *puts shopping bags on kitchen table.*

OLD MAN: Well, I never. I saw you coming out of my shed and I thought –

MARGHERITA: No!

LUIGI: What?

MARGHERITA: No.

OLD MAN: Well, that is a puzzle, ain't it.

ANTONIA: All right. It's just something I picked up at bargain prices at the supermarket.

GIOVANNI: How bargain?

ANTONIA: Very bargain. Look I only paid half price for half the stuff and the other half I half nicked.

LUIGI: What's she talking about?

GIOVANNI: Nicked? Have you started nicking now?

ANTONIA: Yes, I have.

MARGHERITA: No, she hasn't!

ANTONIA: It's no use, Margherita. They had to find out.

GIOVANNI: I can't get over it. I'm going barmy. My wife a tea leaf.

LUIGI: Yeah, well. It's not that barmy. Let's have less of the moral indignation. (*Pointing under couch*)

GIOVANNI: Why not? I'm entitled. It's all right for you, but I'm up to here in debt due to this totally irresponsible tea leaf here.

ANTONIA: That's it. Call me a thief. And what about 'whore' while you're at it? (*Undoes belly, revealing shopping bag*) All this ain't a kid. It's veg, and spag and rice and sugar and spag and spaghetti. All of it nicked.

LUIGI: (*Peering in and under shopping bag*) What happened to the kid? The transplant?

GIOVANNI: The baby tent? The fully automatic –

LUIGI: Belt up for once. Margherita?

MARGHERITA: Yes??

LUIGI: (*Thinks, looks at* MARGHERITA *and* ANTONIA) It's all a con. The whole thing.

GIOVANNI: To think I was worried to death about your health. The whole thing was a pack of lies.

LUIGI: Even me being a father.

ANTONIA: Yeah. It's all lies. The whole thing.

GIOVANNI: I'm not half going to give you one. (*Starting towards* ANTONIA)

LUIGI: Don't be hasty. (*Holding him back*)

GIOVANNI: All right I won't. I'll kill her slowly. I'll mangle her into little pieces.

OLD MAN: Well, I'm off. I think you've had all the news. Look after yourself. Ta ra.

They all wave politely.

GIOVANNI: Ta ta.

LUIGI: Yes. Nice to have met you.

OLD MAN *exits.*

GIOVANNI: Right, let me at her.

LUIGI *again restrains* GIOVANNI *with difficulty.*

ANTONIA: Let him go, Luigi. Let him kill me. I'll just sit here and let him whack my brains out. I'm tired of this shitty life. I'm tired of all the running around trying to scratch a living out of nothing with no help at all. All you get from him is moral indignati . . .

LUIGI: Indignation.

ANTONIA: Yes. That. And a lot of wind. Our kids are chucked on the scrapheap, a whole generation of them without the hope of getting a job. The right laying waste and who's standing up to them? Him and his party. Like a dead haddock. I've had enough of it. Luigi. I've changed my mind. I'm not giving in. Don't let him go after all.

LUIGI: Oh, all right. (*Grabs* GIOVANNI)

ANTONIA: I'm leaving home instead.

LUIGI: That's good.

ANTONIA: I'm going to live round your place, Luigi.

LUIGI: That's bad.

MARGHERITA: Help!

GIOVANNI: You can't leave. You're my wife.

LUIGI: See?

GIOVANNI: Keep out of this! She's my wife.

ANTONIA: I'm your wife. But are you my husband?

GIOVANNI: What are you on about?

ANTONIA: Well, you're not the bloke I married, that's for certain. You're not the Giovanni I knew. You were a fighter then. Don't rock the boat. Where's the real Giovanni Bardi? Millet soup!

GIOVANNI: All right, if that's how you feel. Go on. Go and leave and live at Luigi's. And take the bleeding sugar with you.

ANTONIA: What?

GIOVANNI: Yeah. Might sweeten you up a bit. And the rice and the flour.

ANTONIA: What's he talking about?

GIOVANNI: It's under the sofa. We nicked it today.

MARGHERITA: No that's our stuff. We nicked it.

LUIGI: No. He's right. We nicked it. Three sacks' worth.

ANTONIA *pulls sack from under couch.*

ANTONIA: You blooming old hypocrite. 'I'd rather starve than eat stolen food.' You two-faced sodbox.

GIOVANNI: Leave it out.

ANTONIA: Well, I'm well out of it. Let's go, Luigi, Margherita. (*Exits*)

LUIGI: Don't let's be hasty.

GIOVANNI: Just because you're right you don't have to stand around gloating. Go on, the lot of you.

LUIGI: (*Calling down the hall*) Hear him out, Antonia, you might change your mind.

MARGHERITA: Yeah!!

Re-enter ANTONIA.

ANTONIA: Wait a minute. Did you say 'because you're right'?

GIOVANNI: You heard. I'm not going to repeat myself.

ANTONIA: Are you feeling all right?

GIOVANNI: No I'm not. I feel sick.

ANTONIA: What about?

GIOVANNI: About today. About tomorrow.

ANTONIA: What are you on about?

GIOVANNI: None of your business.

ANTONIA: Suit yourself.

GIOVANNI: It's the women today and Luigi on the train with Marco and Tonino and the youngsters in the canteen (and even the shop stewards) and the guys at the lorry with the sacks of flour and rice.

LUIGI: Anybody you left out?

GIOVANNI: Yeah me.

LUIGI: You don't come into it.

ANTONIA: He does.

GIOVANNI: No. I don't. That's it. That's what gets me in the goolies.

LUIGI: See?

GIOVANNI: What were the women doing?

LUIGI: Nicking.

GIOVANNI: No they weren't.

ANTONIA: He will argue.

GIOVANNI: They were making a stand. Where've I been all my life? I don't know. I'm confused.

LUIGI: No? Really?

GIOVANNI: All right! Twenty years, Luigi. Twenty years to learn what I've learnt.

ANTONIA: And what have you learnt?

GIOVANNI: I don't know!

LUIGI: You are a slow learner.

GIOVANNI: Sneer you may. But I've fell in. (*Tapping temple*) That's what I've done. Fell in, finally. All those people today milling about the streets with groceries up their jumpers are looking for a bit of leadership, that's what. They're saying, 'Get in there, old cock, there's a fight on.' And they're saying it to their unions. The right are on the rampage and they're saying, 'We've had a bellyful of it,' and they're saying, 'If you don't take hold, we will!' And they're saying to the politicians, 'We want the bread *and* the biscuits, so shut your cake'ole!' And us, the so-called opposition, is wobbling in its boots. Well, we're going to have to pull ourselves up by the bootstraps, and roll our sleeves up and get weaving up to our elbows otherwise someone'll nick the carpet out from under our feet and we'll be up the spout without a paddle.

Pause.

MARGHERITA: I know exactly what you mean.

GIOVANNI: Yes, well. Buzz off, the lot of you. I've got some thinking to do.

ANTONIA: What about?

GIOVANNI: About today. About you.

ANTONIA: Are you asking me to stay?

LUIGI: I think he is. Aren't you, Giovanni?

MARGHERITA: I think he is, too.

GIOVANNI: I didn't say that.

ANTONIA: Well, I will.

GIOVANNI: You will?

ANTONIA: Course I will. Don't argue.

GIOVANNI: I'm not arguing. I was just –

ANTONIA: Oh belt up. Give us a kiss.

They kiss.

MARGHERITA: Innit lovely?

LUIGI: It won't last.

Knocking.

MARGHERITA: Oh my God!

LUIGI: Who is it?

INSPECTOR: Police! Open up!

ANTONIA: Quick, hide everything!

MARGHERITA: Aaaaaaooouuu!

ANTONIA: Dozy cow!

*General panic as they run hither and thither concealing
everything.*

GIOVANNI: Hold it. Hold everything. What is this? They've
been giving us the run-around all day. I'm not running any
more. We'll face the bastards.

INSPECTOR: (*Entering from cupboard*) I can see! I can see! St
Eulalia be praised. Merciful Saint! And look at me. I'm
pregnant! Oh what a bonus. I'm a mother! I'm a mother!

GIOVANNI: What's got into him?

Pause. They look at each other.

ANTONIA: There's only one thing for it, Margherita. We'll
sing the song.

They sing the song (vocal and instrumental depending on the cast's musical talents).

Sebben che siamo donne
Paura non abbiamo
Per amori dei nostri figli
In leghe ci mettiamo

E voi altri signorini
Che ci avete tanto orgoglio
Abbassate la superbia
E aprite il portafoglio

They say we should be moderate
Not stirring up class war
But we're bent on being obdurate
We'll take it all we don't ask more

We'll defeat their aims for starters
We'll foil their dastardly plan
Can we have their guts for garters?
We say fucking right we can!

Fade to blackout.

Elizabeth: Almost by Chance a Woman

translated by Gillian Hanna

Author's Note

'Be Careful, This is a Forgery.' This legend should be printed
on the frontispiece of the text of *Elizabeth: Almost by Chance
a Woman*. Certain sentences attributed to Shakespeare are
forgeries; many allusions to historical facts are forgeries;
certain characters who appear on stage are downright forgeries,
to say nothing of those who are referred to from time to time.
Yet the body of the text is, I assure you, laden with
authenticity.

It is an absurd text with great probability of truthfulness.
The first idea was to play a Boccaccianesque practical joke. I
was thinking of having it printed by a friend, a printer, a great
craftsman-artist, on ancient paper with seventeenth-century
lettering, and of entrusting it to a researcher with a great sense
of humour who was to publish it with modern lettering,
footnotes and introduction, and then entrust it to me and
Franca for us to produce. We would have laughed ourselves
silly for years over what the critics would have written. But it
would have been too hard a joke – too cruel.

Another legend to be affixed to this text is: 'Comedy in the
old Italian style' – in particular of the first half of the
seventeenth century. The setting – the fixed interior – is
classical of the period. The restricted number of characters is a
constant of the Italian theatre of that time. The presence of the
pseudo-procuress, pseudo-Celestina* is also a classical

element of the period. One only needs to think of Della Porta's 'Fiorina' or Ruzzante's 'Anconitano'. But the element that makes the greatest reference to the Italian theatre of the seventeenth century is the character of the absent protagonist. As in Macchiavelli's 'Clizia', here, the Earl of Essex never appears on stage. He is announced, he is expected, he is sighed for, but he never appears.

I will refrain from telling you that the drama is that of a woman's conflict in her relationship to power – you can work that out for yourselves.

There is only one particular I would like to point out to you: the final monologue† is constructed like a mosaic, borrowing various phrases from Shakespeare's most famous plays from *Henry IV* to *Henry V*, from *Measure for Measure* to *Julius Caesar* . . . so you can amuse yourselves by recognising them . . . I have put in some phrases of my own to link them up . . . just for the pleasure of masking the sources and to fabricate a genuine forgery.

Dario Fo, 1986

* Celestina is the bawd in a famous Spanish novel in dramatic form – *The Tragi-comedy of Calisto and Melibea* (1499) by Fernando de Rojas.
† The final monologue in Gillian Hanna's translation is also a Shakespearian mosaic although the quotations are not necessarily the same as in the original.

This translation of *Elizabeth* was first staged at the Half Moon
Theatre, London on 3 November 1986. The cast was as
follows:

YOUNG MAN	Nick Bartlett
ASSASSIN	David Bradford
MARTHA	Angela Curran
ELIZABETH	Gillian Hanna
DAME GROSSLADY	Bob Mason
EGERTON	Jonathan Oliver

Directed by Michael Batz and Chris Bond
Designed by Andrea Montag

*Note: Where this translation departs from the Italian is indicated
by a line in the margin. A literal translation is given in the
Appendix at the end of the play.*

ACT ONE

The scene is set in the style of the Italian Renaissance, on two levels, with an open gallery at the back of the upper level, a door in the right-hand corner, and a staircase running down beside the wall. In each arch of the gallery is a window. On the lower level, a door in the right wall, and another in the left.

In the centre, a bed, a facsimile of the famous nuptial bed of Federigo Da Montefeltro. The space on the left is hidden by a double screen on two parallel tapestries, one behind the other, facing the audience. The tapestries can be drawn back. Behind the second one is hidden a lifesize wooden horse on wheels. On the left wall, a large fireplace and a mirror. Near the fireplace, close to the proscenium arch, is a lectern with an inkstand, pen, papers and a sword.

In the centre, clearly visible, a tailor's dummy on which there is a woman's ceremonial dress – black with a white ruff.

A Version of the 'Candy' song

('*Candia*')

When thou dost cease to love me more,
I'll set my ship for Candy's shore,
And on my billowing sail will blow
Thine eyes in glowing colours, so
When water drown the bridge, oh then I'll see
Thee weep those tears thou ne'er didst weep for me.

And on the prow, there will I place
A carvèd figure-head; thy face,
Thy breasts, thy belly, all will drown
Each time my flying ship dips down
Beneath the water; by the sea held fast,
Those arms that twined round me thou never hast.

And when I come to Candy's sun,
They'll ask me why my sail doth run
So swift, all painted with those eyes;
And I'll reply: 'Let me be wise;
I keep my woman, dear, so close above
In hopes perchance I can forget her love.'

The play begins with the song 'Candia'. The light is dark, almost blackout. The tapestries are drawn to prevent the audience seeing the horse. As the song finishes, ELIZABETH enters, papers in hand. Because of the darkness she bumps into the dummy.

ELIZABETH: Well, where's everyone got to . . . ? Martha! Let's get going . . . (*She finds herself entwined with the dummy*) . . . What's this? . . . Martha, why must you keep everything shut up . . . ? (*She draws the downstage tapestry. A ray of light falls on the dummy. ELIZABETH screams*) . . . AAAHH!! Damned Stuart! (*She takes the sword from the desk*) . . . Get away! You don't frighten me . . .

She turns to a curtain on the right which is moving, and lunges at it with her sword.

ELIZABETH: And neither do you! I've seen you . . . you bastard! I'll run you through!

She sinks the blade into the tapestry.

MARTHA: (*From behind the tapestry – terrified*) Help! Stop it! Elizabeth!

ELIZABETH: Who is it? Come out of there or I'll kill you!

MARTHA: (*Entering*) It's me, Martha . . . What on earth's got into you?

ELIZABETH: Martha? What were you up to behind there? Were you spying on me?

MARTHA: Don't talk nonsense. I heard you screaming . . . What's the matter?

Using a pole, she draws back the hanging in front of the window – the ray of light which crosses the room falls full on the dummy. ELIZABETH screams again, and hurls the papers at it.

ELIZABETH: There, there . . . It's Mary! . . . The Stuart woman!

MARTHA: No dear, no. It's only her dress . . . Calm down.

ELIZABETH: Who brought it in here and put it on that headless dummy?

MARTHA: You ordered it to be fetched out of her wardrobe . . . You wanted to give it to someone . . . I don't know who.

She removes the dress from the dummy and takes it off stage.

ELIZABETH: That's not true. As a matter of fact, I asked for it to be got out . . . so it could be aired, that's all.

MARTHA: Well, there's obviously been a little misunderstanding.

ELIZABETH: Misunderstanding, my arse! Someone's done it on purpose. Stuck it there on the dummy . . . without a head . . . to give me a heart attack! Whose charming idea was this? I want him brought here immediately!

MARTHA: Very well . . . I'll get on to it straight away . . . I'll summon all the servants . . . and we'll have a nice inquest. Then everyone will know that the queen is still haunted by the ghost of Mary of Scotland.

ELIZABETH: I am not haunted . . . I couldn't give a monkey's fart about the slag Mary of Scotland!

MARTHA: Well then, prove it. Calm down and get back into bed.

She goes to open the doors of the bed.

ELIZABETH: Leave them alone. Don't open the doors of my bed!

MARTHA: (*Lowering her voice*) Why not? Got a visitor in there? Bloody hell, you must have woken him up with all the squealing you've been doing!

ELIZABETH: There's no one to wake up. I didn't have anyone in my bed last night.

MARTHA: Why don't I open it up then?

ELIZABETH: No, I said. I didn't have anyone in last night, but the one I had three nights ago might still be there.

MARTHA: O for heaven's sake! All right . . . You're being impossible this morning. What's got into you? Look what you've done . . . you've scattered these papers all over the place with your flapping about.

She picks up a few.

ELIZABETH: O yes. Give me those.

MARTHA: What is all this stuff?

ELIZABETH: Why don't you tell me? Who is this bastard? Does he write these slanders all on his own? Or maybe he's just an imbecile? I haven't slept a wink all night, trying to work it out.

MARTHA: Elizabeth, will you please calm down . . . It's me who can't work anything out . . . Who are you talking about?

ELIZABETH: Shakespeare. Who is this Shakespeare?

MARTHA: Shakespeare? Not again! What's he done to you this time?

ELIZABETH: I told you to find all this out at least a month ago. I want to read every page he's ever written . . . I want to know how much of this crap he's managed to get on the stage . . . who prints it . . .

MARTHA: (*Pointing to the papers she's just finished picking up*) Considering all the really appalling problems you've got to contend with, I can't see why you're working yourself into a lather over these silly melodramas. Now really, this is becoming an obsession.

ELIZABETH: Of course: Elizabeth is mad. She's off her head! Sit down here and look at this . . . (*She shows her the papers*) . . . tell me that here in this Henry IV, and again here, in this Richard III, he isn't talking about me . . . my life . . . my system of government . . .

MARTHA: But he didn't make any of this up: it's history.

ELIZABETH: Yes, well, maybe I can't get pissed off with history for copying my life, but I can get pissed off with this creeping bastard for putting it up on the stage as plain as a pike-staff!

MARTHA: So now you're the queen of fairyland too.

ELIZABETH: Fairyland? (*Shows her more papers*) All right then, look at Hamlet: are you trying to tell me it's not an exact portrait of me? Tell me it's not!

MARTHA: Hamlet a portrait of you?

ELIZABETH: Yes. Don't stand there with your mouth hanging open. Have you read it?

MARTHA: No . . . I barely know the plot.

ELIZABETH: Then read it. Very carefully. You'll find my expressions in it . . . my cries of despair . . . my curses . . . things I've shouted here, in this room. How did this Shakespeare know all this? Who's the spy in here? Martha!

MARTHA: Listen, if you're looking at me . . . just say the word . . . I'll start packing now.

ELIZABETH: O stop it . . . you haven't got the imagination to be an informer. Stop it!

MARTHA: Thank you very much. Anyway, if you could possibly learn to shout a little more quietly, you might avoid being overheard by the guards in the corridor and secretaries passing by, not to mention stray villains hanging about outside your door, or even any young layabout who happened to be tucked up in your bed . . .

Points to the closed doors of the bed.

ELIZABETH: So now you're going to gang up with all the muckrakers too, are you?

MARTHA: Well I'm good at muckraking, I'm the one who makes your bed every morning.

ELIZABETH: I suppose that's true.

MARTHA: Anyway, if you really want to find out what's at the back of these plays, why don't you ask your Chief of Police . . . ?

ELIZABETH: Who? Egerton? Where is he?

MARTHA: He's out in the corridor where he's been since daybreak. If you want, I'll let him in.

ELIZABETH: Let him in? So he can find out what a ghoul I am first thing in the morning? If that damn spy-master catches the merest glimpse of me, tomorrow the whole of London will have a detailed description of what a horror I am in my natural state.

MARTHA: Very well. As you wish. He'll have to wait till you've been renovated. (*Ironically*) I'll tell him to come back in four hours. This afternoon.

ELIZABETH: (*Dry*) Ho ho ho. Very witty! All right, let him in. But put something in front of me so he can't see me . . . O never mind, I'll do it myself . . . I'll shift my horse . . . that'll do it . . .

She draws back the second tapestry to reveal the horse which she pushes to the centre.

MARTHA: (*At the door to the top of the stairs*) Please, Egerton. Do come in. Her Majesty is waiting for you.

EGERTON enters. He is holding a folder under his arm.

EGERTON: Thank you. Good morning, Your Highness . . .

Looks around.

ELIZABETH: Good morning, Egerton.

EGERTON: (*To Martha*) Where is she?

ELIZABETH: I am here, behind . . . behind the horse. I'm warning you, Egerton, if you so much as poke your nose round the neck of this animal to try to get a glimpse of me . . . (*She gets a pistol out of her bodice*) . . . I'll put a bullet right between your eyes, you little sneak. (*She points the pistol round the neck of the horse at* EGERTON) What news have you got for me?

EGERTON: Your Majesty, I am mortified. I can see that you are angry with me.

ELIZABETH: 'Angry' . . . that's such a little word, Egerton. I am beside myself with fury. In the first place because you have as yet given me no information about the thugs who fired on me from the riverbank when I was out in my barge: I don't know if they were Irishmen, Puritans, Papists, or hunters who mistook me for a golden cockerel . . .

MARTHA *goes out, and returns with a large basin and towels. She washes* ELIZABETH's *feet.*

ELIZABETH: Secondly: because I am still trying to find out what criteria you use when you examine texts submitted to you to be licensed for performance. And you are supposed to be the head of my Intelligence Service? Imbecile service, you're the head of.

EGERTON: Your Majesty, I am ready to submit myself to any insult. However, allow me to reassure you that the desperado in question has been apprehended and has talked.

ELIZABETH: Of his own free will?

EGERTON: Yes. Once we applied a burning brand to his feet . . .

ELIZABETH: For the love of God, Egerton, still using these criminal devices . . . it's inhuman.

EGERTON: But Your Majesty . . . It's as old as the world itself. If the police force wants to get confessions, it is obliged . . .

ELIZABETH: (*Interrupting him*) Obliged my arse! How can I make you understand? We're not living in my father Henry VIII's time any more. Then, they quite simply regarded torture as out-and-out amusement for the interrogators. No. Nowadays we live in a free, humanitarian state, and it's my duty to be shocked, to reproach you . . . to drag you in front of a court if I catch you in the act. Your duty is to continue the torture nonetheless. But you're not supposed to come running to tell me about it. For God's sake, Egerton, you've ruined my day.

EGERTON: You are right. Forgive me. The one thing we know for certain is that none of this has anything to do with the Earl of Essex.

ELIZABETH: Ah. (*With emotion*) Robert, Robert. (*To* EGERTON) You're just saying that to humour me. You know I love him to distraction.

EGERTON: No, Your Majesty, it is the truth. We have a fanatic on our hands. A single lunatic.

ELIZABETH: How can he be single if there were two of them?

EGERTON: Yes. Two single lunatics.

ELIZABETH: I see. In a while you'll discover there were three of them . . . or four . . . The National Association of Single Lunatics . . . You are pathetic and repetitious . . . Whenever the instigators of any piece of crap look like being discovered, you're terrified in case the names turn out to be well-known ones, so you come up with this ridiculous refrain about the single lunatic!

EGERTON: Perhaps you are right, Your Majesty . . . we are repetititous . . . But I can assure you that in this instance, the Earl of Essex has nothing to do with it.

ELIZABETH: In this instance? Then does he have anything to do with any other instance? Come on. Speak.

EGERTON: I am very much afraid that he may be getting caught up in an enterprise that is truly insane.

ELIZABETH: Is that so? And you, Egerton, along with the rest of my councillors, are gloating.

EGERTON: Your Majesty . . . I beg you . . . we . . . the fact is that the Earl is allowing himself to become the unwitting tool of militant extremists. They are trying to persuade him to organise a serious popular revolt, backed by a supporting invasion.

ELIZABETH: Supporting invasion by whom? From where?

EGERTON: They are trying to involve your cousin, the King of Scotland.

ELIZABETH: James?

EGERTON: Yes. They want him to send his troops to support them when the revolt breaks out . . .

ELIZABETH: They couldn't be such fuckwits . . . bloody . . .

MARTHA: Now, now, Elizabeth. Remember you're a lady as well as a Queen.

ELIZABETH: And I'm the Pope of my own religion as well! And if you don't shut your mouth I'll excommunicate you! Get out.

MARTHA *goes out, taking the basin and towels.*

ELIZABETH: It's not true, Egerton . . . All lies! Proof, I want the proof!

MARTHA *re-enters.*

EGERTON: And here it is, Your Majesty.

He gets some sheets of paper out of a folder and holds them out to the QUEEN *without looking at them. She stays hidden behind the horse.*

EGERTON: It is a letter written in the hand of the Earl of Essex.

He makes a slight movement in her direction.

ELIZABETH: (*She stops him with the pistol*) Stop there, or I shoot!

She reads the letter intently.

ELIZABETH: 'Now is the time to act! Swiftly! A more propitious moment can hardly come again. The whole country is exasperated, convinced that the Queen is now totally at the mercy of her councillors, who, with their disgraceful political actions, are leading England to her destruction.' (*She laughs*) Martha, come here and look at this! (*Shows the letter to* MARTHA) It's a forgery. It's a ridiculously clumsy imitation of Robert of Essex's handwriting. It's a forgery. Intelligence Service!

EGERTON: Is it possible? But the courier was one of our own men . . . He assured us . . .

ELIZABETH: Be quiet! It's a forgery, I said! Or perhaps, Egerton, you doubt my word against that of some infiltrator who is no doubt playing James's game?

EGERTON: O heavens! I don't know what to say . . . well, it's simple enough to check up on . . .

ELIZABETH: There you are! Well done! Check up on it! Question him, yes. Arrest him, this trusty collaborator of yours, and apply the Rule of Repentance.

EGERTON: The Rule of Repentance?

ELIZABETH: Of course. My brother Edward thought it up. First you frighten the hell out of the prisoner by showing him the gallows . . . then suddenly you promise him his freedom, and money if he will grass . . . He'll begin denouncing people like a supergrass before you've had time to blink . . . you'll have to plead with him to stop before the prisons start bursting at the seams!

EGERTON: Of course, Your Majesty . . . I will let you know as soon as possible.

ELIZABETH: Keep me informed, Egerton.

EGERTON: Straight away. (*He bids her farewell*) Your Majesty . . . Your devoted . . .

He bows to MARTHA. *He exits, leaving his folder on a chair.*

ELIZABETH: Your devoted arsehole!

She pushes the horse back to its original position.

MARTHA: Pardon me, Elizabeth, I happened to catch a glimpse of those letters . . . I was struck by your vehemence . . . there's no doubt?

ELIZABETH: No, no doubt at all. I am absolutely certain. That letter was written by Robert of Essex himself.

MARTHA: (*Gobsmacked*) Ah! Now what?

ELIZABETH: Be quiet. Shut up. Do you expect me to condemn him to death? Am I supposed to have his head chopped off? What use is a man with no head to me? I love him, the wretch. And anyway, you said yourself that perhaps it was my own fault if Robert's gone mad like this.

MARTHA: That's right, stand up for him! Protect him! Your Knave of Hearts . . . just watch out he doesn't pick up too many trump cards . . . or the Joker . . . that would really be a laugh!

She goes out and comes straight back, carrying a tray with cups and teapot. She serves the QUEEN.

ELIZABETH: The Joker? You've understood nothing. Robert Devereux already had the Joker. I was the Joker! But the idiot didn't know how to play me . . . he threw me away like the two of spades! What's more, he's organising coups against me, surrounding himself with a bunch of halfwits, each more halfwitted than Robert himself. And Egerton and Cecil and Bacon have completely filled the group with the infiltrators, spies and agents provocateurs . . . And the poor little sod hasn't even noticed! What the hell does he think he's up to? Bloody little bollocks! When I think that last night he started a coup . . .

MARTHA: Who, Essex and his men?

ELIZABETH: Yes. About fifty of them attacked the Armoury in the Old Palace and they filched a whole pile of arms. And it seems as though Egerton knew all about it. But said nothing. Fortunately, I have a second even more secret police force of my own, and I've completely infiltrated his secret police force with my secret secret police force, and they keep me informed about everything, secretly. (*Ironic*) This system is known as 'parliamentary democracy'. So they attacked the Armoury, and whistled out a bunch of weapons. They even nicked two culverins. I'm mad about my culverins. (*Takes up the story again*) I must say, they came up with a rather ingenious trick.

MARTHA: Wonderful!

ELIZABETH: Overjoyed are you? O, look at her . . . pretends to be so hard-hearted, don't you? But I can see you've got a soft spot for the Knave of Hearts too.

MARTHA: No. Just a minute. I was only admiring the courage and intelligence . . .

ELIZABETH: Whose intelligence? Robert of Essex? His head is so empty that if an idea ever did pop into it, it would die of loneliness. (*Hands* MARTHA *a cup*) Drink your tea. You're forgetting Egerton's infiltrators. Now they are intelligent. This attack on the Armoury was planned here in the Palace . . . by my men, sat round a desk, with the intention of screwing Robert once and for all.

MARTHA: All right. It's certain that Egerton must have known about Essex's plan to get the arms out of the Palace.

ELIZABETH: Yes, but he left them alone to get on with it. You always let the victim of a sting win the first three rounds so that you can smash them all the harder in the end. Cecil my beloved councillor . . . Bacon . . . Knollys . . . the whole lot of them, including the Privy Council, they all want to teach me a lesson. They can never forgive me for having showered the boy with gifts and leases and appointments. I love him . . . and I give him presents, I give him presents. When I think of his insolence, that damned pygmy . . . shouting at me . . . 'One of these fine days he'll put a saddle on your rump, this Essex of yours! Like a heifer . . . !' He called me a heifer, do you hear?

MARTHA: Who dared say that? Which pygmy are you talking about?

ELIZABETH: Cecil . . . my adored councillor. I took no notice of him. I was completely indifferent, as if he'd never even opened his mouth. I just spat in his eye. Bullseye, Martha, it was brilliant. SPLAT! And it wasn't just a lucky shot either

. . . I spent three months practising how to put out a lighted candle at ten paces . . . and then I booted all their arses out of the door, swearing like a trooper.

MARTHA: They want to get their own back now!

She takes the tray and begins to go.

ELIZABETH: They will bring me his head on a platter like John the Baptist. If I could only talk to him, the idiot!

MARTHA: (*Embarrassed*) I've talked to him.

ELIZABETH: You? When?

MARTHA: Three days ago. I went to look for him. Now I want to make this quite clear. I only did it for your sake. I heard you weeping all night . . . calling out his name . . .

ELIZABETH: Why did he agree to see you? Come on, be brave.

MARTHA: (*Even more embarrassed and reluctant*) I told him a little fib.

ELIZABETH: What fib?

MARTHA: Yes, but you mustn't be angry . . . do you promise?

ELIZABETH: I promise. Queen's word of honour.

MARTHA: I told him you sent me.

ELIZABETH: (*Kicks the tray that* MARTHA *is holding. The cups smash on the ground*) O, slag . . . bitch . . . you stinking . . .

MARTHA: Now now. You promised. Queen's word of honour.

ELIZABETH: Who gives a fuck . . . I'll split you in two . . . I'll murder you . . .

She snatches up the copper pot and goes to hit her with it.

MARTHA: (*Shouting, trying to block her*) Calm down, Elizabeth. Robert Devereux didn't believe me anyway.

ELIZABETH: (*Complete change of voice. As if nothing had happened*) Martha. What are you shouting about? Say 'He didn't believe me' and leave it at that. There are times when you make me want to smash my copper pot over your head. (*Takes up the story again*) He didn't believe you.

She absent-mindedly picks up the folder that EGERTON *left behind.*

MARTHA: No! He's still sulking about the last time . . . he says you humiliated him in front of everyone . . . am I allowed to know what you called him that was so offensive?

ELIZABETH: Gigolo and rent-boy!

She opens the folder and glances at the contents while she talks to MARTHA.

MARTHA: Rent-boy? Are you out of your mind?

ELIZABETH: But he'd infuriated me. He gave me a shitty little smile and called me 'crooked carcass' and 'withered' . . . What do you say to that?

MARTHA: It's not very nice . . .

She picks up the cups that had fallen on the floor.

ELIZABETH: It's not very nice, no. But I had my revenge. I took back the earring I'd given him . . .

MARTHA: Good for you!

ELIZABETH: Yes. I bit off his earlobe.

MARTHA: That seems a bit excessive to me . . .

ELIZABETH: Well, I gave it back to him . . . the earlobe.

She buries her nose in the contents of EGERTON's *folder.*

MARTHA: Well, the fact is that when I tried to warn him about what I knew . . . the infiltrators and spies . . . you're not listening to me . . .

ELIZABETH: Yes, yes. I'm listening. Go on . . .

MARTHA: What are you reading?

ELIZABETH: It's Egerton's file . . . he forgot it . . . or maybe he left it behind on purpose. They're copies of letters from various ambassadors to their respective masters . . .

MARTHA: Heavens! And Egerton, the spy-master, opened the envelopes?

ELIZABETH: Of course. It's all part of the Intelligence Service! He has solvent saliva . . . one lick . . . he opens them, copies them and sends them off again. O, look at these. They're all about me. Listen, listen, this is how the Venetian ambassador honours me. (*She reads*) 'The Queen of England shows off by quoting Latin and Greek, but more than anything else, she loves to laugh in the most gross and vulgar fashion. She tells filthy jokes that would make a brothel-keeper blush. She swears . . . An Italian clown taught her how to blow the most disgusting raspberries, and these she graciously bestows on those lords who have fallen into disfavour. I have even seen her spit on one of them . . .' (*She laughs. Very amused*) So he was there too!

MARTHA: International celebrity at last . . .

ELIZABETH: (*Still reading*) 'She dances like a madwoman, doing incredible jumps. And she sweats so much that when she does pirouettes she soaks the onlookers, like a wet dog that's just got out of the water.'

MARTHA: Well that's true enough. When you're in a state, you do soak everything.

ELIZABETH: Now the Portuguese ambassador thinks I'm really charming . . . Listen how he describes me: 'A wooden doll. A bloodless puppet decked out in frills and furbelows. A sumptuous gown out of which sprouts a head of glass.' Scumbag! Papist shit! (*To* MARTHA) That's not written down. I said that. Listen. Here's more . . . 'Elizabeth is terrifying, even when she laughs . . . ' All right then, the next time I meet him, I'll laugh for three-quarters of an hour . . . I'd like to see him finished . . . dead! (*Hands the folder to* MARTHA) Here, you carry on . . .

MARTHA: 'They say of her that she's too feminine to be a man . . .'

ELIZABETH: I beg your pardon?

MARTHA: '. . . and not feminine enough to be a woman . . .'

ELIZABETH: I'm a hermaphrodite! Elizabeth, Prince Charming!

MARTHA: 'Like all self-respecting monarchs, she loves funerals . . .'

ELIZABETH: All monarchs love funerals. All right. So what?

MARTHA: 'During the service, she drowns out the choir's top notes with her sobbing . . .'

ELIZABETH: That's because I suffer . . .

MARTHA: 'Then the very same evening she turns up at a feast twined round Essex, and waddling like a . . . *birrocha encalorada . . .*'

ELIZABETH: What does that mean? (*Snatches the letters from* MARTHA) *Birrocha encalorada* . . . I'd say that was some kind of insult. (*Looks intently at the sheet of paper*) O look, there's an asterisk here . . . O Egerton's translated it . . . how kind of him! 'Waddling . . .' N-o-o-o-o! '. . . like a she-mule in heat'!? 'Then she proclaims that she has bestowed the title of Earl Marshal on her lover in recognition of his acts of valour in the battlefield of her bed . . .' (*Very very calm*) . . . This doesn't even touch me . . . Sarcasm is the lowest form of humour. A she-mule in heat!! (*Terrifying scream. She hurls chairs, stools, lectern. She kicks the horse, which rolls forward. She gets out the pistol, fires a shot at it. The horse returns to its position*) Stay where you are! If you don't stop, I'll kill you. It's moving. It's moving. (*To the horse*) Stay where you are!

She puts the pistol back in her bodice.

MARTHA: Don't go mad! Just because this man Foexen writes things that you say yourself all the time . . . and your language is much worse.

ELIZABETH: I love him and I can do as I please! (*She notices all the furniture overturned on the floor*) This place is like a bloody brothel. Tidy all this up, Martha! (*Change of tone*) Here I am dying for love of this wonderful brute who won't even deign to throw me a word . . . a letter . . . and all I hear in my head is his voice. And all I can see with my eyes are his eyes . . . I am dying of love . . . I love him.

MARTHA: Come on, Elizabeth. Come on. It's all right. It will pass.

ELIZABETH: How many times do I have to tell you? I don't want it to pass. You and your 'It will pass.' (*Imitates her voice*) I like dying of passion. (*She touches her breast in the spot where she replaced the pistol*) O my God!

MARTHA: What is it, dear? Do you feel ill? Your heart? Sit down.

ELIZABETH: No, it's the pistol . . . I stuck it down here . . . in my bodice . . . it's slipped down . . . it's going to go off . . .

MARTHA: But it's empty. You fired it just now.

ELIZABETH: It's got two barrels . . . the second one is still loaded . . . it's primed . . . the trigger's cocked . . . it's going to go off . . . Jesùs! I'm going to shoot myself!

MARTHA: Stay calm. Stay calm. Now I'll unlace your corset. Get up slowly. I'll have to start at the waist. Stand on this stool . . . Where do you feel it?

ELIZABETH: This is terrible! (*She gets on the stool very very slowly, moving with great circumspection*) Why do you have to make me get up so high to die . . . I'm on my tomb already.

MARTHA: There. Now it's unlaced . . . We'll have to slide it round under the armpit so we can get it round the back . . . Hold on while I get someone to help me . . . (*Runs towards the door*) . . . Guard!

ELIZABETH: Are you mad? Look at the state I'm in . . . and you're going to let just anyone come barging in . . .

MARTHA: It's your choice, dear: a bullet in the stomach or an indiscreet guard?

ELIZABETH: A fortune teller once warned me I'd have trouble with a cock . . . I never thought it would be my own cocked pistol!

MARTHA *comes back with two* GUARDS.

MARTHA: Now be careful! You could set it off . . . we have to ease it round to the back . . .

ELIZABETH: Two of them? Why didn't you call the whole garrison? Bitch!

The three of them set to the task of getting the pistol.

MARTHA: Be brave . . . now you two . . . stretch your fingers . . . here . . . can you feel the pistol?

ELIZABETH: (*Looks at both young* GUARDS *with interest*) Good morning! Of course . . . Come on . . . feel it . . . touch it . . . run your hands over it boys . . . (*Change of tone: menacing*) If you make me go off, that's it . . . If I survive I'll murder you!

MARTHA: Now be good, Elizabeth . . . O damn . . .

ELIZABETH: There, I knew it . . . it's slipped down . . . It's here, over my stomach . . .

MARTHA: No, it's all right . . . It's even better . . . come on, we just have to turn . . .

The two GUARDS *are now behind the* QUEEN, *continuing the search.*

ELIZABETH: Hey, go easy . . . those happen to be my buttocks . . . O my God . . . (*Languid*) . . . Oh. Oh. You might at least throw me the occasional affectionate remark . . . ! Louts!

MARTHA: Once more . . . come on, it's moving . . . nearly there . . .

A shot goes off.

ELIZABETH: O God! Martha! I've assassinated myself! (*Terrified*) Blood . . . I can feel blood running down my legs . . . O God . . . I'm dying . . . My Essex . . . I want him here . . . now . . . Robert! I want to see him for the last time.

MARTHA: (*To the* GUARDS) Out! Go away! Get out!

The GUARDS *leave.*

ELIZABETH: Shot in the arse . . . What an inglorious end for a Queen! . . . Listen, Martha: say that you did it . . . Take the blame. (*Reaction from* MARTHA) I know they'll cut your head off, but the Catholics will make you a saint! Saint Martha-the-Arseshooter.

MARTHA: Let me see . . . (*From behind* ELIZABETH, *she lifts her skirt*) . . . Help me: come on, lift your skirt up. I can't see any blood . . .

ELIZABETH: Are you sure?

MARTHA: No . . . there's a hole . . . but it's in the dress.

ELIZABETH: (*Melodramatic*) So that means the gun went off into thin air, and I've pissed myself . . . I have, Martha . . . (*Gets down off the stool*) . . . and such a lot! O it's too humiliating! The guards pawing me off-duty . . . the pistol going off . . . pee all over me . . . (MARTHA *goes off and comes straight back with a basin and a towel*) . . . and Robert doesn't love me any more . . . I want to see him . . . (*Snivelling*) . . . Martha, go and find him for me . . . tell him to stop planning attacks on me . . . tell him if he'll come back I'll give him back the monopoly on the sweet wine . . .

MARTHA: Yes, yes, dear . . . I'll find him for you . . . I'll bring him here . . . First of all, come here so I can wash you.

ELIZABETH: (*Takes the basin from* MARTHA) Leave me be. I can manage on my own . . . You go on . . . Look for him . . . But don't tell him that I sent you . . .

MARTHA: Well what shall I say then?

ELIZABETH: Tell him I'm ill . . . that I'm dying . . . Yes, that's it . . . I've shot myself with a pistol . . . but don't tell him about the pee . . . for God's sake. (*She goes out, puts down the basin and shouts*) Martha, stop! (*Re-enters*) I can't let him see me looking like this. I just caught sight of myself in the big mirror! . . . It gave me such a shock! Where is my little mirror . . . I want to see if it makes any improvements. (*Looks in the small mirror*) No improvement. No improvement at all. Martha, why have I grown so old these last thirty-five years? . . . I can't let him see me like this . . . like a wreck . . . just so he can call me a 'crooked carcass' again . . . no, I can't . . . I'm ugly, horrible, old . . . (*She's stuffing little leaves into her mouth: she takes them out of the pocket of her dressing gown*) . . . I'll kill myself . . . O what a life!

MARTHA: Well to begin with, you can spit out that disgusting mess of leaves . . .

She goes to get a basin.

ELIZABETH: They lift my spirits . . . make me feel better . . .

MARTHA: They knock you out is what they do . . . and they make your teeth turn black so they look rotten . . . come on, spit them out!

She offers her the basin.

ELIZABETH: No I won't spit them out.

MARTHA: Come along, otherwise you'll have breath that stinks like a captive dragon's! Spit!

ELIZABETH: (*She spits in the basin*) A captive dragon's breath is just what I need . . . I've already got the skin . . . if I bumped into Saint George, he'd use me for target practice.

MARTHA *takes the basin off and comes straight back.*

MARTHA: Yes that's right . . . come on now, why don't you do something to pick yourself up a bit . . . a nice astringent poultice . . . a good massage to tone you up . . .

ELIZABETH: Not again . . . Not that old hag again . . . what does she call herself?

MARTHA: Dame Grosslady . . . yes, she's the one . . . the only one who can save you . . .

ELIZABETH: Yes. Save me with dung . . . that's what that old hag puts in those miraculous poultices of hers. She's disgusting!

MARTHA: Don't talk nonsense. What do you mean, dung? It's organic mud. Decomposing matter and putrefied vegetable detritus.

ELIZABETH: There you are. You said it! The scientific definition of shit! Yes, I've been told all about her: she comes and slaps these poultices of organic dung – that's what you call it – on you; and you look younger – twenty minutes younger at the most . . . and in return you can't go out of the house because of the filthy stink you give off . . . so people say: 'Ah, doesn't she look young!' . . . and then SMACK! Out cold. For the love of God. And then I've been told, to lift the skin on your face, she pulls your hair back so hard you end up looking like a skull. A young skull, but a skull! And then she massages with her great meaty hands, she wrings your fat . . . and thumps you . . .

MARTHA: I understand. You don't feel like it . . . You're right. All that torture, and for whom? We won't bother . . .

ELIZABETH: (*Decisive*) Yes, we won't bother. (*Same tone of voice*) Go and summon Dame Grosslady straight away.

MARTHA: Yes but . . . hold on a moment . . .

ELIZABETH: Obey me!

MARTHA: You won't change your mind and make me send her away like you did last week?

MARTHA *goes and fetches a cloth.*

ELIZABETH: I told you to obey me . . . Damn chatterbox . . . how did I end up living with you? . . . What are you doing now?

MARTHA: (*Pointing to the wet floor*) Wait a second, let me mop this up.

ELIZABETH: Have you gone mad? It's holy piss. I did it. I am the Pope. Shift yourself!

MARTHA: All right. Shall I bring her in then?

She goes towards the door.

ELIZABETH: Bring who in?

MARTHA: Dame Grosslady. She's waiting outside.

ELIZABETH: Already? How on earth did that happen?

MARTHA: I thought it might be a good idea. I sent for her.

ELIZABETH: Stop! Just a minute! Wait . . . I'm not ready . . . I'm afraid . . .

MARTHA: Just think of all the agony a hen has to go through just to lay an egg . . . Why, you'll be able to produce a new Queen! (*She goes to the door and shouts*) Open the door! Send Dame Grosslady in!

A gigantic woman comes in. She's wearing a white mask – a Venetian domino: DAME GROSSLADY. She has a basket on her arm and other objects.

GROSSLADY: Maxima domina te exelle nobis . . .

ELIZABETH: Stop right where you are! What's this mask you've got on?

GROSSLADY: I apparel it pimply to misguise the brutissimo mush undersotto it, Your Ladleship.

ELIZABETH: Take it off at once . . . I like to look people in the face.

MARTHA: What difference does it make? She only does it to help you. She doesn't have a very savoury reputation. If anyone found out that you used her to fix yourself up . . . her, next best thing to a witch . . .

ELIZABETH: I said the mask has to go!

GROSSLADY: God wot thee won't be squittered, Your Madge. (*Takes mask off*) Allora, ecco the vero me.

ELIZABETH: Dieu sauve moi, qu'elle est horrible!

MARTHA: Je t'avais prévenue.

GROSSLADY: Dinna fadge with the parleyvoo frog . . . I be perfetto conversazionie in frog, signora magnifica. Si, I sembro a bloke, I savvy, a clapper dudgeon . . . and not too graziosa or snoutfair . . . Per favore, dinna facket me to feel blushful . . . And dinna be fritted of me, sweetling Queenie. I be a bona pimple copesmate, and I be come to aid and abatter you.

She goes to the door and pulls in strange wooden contraptions.

ELIZABETH: I certainly hope so, my dear Dame Grosslady. (*To* MARTHA) What language is this loony speaking?

MARTHA: How should I know? Sounds like a mish-mash of slang and some dialect or other . . .

ELIZABETH: And what is this round contraption?

GROSSLADY: Questo rattletrap we calliamao a strutter or stroller . . . and we serve it to apprentice you to trot on bawdyshoon without going tumblyshanks arsy-versy.

ELIZABETH: Bawdy shoon?

GROSSLADY: Take a squint. (*Shows her two things made of cork and skin*) Pattens con sole mios altissima three footsies.

ELIZABETH: Why don't you just call them stilts and have done with it?

GROSSLADY: The bawdybaskets in Venezia apparel them to look Monty-Blancy and skinny malinky.

ELIZABETH: Did you hear that, Martha? What a career I've had. From a Queen to a whore! Happy at last.

GROSSLADY: But Your Madge, those bawdybaskets pocket piles of loot.

ELIZABETH: I don't need to look any taller. I am fine the height I am.

GROSSLADY: Queenie, ifn tha preferishies we can leaviamo thee thus with a bucket of lard for an arse.

ELIZABETH: Really! What language. I can kick you out, you know.

GROSSLADY: Dinna fash thyssen, Magnifica . . . (*She slips*) Ooops a daisy! What hath I glissaded sopra? . . . What be all this slipsloppy? Mayhap my peepers mistook me, but it doth semble like . . .

ELIZABETH: Yes . . . it was . . . my horse . . .

GROSSLADY: Hissen? A wooden prancer that pisseth? That be bona fortuna!

ELIZABETH: What do you know about anything? It's a royal horse.

MARTHA *and* DAME GROSSLADY *strap the clogs onto* ELIZABETH.

GROSSLADY: O marry then . . . The Royal Wee . . .

MARTHA: Be brave, Elizabeth, get up.

She moves clumsily on the clogs.

GROSSLADY: Bestir thyssen, Magnificence . . . Quetch! Opla! Quicketty presto into the strutter . . . (*They help her into it*) . . . Bene . . . That's the way to do it . . . Allora we shuttiamo thee in, snug as a bug in a rug . . . Assissta, assissta, Lady Martha.

MARTHA: Of course.

GROSSLADY: O guarda the Queenie! The bona lallies! Commandatore of tutto! Miracolo di largesse!

MARTHA: You look slimmer already.

ELIZABETH: (*Amused giggle*) In a baby walker at my age!

GROSSLADY: Does tha desideri a dummy to suck, My Ladle?

ELIZABETH: (*She doesn't react*) Don't I look rather ridiculous, stuck up here like this? I'm taller than my horse . . .

GROSSLADY: O dinna caparison thyssen to the wooden pisser.

MARTHA: Walk. Practise.

ELIZABETH: Take it from me, I'll learn to walk on these whores' clogs, and at the very first opportunity, when I meet the Portuguese ambassador, the 'mula encalorada' one, I'll fall down on top of him . . . I'll use him as a doormat!

While ELIZABETH *practises walking in the machine,* DAME GROSSLADY *brings on a dais on which she puts an armchair.*

GROSSLADY: Foot it, foot it, my sweeting beanpole . . .

ELIZABETH: When I'm in Essex's arms, as soon as he's given up these rebellions against me, won't he be amazed to see how tall I've grown . . . I'll ask him for a kiss . . . (*Laughing*) . . . and he'll be kissing my belly button. (*Changed tone*) Get me out of this thing . . .

GROSSLADY: Beneship, beneship dearlie. Settle thine arse sopra this chaise the whiles I preparare the wrinkle-mousse to smoddle thee in.

MARTHA: Why don't you take it easy, and play your lute for a while. I'll go and fetch it for you.

ELIZABETH: No. Pass me those papers on the lectern.

MARTHA: The ambassadors' letters?

ELIZABETH: No, the manuscript of *Hamlet*.

MARTHA: Not that stuff again.

She brings the manuscript to ELIZABETH.

GROSSLADY: O. *Omelette*! I familiar him . . . I vide that at the Globule . . . Actored by that coneycatcher . . . quando whuffed out that . . . 'Scarper! Scarper into a convict house O-feel-a-me! Thy old man had been cozened and catched by thy bawdy parts else! Capricornified . . . ! Scarper into a convento . . . !' Ha, ha, ha, ha . . .

She gets a jar out of her basket and mimes spreading cream on the QUEEN's *face.*

ELIZABETH: Do you always laugh like that?

GROSSLADY: Nay, nay, my voce be a bit ginger beer just now.

ELIZABETH: What is it you've put on my face? . . . It's pulling my skin.

GROSSLADY: Flowers of fartleberry.

MARTHA: What on earth are you looking for in that manuscript?

DAME GROSSLADY *makes little plaits out of the* QUEEN's *hair and then ties them together at the back.*

ELIZABETH: The proof that this hack isn't writing just to make a fool of me; but that the brains behind Robert Devereux's plot are here!

MARTHA: What are you saying? That *Hamlet* is a piece of propaganda against you?

ELIZABETH: Martha, don't make fun of me. (*To* DAME GROSSLADY) And go easy you, you're not skinning a rabbit . . .

GROSSLADY: It be perfetto normalo, My Leeryship.

ELIZABETH: Listen, get it into your head, will you . . . (MARTHA *takes the clogs off* ELIZABETH) . . . I'm not talking nonsense. This entire work is a fiendish attack on my person and my politics. This thespian guttersnipe is slandering me every single night at the Globe.

MARTHA: Listen Elizabeth, I happened to be at a performance of *Hamlet* at the Globe a few days ago, and I swear I didn't see any attack on you. None at all.

ELIZABETH: You saw it, and you never even had a suspicion? 'The frog lay deep at bottom of the well, perceived the pail above her, circlèd by the light, and took it for the very sun.'

MARTHA: What are you talking about?

ELIZABETH: It's a quotation from Shakespeare.

GROSSLADY: Bellissima! How doth it trip? 'The froggie in the fundament of the well tort the arsehole of the bucket was the sole mio . . .' Splendido!

MARTHA: Be quiet! The only thing I understand is that she's calling me a frog . . . The rest is as clear as mud . . .

ELIZABETH: But it's Hamlet himself who says that.

MARTHA: Are you sure?

ELIZABETH: He could have said it. Even if I made it up, that's the way he talks.

GROSSLADY: Ulrika! It be like tha vidis a defection in a puking glass! Arse about face!

MARTHA: Hold your tongue!

ELIZABETH: No, no . . . she's right . . . that's exactly what it is . . . a mirror image. Exactly!

GROSSLADY: Chop on you, biggedy show-off!

MARTHA: How dare you talk to me like that.

GROSSLADY: Shut thy clapper, pinchfart! Pickfords they stampers. (*To* ELIZABETH) Marry come up, I dinna ken where tha finds thy servitudes, Queenie.

ELIZABETH: To put it precisely, this cunning shyster William Shakespeare . . . in order to disguise . . .

GROSSLADY: Pluck off thy shift. Scoot thy duds.

ELIZABETH: Never. Absolutely not.

GROSSLADY: No need for blushful. We be tutti feminies. The solo erectus here be the pissing prancer.

ELIZABETH: All women. I'm not so sure . . . (*Looks closely at* DAME GROSSLADY) . . . I have my doubts about one of us three, my dear Dame Grosslady.

GROSSLADY: Naughty, naughty. Dinna abuse thyssen. Th'art a reet good looking femina yet.

ELIZABETH: I just don't feel like it.

MARTHA: I've got an idea.

MARTHA *goes out and returns with a kind of screen which she sets up in front of* ELIZABETH, *covering her body but leaving her head sticking out over the top.* ELIZABETH *takes off her dressing gown and shift, helped by* MARTHA *and* DAME GROSSLADY. MARTHA *goes off with* ELIZABETH's *garments and returns with a large sheet in which she wraps her.*

ELIZABETH: As I was saying, Shakespeare, in order to disguise the obviousness of the political allusions . . . has simply reversed the sexes of the characters.

MARTHA: What do you mean?

ELIZABETH: I mean that he has changed the female characters into males and vice versa.

GROSSLADY: He be untowardly pranking a drag act: dressing up in the puking glass.

ELIZABETH: Yes.

MARTHA: Give me an example.

ELIZABETH: That's simple: I'm female . . . Hamlet is male . . .

MARTHA: Yes of course, because Hamlet is a parody of you. I was forgetting.

GROSSLADY: Oy, Mistress Minx, stop that pulling the lallies. Don't make a pish at her.

ELIZABETH: Take no notice of her . . . (*To* MARTHA) . . . Now then, are you listening to me? I am Hamlet! Sweet Ophelia is female . . . and my beloved Robert is male. Hamlet's father has been assassinated . . . my mother was assassinated. The ghost of Hamlet's father pursues him night and day . . . likewise my mother has continually cried through my dreams for vengeance.

GROSSLADY: Vide how it all balenciagas out? Tat for tit.

ELIZABETH: Hamlet's mother marries her brother-in-law . . . And my father too, Henry VIII, married his brother's widow. That is, his sister-in-law.

GROSSLADY: Che famiglia hotch-potch . . .

ELIZABETH: It is my own story . . .

MARTHA: Wait a minute, don't cheat. Your father was personally responsible for Anne Boleyn's death . . . but Hamlet's mother is innocent.

ELIZABETH: Who told you that? Read the text carefully . . . The Queen plays innocence, but Hamlet finds that she's guilty . . . And my father Henry was the same . . . he pretended to oppose the lords who condemned Anne Boleyn to death. O you should have seen him raving and weeping tears of blood over my mother's headless corpse . . . Just like Hamlet's mother!

GROSSLADY: The puking glass imago! Esattamento! Esattamentissimo!

MARTHA: Elizabeth, I'm sorry, but really you're carrying on like one of those barrow boys who sell glue that's supposed to stick anything to anything. I'm sorry . . . Tell me this: what straightforward concrete reason have you got for saying that you are Hamlet in the play?

GROSSLADY: Rispondo mio? But this be the finale time, mark you.

ELIZABETH: Go on, try. We're listening.

GROSSLADY: Allora, Queenie here, Lizzie of Angleterror, it be advised abroad, be possessed of a shockissimo obfuscation: videlicet: when she vidis curtains or tapezzeria stirring . . . she semper hath an excalibur to hand . . . 'A bogey!' she brabbles . . . 'Thwack!' . . . And devil care who may be prinking behind.

She mimes running someone through.

MARTHA: Well yes, actually she nearly had me this morning.

GROSSLADY: By my troth, and she never poniarded thee? Queenie, tha must needs practicare a bit more . . . Fancy missing this doxydell . . . Anyroad up, Omelette hath this same obfuscation . . . There be a scenario wherein the tapezzeria stirs and Bolonius be dietro . . .

ELIZABETH: Polonius, who represents my chief councillor, Cecil.

GROSSLADY: O what an allergy! Disna tha vidi? Dunque: here we haviamo questo Bolonius who be the allergy for Cecil, and he be dietro a tapezzeria, and here be Omelette parleying to his mummikins, prating her the mostissimo hoggish rude: 'How couldst tha matrimonial that pelting pinchfart – thou dishclout!' . . . Si, si. That be his modus of parleyvoo to her. And then at a certo momento the arras stirios . . . AAARGH!! A rattus! Thwack! You savvy, overby in Lurpak-land, they have rattuses five and a half feets alto . . . five feets nine at least. SPLAT . . . Stab with the excalibur! THUNK! She jerrycumumbles him! Bolonius the allergy thrummed on the parterre. (*To* MARTHA) And the proxy allergy be thee . . .

MARTHA: (*To* ELIZABETH) O, you see, what a brilliant proposition . . . Irrefutable!

GROSSLADY: Ah, tha doesna accordian with me? Okey dokey, I must needs presentarey thee a secondo examplo. At the finish of *Omelette*, who trolls up to puttiamo some orderaro dentro the shit heap?

MARTHA: Fortinbras.

GROSSLADY: Shortinarse of Doorway. Bono. And who, so the puritani whiffle it abroad, be the Shortinarse from out the northo who will puttiamo some orderaro dentro the shitheap we calliamo Angleterror?

MARTHA: James.

GROSSLADY: Jams of Sconeland, perched on Hadrian's wall pronto to crash down on thy bonce, Queenie.

She gives a violent tug to the QUEEN's *head.*

ELIZABETH: Just be careful there, Dame Grosslady, you're the one who's crashing down on my head.

GROSSLADY: It be pimply on account of I be all eager beaver.

ELIZABETH: You're pulling my ears and eyes back so hard, I'll end up looking like . . . a mongol!

GROSSLADY: Pish! Mongrel! Thee comes up bellissima . . . Guarda, I've completamente disappeared thy bubble chin.

ELIZABETH: How dare you. I have never had a . . . double chin . . .

GROSSLADY: Tha be correcto. Tha had a bubble neck.

MARTHA: You must forgive her . . . she was getting mixed up with Hamlet. He's the one with the double chin . . . and the little pot belly . . . and the flat feet.

ELIZABETH: The subtle irony of your remark quite escapes me.

GROSSLADY: I comprehensived it! Shall I explicare?

MARTHA: No. Be silent!

GROSSLADY: Nae. I will story it to her. The nub is: the thesp who actors Omelette be nominato Richard Garbage. I savvy him bene. A cove of forty-two . . . under a bono lamp he doesna sembra a day beyant sixty-two . . . sixty-four . . . He be a thumping great pudding . . . moltissimo wheezing . . . and peach time he actors, he attracts an ashma . . . and in the duello with Layherpes – Layherpes be molto juvenilia, he flipflaps, he jumpers great saltos. Vidi what Richard Garbage fadges in the duello . . . he twiddle twaddles . . . he knits . . . (*She mimes knitting*) . . . so at a certo punto . . . though he be never shifting . . . he whoofs out 'Arrgh, arrgh, arrgh'. (*Panting sound*) And the Queenie dickets him 'O Omelette, that's no a bairn nae more . . . Tha be brething through thine arsehole.' Shakespeare, eh? But they censoried that pronto . . . but that be what he scrivened . . . Allora, this Garbage be covered in sweater . . .

MARTHA: (*Interrupting her*) Covered in freckles too . . . and he's not got one, but two double chins . . . and he waddles and minces around halfway between a hen and a Muscovy duck.

GROSSLADY: Si. That be veritabile. He be all sidlewry. He trips all arsey versey with his trotters turned out. But when he actors . . . such forzio, he drunks tutti the spectatori . . .

She acts out in nonsense talk – grammelot – the soliloquy, 'To Be or Not To Be . . .' with all the intonations of a dramatic recitation.

GROSSLADY: And tha comprehensives tuttithing he parleys . . . he be a forza of natura . . . even though he be a bit campy fribble.

ELIZABETH: A bit? He's a raving pansy.

MARTHA: Well it doesn't show.

GROSSLADY: It vidies, it vidies . . . It lacks him but the plumes cultivating out of his arsehole. And forwhy did they

presentare the part to this Monsieur Mingo de Mousetrap?
There needs be five other tractors in the compagnia who had
made a buonerer dog in a doublet . . . juveniler, spindlier,
fitter tractors . . . and perche did they choosie this ham
barm cake?

ELIZABETH: They chose him deliberately. A sour old clumsy
has-been . . . They did it deliberately so there could be no
mistaking that he's supposed to be my exact double . . .
'Queen of shining beauty . . .' That's what those creeps at
court say to me; and all the while my face is crumbling away
. . . 'Goddess of Youth and Freshness . . .' and I'm falling
to bits.

GROSSLADY: Marry, tha canst not dicket that nae more. Not
for thy mush anyroad up. Tocca how thrumming it be.

She gets ELIZABETH *out of the armchair and takes it off the
dais.*

ELIZABETH: What are you up to now?

GROSSLADY: We must needs slenderise thy tripes and
trullibubs, mustn't we?

ELIZABETH: Tripes? What filth have you got this time?

GROSSLADY: Slugslurpers.

She shows her a pair she's taken out of the basket.

ELIZABETH: Leeches?

GROSSLADY: Nay. Leechies suckie gore. Ye grubbies suck
blubber. Oooh . . . suck like . . . Guarda how bellissima
they be . . . and the teensie blue sparklers . . . perky little
capons . . .

ELIZABETH: They're disgusting. No, no. For heaven's sake.
You want to put those revolting worms on my stomach?

MARTHA *makes* ELIZABETH *stand on the dais while*
DAME GROSSLADY *puts the 'slugs' on different parts of
her body.*

GROSSLADY: Si. And the hams and haunches also.

ELIZABETH: O for God's sake!

GROSSLADY: And the boulders, and the smiters . . . and the widow's hump dietro thy neck.

ELIZABETH: O God, I'm going to vomit.

GROSSLADY: And thy kidney-platz and thy botty. They'll slenderise thee dimber damber . . . Guarda the beasties! Guarda this little oinker! Attila! Caligula!

ELIZABETH: All right. Get on with it then. Just don't let me see them. Where were we?

MARTHA: Old Hamlet with his pot belly.

ELIZABETH: Yes, and he's probably impotent as well. He goes around saying he's turned on all the time, but he never does any fucking . . .

GROSSLADY: By my troth, such vulgaritude! The F-word from a Queenie. And difronto of ye timidi little sluggles. Guarda this one. He's gone tutto pallido . . . Slurp away, Genghis.

ELIZABETH: But the thing that really gets up my nose is the way this bastard slanders me, saying I'm bringing the country to ruination. His: 'Something rotten in the State of Denmark' . . . What he means is my sewer, here, in England. Don't you see? Denmark! Who does he think he's fooling?

GROSSLADY: Ah, now I comprehensive this whole puking glass imago business . . . Quando he dicket: 'Lurpak-land be a dungeon' he intends: 'Angleterror be a dungeon . . .'

MARTHA: You've got doubles on the brain!

ELIZABETH: Is that right? All right then, listen: what happens at the end of Hamlet?

MARTHA: A massacre.

GROSSLADY: O si. At the finale there be dead corpuscles here there and tupperware. Layherpes excalibured par ici, the arsenickèd Queen par là . . . the King shite-ing through his denturas ici, Omelette gasparding his ultimo breathe par la . . .

ELIZABETH: And whose fault is it?

GROSSLADY: Omelette's. We all savvy it be Omelette's salt on account of he canst not make up his nous box. He dithers and dathers . . . He oughter've sorted it all long since. Excalibured the poxy nuncle pronto when he was down on his mary-bones jabbering prayers in the gospel shop. 'Now I'll excalibur him . . . no, half a mo' . . . dicket to hissen . . . 'I'll be doing him a flavour . . . cos he'd mort scusied of tutti his sins, and he'd locomote diretto to paradiso . . . My old man morted stuffoed full of sin and Boom!, locomoted to hell . . . I'll attend till nuncle locomotes into the chamber with mamma mia and they start playing at rantum scantum' . . . And then he sorties the excalibur . . . 'No, I willna fadge it today . . . tomorrow . . . we'll see . . . day dopotomorrow . . . I dinna ken . . . mayhap next week . . . ' Odds plut and her nails, he oughter've ordinated the whole shebang in the primo scena when the bogey of Omelette's dad poppied up and dicket: 'O-o-o-m-le-e-e-e-tte . . .' The bogey dad parleyed an echo like all proper bogeys . . . 'O-o-o-omle-e-e-ette . . . i-i-it . . . be-e-e-e-e thy-y-y-y-y nu-u-u-u-ncle . . . he-e-e-e-e be-e-e-e-e the-e-e-e-e a-a-a-a-ssa-a-assi-i-n . . . mo-o-o-o-ort hi-i-i-im . . .'

ELIZABETH: But if he'd killed the King in the first scene, then he wouldn't have been able to write a tragedy with five acts.

GROSSLADY: Mine arse on a bandbox for five acts . . . Then there be O-feel-a-me passing over . . . and then the nick ninny locomotes to Angleterror and retornaries . . . and then the duello . . . Phew! I preferishi things clear. One action but clear. Clearissimo. The bogey dad poppy up, dicket: 'Omelette, he be the villain . . .' 'O be he? . . . Okey dokey then . . .' Sort the excalibur . . . 'Assassin' . . . But noo. It be 'Now I thinkiamo I'll waiter a bit . . . I'll circumbendibus . . . I'll draggie the trotters . . . I'll do it one of these odd come shortlies . . .'

ELIZABETH: And isn't that what I'm accused of too?

She turns round suddenly and squashes the worms.

GROSSLADY: Noooo!

ELIZABETH: What happened?

GROSSLADY: Nay, tha buffle-headed blowsabella. The slugslurpers be all squished . . . quel desastro . . . Just like the finale of *Omelette* . . . Tha's squished the Queenie . . .

ELIZABETH: And isn't that what I'm accused of too . . . ?

GROSSLADY: Squishing slugslurpers? They be correcto.

ELIZABETH: No. Of not eliminating my enemies . . . of not doing anything . . . You know what the Puritans accuse me of: 'The Spaniards are throttling the Dutch right on our doorstep . . . and I, fainthearted Queen, let them get on with it . . . the Irish are in open revolt, and I . . . instead of undertaking a proper scorched earth repression, hesitate, negotiate, fiddle around and keep changing my mind. I talk to the Pope who has excommunicated me, and I refuse to talk to the Protestants who have elected me to be their Pope . . .'

DAME GROSSLADY *is fiddling with* ELIZABETH's *ear.*

GROSSLADY: It be on account of tha be troppo genteel . . . Tha dost license them to prittle and prattle . . . If I were thee . . . WHACK!!

Makes a gesture of chopping off someone's head.

ELIZABETH: (*To* DAME GROSSLADY) What do you think you're up to, poking your finger in my ear?

GROSSLADY: It be not mine digit . . . It be uno of the grublets creepied into thy lughole.

ELIZABETH: Martha, help!

MARTHA: O, Holy Mary, get it out!

GROSSLADY: It isna culpa mia ifn the grublets like greaseball lugholes.

ELIZABETH: O my God, I feel sick!

GROSSLADY: I canna gripper him . . . O here he be . . . Ooop-la! Gotcha. Guarda how blubbered he be . . . bellissimi little peepers!

ELIZABETH: Damned hag . . . Get away from me . . . Get away . . .

GROSSLADY: Tutti the novelty grublettes parterre . . . ! Guarda . . .

ELIZABETH *goes off, followed by* MARTHA, *to get dressed.*

GROSSLADY: Ey, but guarda the pastance and beverage this one hath gluggered down before he snuffled it. So blubberchumps! And yet his sparklers be peepless. Alas! Poor grublette! Here hung that wibble I have wobbled I know not how soft. Where be your soupsucks now? Your slipslimes so slushful and sweatsweet? O well, so it goesio. I will e'en hike him off incontinent chez moi to my hubby. He be a Capitano Birdseye. And quando I show him ye blubbered grublettes he'll be betwattled. He'll locomotor quick coarseyfishing. He'll sticky ye grublettes sopra his anglehooks and hurl them to the fundament of the brook . . . And quando they vidi ye blubbered grublettes . . . Entrare the codpieces! 'What grublettes!!' . . . SCRUMP!! And this even we haviamo a thumping great codpiece to nosh. Ha ha ha. But if'n you think on't, we'll not be noshing cod. Forby the grublettes hath noshed the Queenie and the cod hath noshed the grublettes. So in vino veritas, we'll be noshing the Queen!! Mine arse but that be a frisking dab think, eh? Howzat for an allergy? (*Pause*) To dicket the verity, I didna trade up that little parabola. It be Shakespeare veritably. It be his think, quando he facket Omelette to parley: 'Your grublette be your only imperator for diet . . . Your blubberchumps imperator and your low life bugger be but variable servizio . . . Vido how a Queenie may make a processione through the tripes of your low-life poverty man.' It be sufficiently to give thee the frighteners! Quel idea pot, that Shakespeare! Tha canst not think one think he hath not thinked before!

ELIZABETH: (*Behind the tapestry*) Dame Grosslady! It might be my imagination, but I really do have the feeling that I'm thinner.

GROSSLADY: Nay, nay. Veritablymenty, it be not thy imaginaziony, Queenie. Tha must needs be slenderised. Guarda how puffed and blubbered the beasties be from sucking at thee . . . sembra in the pudding club.

She shows her. Passing one of the worms round the curtain with her hand.

ELIZABETH: (*Still behind the tapestry*) Aaargh! I told you not to show them to me! Stupid bitch! (*Change of tone*) Listen, could you work another little miracle . . . on the breasts . . . they're like two dried up lemons.

GROSSLADY: Tha kleps that a 'little' miracolo!! An tha gies me tempo sufficienty I can resurrectio the dumpling bubbies . . . I'll gie thee twa titties so gollumpus, quando tha crosses thy strappers 'twill sembra a mantelpiece – tha canst rest a varse of floribundikins sopra and sprinkle them each matin . . . O che bellissima! Bellissima duds!

ELIZABETH *enters wearing a dress and a court wig and a suitable crown.* MARTHA *follows her.*

ELIZABETH: It's just a little something I put on for wearing around the house . . . How do I look? Do you think Robert will like me?

MARTHA: He will be stunned.

GROSSLADY: He must needs be bog-eyed . . . As I be, over thee and Shakespeare's double omelette!

MARTHA *and the* DAME *put the pattens on* ELIZABETH.

MARTHA: And me!

ELIZABETH: Ah, so I've finally managed to sow a seed of suspicion in that head of yours!

MARTHA: I'm more puzzled than anything . . . You know that if what you suspect is true, it means there's an organised conspiracy behind the whole thing?

ELIZABETH: Of course there is.

GROSSLADY: Marry come up, I dinna convocate. Odds bodikin! Revoluziony organizzato by thesps? Canst tha vidi them, tutti the tractors with their wooden excaliburs and their canoni stuffoed with talcum and mush powder? 'Pronto for the revoluziony! Stuffo the canoni! Fire!' BOOM BOOM!! (*She mimes the explosion of a cannon loaded with talc. Has a coughing fit*) Finito the revoluziony!

ELIZABETH: Really. These thespians are just the chorus. There's someone behind them, firing real bullets. And I'll prove it to you. Give me the manuscript of *Hamlet*, and I'll read you this monologue replacing the male with the female. Instead of 'Prince', I'll say 'Queen'.

'Why what an ass I am. This is most brave,
That I, the daughter of a dear mother murdered,
Prompted to my revenge by heaven and hell,
Must like a whore unpack my heart with words
And fall a-cursing like a very drab . . .'

EGERTON: (*He comes on with another folder*) Excuse me. Am I disturbing . . . ?

DAME GROSSLADY *goes towards* EGERTON *and makes signs at him to be quiet.* ELIZABETH *gets up and walks on the pattens.*

ELIZABETH: Quiet backstage!

She continues the recitation.

ELIZABETH: 'How stand I then, that have a mother killed, a father stained,
Excitements of my reason and my blood,
And let all sleep? While to my shame . . .'

EGERTON: Who is she so angry with?

GROSSLADY: (*Under her breath, but getting louder*) She be actoring the party of Omelette. He be a wibble-wobble ambodexter transvest; portas plumes in his arse, and he takes the pish fuori the Queenie . . .

ELIZABETH: (*Trying to interrupt* DAME GROSSLADY) 'Bloody, bawdy villain . . .'

GROSSLADY: (*She explains the plot of* Hamlet *to* EGERTON *in nonsense language – 'grammelot'*) . . . ecco the finale of

Action One! (*To* ELIZABETH) Your Infernalship, it
behoves me to explicary this to him on account of he doesna
ken sweet F.A. from *Omelette*. He must needs be one of the
Old Bill . . . Paolizia . . . (*Continues to 'explain' the plot of*
Hamlet *to* EGERTON) . . . finale of the Quarto Action!

ELIZABETH: Hold your tongue, Dame Grosslady . . . !
'Bloody, bawdy villain . . .'

Behind ELIZABETH's *back,* DAME GROSSLADY *mimes
the plot of Act Five.*

ELIZABETH: Give me your hand!

GROSSLADY: I be quasi finito Action the Fist!

ELIZABETH: (*To* DAME GROSSLADY) If you say one
more word, I will summon the guards and have you thrown
out.

'O most pernicious woman!
O villain, villain, smiling damned villain! . . . It cannot be
But I am pigeon livered, and lack gall
To make oppression bitter . . .'

Why are you looking at me like that, Egerton? Do you think
I've grown? (*Indicating the clogs*) You probably didn't know
that you go on growing until you're seventy years old, did
you! (*Serious*) Tell me something, if someone had the
impudence to mock your Queen in like fashion, making a
fool of her with such insults . . . what would you do?

EGERTON: Your Highness, who has dared to show such a
lack of respect towards your person?

ELIZABETH: (*Hands the manuscript to* EGERTON) Here he
is: name and surname . . . and the vile speeches, word for
word. If you, my dear Egerton, went to the theatre a little
more often . . . to the Globe, for example . . . this very
evening . . . you would hear them being repeated.

GROSSLADY: Tha'd vidi that Omelette be a kinder dragging
act . . . he fakes pun o' the Queenie . . . And he be
clubbered in the fundament of a well, transvested as a frog,

regarding the arse end of a bucket, and he dicket: 'O che sole mio bellissimo!'

EGERTON: This is impossible!

MARTHA: It's true. These crude theatrical guttersnipes are insulting her . . . and the audience applauds it.

ELIZABETH: And all you're interested in is setting traps for Essex and his bunch of useless idiots to fall into.

EGERTON: Can it be true that they're saying these kind of slanders at the Globe? Sheriff Golber is there every evening. He hasn't noticed anything. He never told me they were making references to you.

ELIZABETH: Is that so? My wooden horse has more brains and imagination than you and Sheriff Golber put together.

GROSSLADY: And he pisseth also!

ELIZABETH: Give me that manuscript. Listen to me Egerton, and try to understand the real meaning of what I'm going to read to you.

GROSSLADY: Nay, miladly, he doesna comprehensive . . .

She's referring to the astonished look on EGERTON's face.

ELIZABETH: Silence, Dame Grosslady!

GROSSLADY: But guarda the expressiony on his mush. He doesna comprehensive. There be nae sparkle in his peepers . . .

ELIZABETH: That's enough . . . Hamlet speaks: 'To die, to sleep . . .' O, Dame Grosslady, I am reading Shakespeare here, don't interrupt.

GROSSLADY: I dinna interrupto – but he doesna comprehensive.

She makes fun of the perplexed look on EGERTON's face.

ELIZABETH:
'. . . To die, to sleep –
To sleep, perchance to dream. Ay, there's the rub;
For in that sleep of death what dreams may come

When we have shuffled off this mortal coil
Must give us pause – there's the respect
That makes calamity of so long life . . .'

EGERTON: I don't understand.

DAME GROSSLADY *is very pleased.*

ELIZABETH: Well done, that's right . . . that's a good line for
you . . . keep saying it . . . Just throw it in every now and
again. It helps me. Go on, say it.

EGERTON: I don't understand.

ELIZABETH: 'You don't understand? If it weren't for terror
of the beyond, everyone would slaughter themselves!
Thousands and thousands of people would put an end to
themselves . . . they would hurl themselves off high cliffs, or
into the sea . . . or they would throw themselves into
fire . . .' Now say your lines again, please Egerton.

EGERTON: I don't understand.

GROSSLADY: So what be new!

She goes over to ELIZABETH *and glances at the manuscript.*

ELIZABETH: Well done! You don't understand? But it's
perfectly clear, wouldn't you say?

'For who would bear the whips and scorns of time:
Th'oppressor's wrong, the proud man's contumely,
The pangs of disprized love, the law's delay,
The insolence of office, and the spurns
That patient merit of th'unworthy takes . . .'

You can check I'm not making any of this up, Egerton . . .

GROSSLADY: Ecco me, checking it punctilio dicky bird for
dicky bird. I spy it finigraphically to vidi tha doesna
inventory any . . .

ELIZABETH:
'. . . who would fardels bear,
To grunt and sweat under a weary life . . .'

EGERTON: O yes. He's really got it in for us.

GROSSLADY: He'll squeeze our brains to a snivel!

ELIZABETH:
'But that the dread of something after death,
The undiscovered country, from whose bourne
No traveller returns, puzzles the will
And makes us rather bear those ills we have,
Than fly to others that we know not of?'

GROSSLADY: 'Tis terribil-ay! I comprehensive his stratagemical acts and monuments! Questo Shakespeare dicket to the rabblement: 'What do you fadge? Shift your ways! Go to! You perfect to be put upon like slaveys, like dumbo bruttoes – pimply on account of your terrorizzato of tripping off to hell? Arseholes! Dandiprats! Hell be here, here sopra terra . . . not underbeyant. Divven be frit. Be a bravery! Arise! Shuffle off this governo of turd. Batter it to a tripes!'

She begins to sing a revolutionary protest song.

EGERTON: (*Shouting*) You're right, you're absolutely right! This is an incitement to rebellion, to revolt!

GROSSLADY: Tranquil thyssen! Thy nous box will explosive else. 'Tis too gross to swallow all at a catch! Go at it piano piano . . .

MARTHA: Just a moment. Now I think you're going a little too far . . . I don't see any real incitement to rebellion in this. Perhaps a tendency towards a sort of ill-humour . . . discontent, let us say . . .

GROSSLADY: (*She mocks* MARTHA's *attempt to play things down – mimes a chicken laying an egg*) PLOP! The ovum of harmonia! And a teensy Paisley inside!

She mimes something small running away.

EGERTON: Come what may, Your Majesty, I will arrest him and close down the theatre immediately . . .

GROSSLADY: And then tha canst fire and brimstone it . . . A puff of wind . . . some ambulating sparks . . .

ELIZABETH: You will do nothing of the kind, Egerton. What you will do is make enquiries and find out whether this Shakespeare is part of the Earl of Essex's plot . . . then we will see . . .

EGERTON: I will set up an inquiry straight away.

ELIZABETH: While we're on the subject of enquiries, have you been able to authenticate that letter to James of Scotland? The one that according to you was written by Robert of Essex?

EGERTON: Your Majesty, I am mortified, but I am obliged to tell you that you were right: the letters have been found to be forgeries . . . even the seals were forged.

ELIZABETH: You've been able to conduct a thorough inquiry in so short a time?

EGERTON: No – we simply hung the courier who gave us the letter up on a hook . . . After a while he retracted everything . . . he admitted that it was all a libel he'd made up on the spur of the moment.

ELIZABETH: Perfect! You see Martha, in our country, the quality of justice is now strained, it hangeth balanced from a butcher's hook.

GROSSLADY: Bella! Bellissima! What a metaphorical! Shakespeare, Shakespeare . . . Shakespeare . . .

ELIZABETH: No, Dame Grosslady. It's not Shakespeare's, it's mine.

GROSSLADY: But 'twas Shakespeare's stylo!

ELIZABETH: Well I dare say it will turn up in one of his pot boilers sooner or later . . . He steals all of his best lines from me . . . Now what is it, Egerton? What are you hiding in that folder? Bad news, I would imagine.

EGERTON: It is proof, Your Majesty.

ELIZABETH: Proof of what?

EGERTON: That certain bands of Puritans are preparing to give aid to the plotters.

ELIZABETH: (*Amused laugh*) Ha ha . . . Your trap turning against you, Egerton? You dangled the bait of the Armoury so the plotters would be well armed, and Essex would be provoked into an attack . . . You intended to screw him once and for all. And now, bands of Puritans are snapping at the same line. Oh! It is great sport to see an Egerton preparing the powder, and then on account of the mistakes he has made, to see him hoist with his own petard . . . BOUM!

GROSSLADY: Ha ha! Bona! Shakespeare!

ELIZABETH: It's mine, Dame Grosslady.

GROSSLADY: And what dost Shakespeare e'er scriven of his own? What? (*Pause*) Tealeaf!

EGERTON: I am at a loss to understand your extraordinary satisfaction, Your Majesty. One might think you were savouring the prospect of our possible undoing.

MARTHA: He's right. You must be mad. You forget it would be yours too.

ELIZABETH: All right, all right . . . I went a bit too far. Very well then, what is keeping you from stepping in?

EGERTON: Your Highness, at the moment they are all dispersed in small groups . . . we are waiting for them to join forces. We will attack them before they can reach the Houses of Parliament or the Palace.

ELIZABETH: Which Palace?

EGERTON: This Palace. Your Palace.

GROSSLADY: Dost tha no comprehensive, Queenie? Questi abscotchalators be furnished with the brass neck to come here and mort thee.

MARTHA: Exactly!

EGERTON: So, Your Highness, I feel, and Secretary Cecil is of the same opinion, that you would be safer in some other place than this.

ELIZABETH: In other words, I've got to make a run for it.

GROSSLADY: Afterwards that I've confectionated the mantelpiece with the varse of floribundikins for you to sprinkle . . .

ELIZABETH: Be silent!

EGERTON: Yes, Your Majesty. The Lords of the Privy Council, and the Commons and Bacon above all, they all insist that you take shelter in Kenilworth Castle . . . You will be escorted under armed guard, naturally . . .

ELIZABETH: Under armed guard? Why me? What have I got to do with this? With my own eyes I have read dozens of abusive scrawls on walls in London these last few days . . . and in none of them have I seen incitements to rise against the Queen and skin her alive. What I have seen are insults and death threats primarily to you, Egerton . . . to Cecil . . . to the Lords . . . not to mention Bacon . . . According to the people, it is you are giving me ill council . . . to them, I am still their Good Queen Bess. Allow me to offer you a piece of advice: why don't you move, the whole lot of you, to Kenilworth Castle under armed guard . . . it's safer there.

GROSSLADY: Ah! Terribil-ay Queenie!

MARTHA: Elizabeth, you are pitiless. Tell me when you saw these scribbles on the walls? . . . I know it's weeks since you've been out.

EGERTON: Quite. Unless, Your Majesty, you've been wandering the streets at night alone?

ELIZABETH: Dame Grosslady, pass me that cylinder. (DAME GROSSLADY *passes her a telescope which is leaning against the bed*) I've been out with this.

EGERTON: What is it?

ELIZABETH: (*Hands the telescope to* EGERTON) It was a present from the Venetian ambassador. It's called a telescope or spy-glass. Hold it up to your eye. It's an amazing contraption. Don't be alarmed.

EGERTON: It's extraordinary . . . (*Points the telescope to the back of the auditorium*) . . . incredible how everything looks so close. It's remarkable! It feels as if you could reach out and touch those people down there.

MARTHA: Would you mind passing it to me for a moment?

EGERTON: O I'm so sorry . . . Of course . . . Please do . . . It would certainly be delightful to have some of these contraptions for the police.

MARTHA: It's stunning!

ELIZABETH: Of course. I've already ordered a trunkful for you. Then you can keep an eye on all the citizens, all the time: what they're doing, who they're with . . . even behind their windows, in their own houses . . . You can watch them in bed, making love . . . or even when they're on the jakes . . . Watching everything! A truly modern state! The watchdog state!

GROSSLADY: (*She snatches the telescope from* MARTHA) O Jesu! I must needs vidi doublet. I canna credit my peepers!

ELIZABETH: What is it?

GROSSLADY: Down beyant. At the fundament of the frog and toad . . . It guardas like thy lambkin, the Pearl of Yessex, gorgioso, vero? They be arrivarying in processiony . . . with all his rabblement . . . some few spectatori be giving them the clap . . .

MARTHA: Give that to me . . . (*She looks through the telescope*) . . . Yes . . . they're armed . . . they're waving . . . they're appealing to the people to join them.

EGERTON: Goddammit . . . we didn't expect them so soon. Excuse me . . . (*He takes the telescope from* MARTHA) . . . let me have a look.

ELIZABETH: (*She snatches back the telescope*) The contraption is mine. I take precedence.

EGERTON: You are right. Pardon me.

GROSSLADY: (*She gets another, smaller telescope out of her basket and points it into the audience*) Grab a vidi, Queenie, grab a vidi . . . I be frit we be battered to dirt this time.

ELIZABETH: Where did you get that telescope, Dame Grosslady?

GROSSLADY: 'Tis mine. I fetched it from Venezia . . . they do market them sopra barrows in the piazza. A free peeper with every ten wooden gondolas! Secreto militare!

ELIZABETH: (*Looking through the telescope*) Look, there's another group crossing London Bridge. And more coming down the Strand from Temple Bar . . .

EGERTON: Excuse me, but I must leave immediately. I must find Hellington and prepare the counter attack.

GROSSLADY: I will companionate thee to the sorty.

ELIZABETH: Stop! You will prepare nothing whatsoever! The orders are: no one moves. Let them let off steam for a bit; let them enjoy the applause of the shopkeepers and market apprentices.

GROSSLADY: Bona dicket, Queenlie! At the primo whuff of explosionary cannon they'll piss theirsen wuss than thy prancer!

ELIZABETH: There is one thing I want you to do, Egerton . . . Go to Secretary Cecil and order him to send Sir William Knollys and the Lord Chief Justice to Essex with this message . . . take notes . . .

GROSSLADY: (*She has taken a pen and some paper from the desk*) I be pronto to takiamo notey. I will facket the scrivening, Your Burblyship.

ELIZABETH: (*Makes a sign of agreement*) 'We come from . . .'

GROSSLADY: Pull thy prancers . . . I must needs scriven the addressio . . . 'To the Pearl of Yes-sex, Yes-sex House . . .'

ELIZABETH: I am sending two of the Lords to take the message . . . There is no need to write the address . . .

GROSSLADY: Your Queenship, ifn the lords miss their way . . . the messagio would go adrift . . . It doesna fadge o'ermuch to scriven the addressio.

ELIZABETH: Well, hurry up then.

GROSSLADY: 'To the Pearl of Yes-sex – to be meted into his veritable mitts . . .'

ELIZABETH: 'We come . . .'

GROSSLADY: (*She repeats mechanically*) 'We come . . .'

ELIZABETH: '. . . from the Queen . . .'

GROSSLADY: '. . . from the Queen . . .'

ELIZABETH: '. . . to understand . . .'

GROSSLADY: (*As before*) ' . . . to blunderstand . . . French . . .'

ELIZABETH: Don't talk rubbish! ' . . . to understand . . .'

GROSSLADY: '. . . to blunderstand . . .' Pull stop! Well, that be translucent . . .

ELIZABETH: Why have you put a full stop. I didn't dictate that.

GROSSLADY: 'Twas the finish of the phrase.

ELIZABETH: It certainly was not. Go on.

GROSSLADY: Allora, bomber!

ELIZABETH: No comma!

GROSSLADY: Semi bomber!

ELIZABETH: No semi-colon!

GROSSLADY: Excommunication mark!

ELIZABETH: No. I said no! There is no punctuation there!

GROSSLADY: But now I must needs tornare ye pull stop into some other fadge, savvy? Preferishy a floribundikins sopra? A strangleman's noose? Sanctus Giorgio sopra his prancer?

ELIZABETH: Be silent! 'We come from the Queen to understand . . .' O all right then . . . comma.

GROSSLADY: Bomber.

ELIZABETH: '. . . why certain articles of faith . . .'

GROSSLADY: '. . . why certo tickles i'faith . . .'

ELIZABETH: (*Obstinate*) 'Articles'!

GROSSLADY: 'Tickles . . .'

ELIZABETH: *Ar*ticles!

GROSSLADY: (*As one to whom everything is suddenly clear*) 'Ah! Tickles!' . . . I vidi the game now . . . (*Begins to write again*) . . . Ah! Ah! 'Tickles!' Ah! Ah!

ELIZABETH: 'Between you and your Queen . . .'

GROSSLADY: Another Queen?

ELIZABETH: No!

GROSSLADY: The same Queenie as previous! 'The Queen . . . the same Queen as previous . . .'

She writes.

ELIZABETH: No. They'll know that.

GROSSLADY: Must they needs guessy?

ELIZABETH: Silence! '. . . Are at issue . . .'

GROSSLADY: 'A tissue of lies . . .'

ELIZABETH: (*Correcting her, repeating the word but emphasising the 'A'*) *At* issue!

GROSSLADY: (*As if to say 'It's the same thing'*) Of lies.

ELIZABETH: *At* issue!

GROSSLADY: Bless you!

ELIZABETH: 'And need to be . . .'

GROSSLADY: 'Or not to be that be the question mark . . .'

ELIZABETH: That's enough! 'And need to be addressed . . .'

GROSSLADY: 'Dressed . . .'

ELIZABETH: *A*-dressed!

GROSSLADY: 'Ah! Dressed!'

ELIZABETH: Not 'ah' . . . 'and' . . .

GROSSLADY: 'Undressed . . .'

ELIZABETH: 'You shall have law . . .'

GROSSLADY: Ah! You shall have more. Ah! More tickles!

ELIZABETH *looks at her threateningly. She begins to write again.*

ELIZABETH: 'Justice and the law . . .'

GROSSLADY: Just as before. More tickles just as before.

She has got to the bottom corner of the paper and can't fit all the words in.

ELIZABETH: '. . . Justice . . .'

GROSSLADY: 'Just a . . . just a . . .'

Turns the paper round.

ELIZABETH: What are you doing. Dame Grosslady?

GROSSLADY: There be no room remaining for justice!

She goes up to EGERTON *and re-reads the whole letter – including the punctuation, in nonsense language – grammelot.*

ELIZABETH: (*Tries to interrupt her several times, and finally shouts*) Dame Grosslady! Fucking cow! The signature!

GROSSLADY: Si, I scrivened that . . . 'Fucking cow!'

She gives the letter to EGERTON.

EGERTON: With your permission, Your Majesty. I will return later. (*Glances at the letter and turns to* DAME GROSSLADY) What language is this written in?

GROSSLADY: Stepnitalian! It be comprehensived by rebels everywhere!

ELIZABETH: Egerton, declare a twenty-four hour truce. As soon as the Lords have spoken with Essex, bring him to me. Thank you!

EGERTON: Of course, Your Majesty. I will bring you news as soon as possible.

Exits.

GROSSLADY: Ah Queenie, did'st tha no vidi the pallidity of Sir Thomas when tha recked him of the graffiti against his scurviness? I wager Cecil and Bacon be cacking their kecks.

MARTHA: Dame Grosslady, please . . . speak in a more seemly fashion!

GROSSLADY: I apprehended to parley filth by neighbouring Queenies . . . fucking cow!

ELIZABETH: Dame Grosslady, you heard . . . Robert will be here before long. He might even decide to come this very evening. You promised me some miracle or other for my breasts . . .

GROSSLADY: I can fadge it . . . But I must needs apprehensive thee . . . Perchance 'twill single a bit.

ELIZABETH: Sting?

GROSSLADY: Si, forby questi.

She holds up a glass jar.

ELIZABETH: What's in there?

GROSSLADY: Buzzies.

ELIZABETH: Buzzies? Do you mean bees? And what are you going to do with them?

GROSSLADY: Primo, Martha, take ye twig of sandalwood. That be to facket fumo. I cleave the open pottle, and the buzzies indentro, sopra the dumpling . . . Then I license a smidge of fumo dentro . . . the buzzie frantics a fury – and FATANG! He stabs thee! Then incontinent tha'll vidi the bubby to get all blubberful! Plumptious! Unplumping! Sillyconey!

ELIZABETH: You are completely mad . . . my breast swollen by a bee? Those animals really hurt.

MARTHA: What an amazing discovery! I would never have thought of that!

ELIZABETH: So why don't you let it bite your titty then if it's so amusing?

GROSSLADY: (*Referring to* MARTHA's *flat chest*) Tha would'st need a gorilla sting for that mopsqueezer.

MARTHA: I don't have a Robert to cradle on my firm breasts, my dear. In any case, you can always say no. We'll stuff your bodice with cotton rags . . .

GROSSLADY: Si, we can certo stuffy the camisa with cottone – but it never be similar . . . Dost tha no ken the ancient posy: 'Titties of cotton sempre feel rotten' . . . ? And what if perchance Roberto should desidera to stroko thee? Anyroadup, a buzzie stab doesna pain o'ermuch . . . for that since I'll smurch a peck of honey and myrrh sopra the bubby to take off the hurt.

ELIZABETH: Are you sure they'll be really plump and firm?

GROSSLADY: Well . . . they willna sembra balloonios . . . but I can prometto thee them bellissima.

ELIZABETH: All right then . . . Let's get on with it! We might as well go stark raving mad while we're about it.

DAME GROSSLADY *begins to get all her bottles and jars out of her basket.*

MARTHA: Good girl! Come on then, Dame Grosslady.

GROSSLADY: Buona. Attend whilst I smurch on the honey and myrrh . . . Assista me.

She hands MARTHA *a piece of sandalwood, signalling to her to light it.*

ELIZABETH: Just a moment. How long is this swelling going to last?

GROSSLADY: O . . . tray days . . . mayhap five . . . it be dependable on how long we leave the stabbie dentro the bub.

ELIZABETH: I see. So if you pull the sting out after half an hour . . .

GROSSLADY: Nay, nay. Mezz'ora is troppo lungo. Tha'd sprout a bubby like a water melony. Cosi!

ELIZABETH: That's all I need!

GROSSLADY: Lambkin Queenie, prendy a buona inhale.

ELIZABETH: Robert, love of my life, I am doing this for you.

GROSSLADY: Go to't, Martha. Facket the fume.

She puts the jar to the QUEEN's *breast.*

ELIZABETH: AAAAAARGH! O my God, that hurts . . . !

GROSSLADY: Splendido! That be marveloso! It stabbed her Giovanni Robinson! Hurrah!

MARTHA: Wait, let me blow . . .

ELIZABETH: I'm going mad here . . . it's burning me . . .

GROSSLADY: Dinna give in, dinna give in . . . Majestical, I be fit to pose some camphor sopra.

We see her put down the jar full of bees.

ELIZABETH: That's enough, that's enough . . . pull the sting out . . .

GROSSLADY: Nay nay . . . A wee whiles more . . . attend my sweetling, dinna give in . . . guarda, guarda . . . it be blubbering up sudden!

ELIZABETH: (*Happy*) It's swelling, it's swelling! OOOOH! but it hurts!

MARTHA: Don't give in yet . . . think about how beautiful you'll be afterwards. I'd almost consider having it done myself. (*Pointing to the jar on the stand*) What's that bee doing in the jar?

GROSSLADY: O he hath mistook his stab now . . . he be morted. Attend the whiles I preparare another pottle . . . a novelty buzzie.

ELIZABETH: Wait . . . let me get my breath back, at least.

GROSSLADY: Nay, the bubbies must needs blubber up equaliter . . . so tha canst keep a squint on them . . . Tha musna have one to blubber up and up, and t'other rest as flat as a plancake.

ELIZABETH: All right . . . get on with it then . . . (*She stops, very embarrassed*) . . . O MY GOD . . .

MARTHA: What's the matter?

ELIZABETH: (*Very ashamed*) I'm pissing myself again.

GROSSLADY: That be perfetto normale . . . that be what buzzie stabs always effect. Piss thyssen dry . . . we will accusiamo the pissing prancer . . . allora . . . here we go the secundo! (*She applies the second jar to the breast*) Doth he stab?

ELIZABETH: No, it's not stinging.

GROSSLADY: (*To* MARTHA) Facket fume . . . fume . . . (*Turns back hopefully to the* QUEEN) Doth he stab now?

ELIZABETH: No, it's not stinging.

GROSSLADY: O thou buffle-headed buzzie! Tha doesna desideri to stab, eh? I'll apprehend thee a lezione.

She shakes the jar.

ELIZABETH: (*Preoccupied*) What's going on now? Am I going to be left with one breast swollen up like a melon and the other one like a dried-up lemon?

GROSSLADY: Nay nay . . . Guarda . . . I've clapped Macnamara, the Vengeancer.

She gets another jar out of her basket.

ELIZABETH: What's that?

GROSSLADY: An Irish hornetto . . .

ELIZABETH: An Irish hornet? (*She stands up*) O now I understand . . . You're in on this plot . . . You want to kill me with hornet stings!!!?

GROSSLADY: Dinna be frit, sweetling splendiforousness . . . it hath a stab more delicato than the buzzie . . . Now, now, dinna agitational thyssen.

Without realising what she was doing, MARTHA *put the taper on the chair when* ELIZABETH *got up.*

GROSSLADY: Grabble her, Martha!

MARTHA *pushes the* QUEEN *back on to the chair.* ELIZABETH *leaps up, shrieking.*

ELIZABETH: AAAARGH!! What's that? AAARGH! That's burning!

MARTHA: I am so sorry, my treasure . . . it's all my fault . . . I put the taper down there . . .

GROSSLADY: Gollumpus! Careless trapes! Firing the Queenie's fundament . . . (*Takes a basin*) . . . Settle thee here, lambkin . . . settle in the basinetto . . . the acqua will colder thee.

In getting the basin, she inadvertently puts the jar with the Irish hornet in it on ELIZABETH's *chair.*

ELIZABETH: Get away . . . that's all I need, to get my backside soaking wet . . . (*She sits down*) AAAAARRGH!

MARTHA: What's the matter?

ELIZABETH: Did I sit on the taper again?

GROSSLADY: Nay . . . Now thee be settled sopra the pottle of buzzies . . . Addlepated buzzie! He didna desideri to stab thee on the bubbie, but he hath stabbed thee on the fundament . . . Catholico! Republicano! Scargillimus!

ELIZABETH: O my God! What a bloody mess! I've got one buttock like a melon, and one breast like a balloon, one titty like a dried-up lemon and the other buttock scorched . . . What a sodding state for a Queen to be in . . . And I'm still pissing myself . . .

The lights go down as the song begins.

SONG:

Elizabeth the Loony Queen

Loonie Lizzie took a fit
Said she wanted young girl's tits.
Wanted to be gorgeous, see
Had herself stung by a bee.

Had her titty stung, O cripes!
By a wasp with yellow stripes.
Knockers knocked, O rat-tat-tat-!
One is swollen, one is flat.

Refrain:
Mamma mia mamma mia mamma mia it don't half hurt
Mamma mia mamma mia mamma mia it don't half hurt.

One boob puffed up like a marrow
T'other flat as Harold's arrow

Waspie will not bite a bit
Will not bite the flabby tit
Will not take a bite of it.

Lizzie sat on that damned bee
Queen with one big boob to see
Had one buttock like a boulder
(This to stop her looking older!)
One boob up and one boob down
Bum lop-sided – don't she frown
Arsy-versy, what a fright
Then she pissed herself all right.

Refrain:
With one tit no, the other yes
The Queen does peepee down her dress.

ACT TWO

SONG:

A Version of Isabella with the Red Hair
(Isabella La Rossa)

The prisoner from the tower is taken
Ah! Dear God, my heart is broken
Now my foolish life is over,
Gone for ever, gone my lover.

Isabella had three lovers,
Came to woo her red hair, ever,
The first one lingered near her door at night
The third came singing in the fading light
The other, hidden in her bed
Made love with her whose hair is red
Made love with her to give her pleasure
But now she will repent full measure.

Isabella, ah, don't do it
Now you're blushing, now you'll rue it
Making love with secret breath
Will bring this young man to his death
Your love is gone, young man so brave,
Love is a stone weighs on your grave.

Away, soon now the dawn will break
They'll kill you, hang you for love's sake

The first one lingered near her door at night
The third came singing in the fading light
The other, hidden in her bed
Made love with her whose hair was red
Made love with her to give her pleasure
But now she will repent full measure.

When the song Isabella La Rossa *ends, the light comes up very slowly. The* QUEEN, *centre stage, is sitting in the saddle of the wooden horse. She is looking through the telescope, which is pointed towards the audience. She is dressed as she was before: she has no wig on.*

To one side, clearly visible, on the tailor's dummy with which we are already familiar, is a sumptuous white ceremonial dress. On one of the chairs, a hooped petticoat, a cap, a dress. On the bed, clearly visible, a wig identical to that which ELIZABETH *usually wears.*

ELIZABETH: Are you still awake? Yes, yes. Those are your windows with the lights on. (*Into the wings*) Martha! For the love of God, Robert, that's enough! I can't take any more! (*Her voice getting louder and angrier*) MA-A-A-RTHA-A-A!

MARTHA *enters, running, and goes towards the bed.*

MARTHA: Here I am, sweeting. What's the matter?

ELIZABETH: Where do you think you're going? Can't you hear I'm not in bed?

MARTHA: (*Amazed*) What are you doing up there?

ELIZABETH: I got up here because it's the only way I can get to see Robert's windows.

MARTHA: Haven't you been to bed at all?

ELIZABETH: No! I can't close my eyes . . . I am all tense . . . like a drumskin!

MARTHA: Now then, dear, try to relax. Would you like some herb tea?

ELIZABETH: Herb tea be damned! Don't be such a fool. I can't close my eyes, I'm as tense as a drum because you've

pulled back the skin on my forehead too tight. Look at me,
stuck up here like a stuffed owl! Fetch the Dame.

MARTHA: Yes, straight away.

ELIZABETH: Tell her to bring something to cool my breasts
down. They're boiling. You could fry an egg on them!

MARTHA: (*Upstage*) Get a move on, Dame.

DAME GROSSLADY *enters. She has another basket with
her.*

GROSSLADY: Eccomi, lambkin . . . Che splendiforousness!
Up sopra the pissing horse so betimes in the matin . . . She
sits like a toad on a chopping block!

ELIZABETH: What have you got in that little basket?

GROSSLADY: Novelty hornybuzzies, carissima.

ELIZABETH: (*Terrified*) More? Go away, for the love of God.
That last wasp sting felt like a stab wound . . . it's left me
with a lump on my left breast.

GROSSLADY: Bona. We calliamo those Venuses bumpy
d'amore . . . tha must needs cleave cunning to the prancer,
we be locomotoring beyant.

She pushes the horse to the left.

ELIZABETH: Besides, you've made the breasts round, but
they're very odd. They go up and down, up and down: they
undulate!

GROSSLADY: O che meravigliosa Queenie! 'Tis a festive
erotico . . . Blokes go berserko for that! Allora we pulliamo
out tutti they pinnikins.

DAME GROSSLADY, *helped by* MARTHA – *the two of
them getting up on stools – take the pins out of*
ELIZABETH's *hair, and undo the plaits.*

ELIZABETH: Thank you. Just let me close my eyes before I
expire . . . God! What a night I had! I feel so good! (*Change
of tone*) Dame Grosslady, I feel dreadful! I had such a
terrible night! During the night I heard shouts coming from
Essex's house . . . it sounded like a pitched battle . . .

MARTHA: Pitched battle?

GROSSLADY: Nay, signora, there hath been no battaglia. I footed it hither and thither. I traversed the entire of London, truffling out buzzies . . . and my lugs harked nought – not e'en the woof of a pooch . . . It hath been tanto tranquillo, thou could'st have heard a bluebottle buzz . . . Oh! The blowsy bluebottles buzzing in London yesternight!

ELIZABETH: But I heard gunfire too. Caliver shots.

MARTHA: It must have been a nightmare.

ELIZABETH: That's right. I had a nightmare: a terrible nightmare! I dreamed about Mary Stuart!

GROSSLADY: Nay?!

ELIZABETH: Here. Walking around my room as if she owned it . . . with no head.

GROSSLADY: Nay?!

ELIZABETH: And she was holding her head in her hands.

GROSSLADY: Extant? The noddle was extant? Come Saint Johnnie the Baptist . . . Che prinking useful, what? Sans mumping thy noddle, tha could'st vidi . . . (*Miming holding a head in her hands and turning it round*) . . . par here . . . par there . . .

ELIZABETH: It was terrifying. The eyes moved, the mouth spoke . . . it was laughing and sneering, saying: 'Filthy bitch . . . Filthy bitch'.

GROSSLADY: O no!

ELIZABETH: 'Things have turned out bad for you, it's not my head that's rolling, but Robert's! Ha, ha!' And then: PRRRTH! She blew a raspberry at me.

GROSSLADY: A gobfart from the noddle decapitato!

MARTHA: O how dreadful!

ELIZABETH: And then suddenly she began to play with the head like a ball . . . she threw it up in the air . . . and she caught it. And then . . . boum, boum, boum, she was bouncing . . .

GROSSLADY: Trouncing?

ELIZABETH: The head!

GROSSLADY: Then che?

ELIZABETH: Then the head escaped from her and yelled 'Christ . . . you're killing me . . . I'm not a bloody football!'

GROSSLADY: God's blood and tonsils, the noddle was correcto! And par where be the Signora's noddle? She did cleave to it! Okey dokey. Smite me with a smicket, I comprehensive the intendio of this nocturnal emission . . . It intendios that ye Pearl of Yes-sex hath tossed his noddle.

ELIZABETH: (*Appalled*) What are you saying?

GROSSLADY: He hath tossed his noddle for amore . . . of thee.

ELIZABETH: Ah, if only that were true.

MARTHA: Yes, everything will turn out for the best, you'll see.

GROSSLADY: (*To* MARTHA) Whilst we parley-voo of amore, dicket her who be en voyage to vidi her . . .

MARTHA: O yes, I was forgetting . . . the ringleader of the conspirators will probably be coming here some time today.

ELIZABETH: Robert?

GROSSLADY: Roberto of Yes-sex hath confectionated his nous-box to come to thee to pay his respectuosos. Isna thee oversopra the moon?

ELIZABETH: (*Aggressively*) Why didn't you tell me this before?

MARTHA: With all this business about nightmares . . . It went right out of my head . . .

GROSSLADY: Thee facket attenzione tha doesna locomotive out of thy noddle for real . . . tha savvies what arrives to those folk . . . (*Mimes heads being chopped off and bouncing them like balls*) Trouncy! Trouncy!

ELIZABETH: Come here, Dame Grosslady, get me down.

GROSSLADY: Si, Your Infernalship.

MARTHA *helps her to get the* QUEEN *down.*

ELIZABETH: Put my hair up . . . Robert will be here before long, and I want my skin to look smooth. And Martha, you keep watch with the telescope.

Knocking at the door.

ELIZABETH: Someone's knocking . . . don't let anyone in while I'm in this state.

GROSSLADY: (*Going to the door*) Dinna flitter thy twitters wi' banging. The Queenie isna making audience. She be all awry, and sembras an owl in an ivy bush. (*She peeps round the door*) Your Hellhoundship, it be the Chiefo Pig of the Old Bill . . . The spy-glass whisker splitter.

ELIZABETH: Egerton? Let him in. Perhaps he's bringing news about Robert.

GROSSLADY: Facket him entrare to vidi thy slubberdegullionness, Your Ladle?

ELIZABETH: Blindfold him.

GROSSLADY: Darkness the chiefo Pig of the Old Bill. That had given him a fart attack!

ELIZABETH: Pull his hat down over his eyes.

GROSSLADY: Buona intelligence! Entrare, entrare, Sir Thomas! (*Pulls his hat down over his eyes*) It be the Queenie's orderaro I must needs tweak thy titfer sopra thy peepers for that since . . . O damnwit! What a noddle! Your Leeryship, he hath such a mumping great noddle, it willna locomotive in the titfer . . . The executionaro woulds't twist his knickers o'er that noddle . . . ah, I arrived . . . that be it. Off tha wends . . .

ELIZABETH: Help him down. Don't let him fall. I don't want him damaged.

GROSSLADY: There be many more mickles where he muckled from.

ELIZABETH: What news do you bring me, Egerton?

EGERTON: Your Majesty, I trust you passed a . . . (*He stumbles*) comfortable night . . .

ELIZABETH: I passed a terrible night! I wish to know why I have seen no sign of the delegation of Lords on their way to Essex's house. Why is that?

GROSSLADY: Rispondi the Queenlie, your boredship.

EGERTON: Your Majesty, Sir William Knollys was nowhere to be found, and as there was no one who could take his place, we thought it best to put it off until today.

GROSSLADY: Smoothie tongue bastardo!

She pushes horse back to original place.

ELIZABETH: Is that so? You propose, you dispose, and you say nothing of all this to me? What are you hiding in that folder?

EGERTON: I am mortified, Your Majesty, but I have to concede once again that your suspicions were well founded.

He opens the folder.

ELIZABETH: What suspicions?

EGERTON: This mountebank . . . (*Tries to read, squinting under his hat*) . . . what's his name . . . ?

ELIZABETH: Is he called Shakespeare?

EGERTON: Yes, that's it. He is the one . . . he is one of the company.

ELIZABETH: Which company?

EGERTON: Of conspirators.

GROSSLADY: Conspiratori? Shakespeare be a revoluzione? Well, that be a burn up for the hooks!

ELIZABETH: Are you certain of this?

EGERTON: More than certain, Your Majesty. This Shakespeare is some way or another dependent on the Earl of Southampton . . . besides which, Southampton is his theatrical patron, since he is joint owner of the Globe.

ELIZABETH: So what?

EGERTON: But Your Highness, Southampton is one of the ringleaders of the plot.

GROSSLADY: (*Gobsmacked*) Nay! Your Leeryship! Tractors and theatricals dabbledoing in politicko? Incredible! What next!

ELIZABETH: (*Becoming more and more upset*) Southampton, my only living relative. I have always shown him affection and sympathy, and now he's joined those pigs who want to screw me . . . he must be mixed up in this business of the letters to James of Scotland too . . .

MARTHA: Now Elizabeth, keep calm . . .

ELIZABETH: BE SILENT! I'll kill them . . . I'll hunt them down from house to house . . . myself! I want them hanged! Drawn! Quartered! (*She can no longer control herself*) I want them left to dangle until they rot! I want to see all the birds in England flocking to rip out their entrails! I feel sick. Martha, I'm going to vomit.

She doubles up, holding her stomach.

MARTHA: There we are. I knew it . . . Come on, come with me . . .

They exit.

GROSSLADY: She be vamoosed. (*She lifts EGERTON's hat*) I'll elevate the titfer. Get a bit of a breathe.

EGERTON: I am so sorry to have been the cause of this extremity . . .

GROSSLADY: Thou wast fortunato tha didna cop the sparkle in her peepers . . . Something scutcher! . . . Horripilant . . . just like her skin and blister, Bloodful Mary, when she made bonfires o' all the Prods . . . But there be no ho with her.

She be a carroty pate . . . Like her dad, Henry the Carrot-Top . . . horripilant! An entiro famiglia of carrot-tops. All scutchers!

EGERTON: What are you babbling about?

GROSSLADY: There be a snotto in my land that locomotives: 'Red head at night, Henry's delight. Red head in the morn, prepare to be shorn . . .'

EGERTON: I feel sorry for Southampton. His days are numbered, poor man. And Shakespeare too . . .

GROSSLADY: THWACK!! The scrivener's noddle into the pannier also! Sir Thomas, dost thou savvy forwhy the English eternity boxes be tiddlier than anyplace else?

EGERTON: No, why?

GROSSLADY: Forby in Angleterror, nearly all the omnumgatherum of folk be buried wi' their noddles in their mitts!

EGERTON: Very witty . . .

ELIZABETH *and* MARTHA *return.*

GROSSLADY: (*Swiftly pushing the hat back down over* EGERTON's *eyes*) Divven laugh so broadcast. Here be the Queenly. (*To the* QUEEN) How dost tha go? Fitter?

ELIZABETH: Much better, thank you. Egerton: enough of this. I cannot take any more. I am sick to the teeth of these plots, these impudent plans . . . Do we understand one another, Egerton? How is it possible that every time one faction wants to eliminate another, they never fail to drag me into the middle of it? What has it got to do with me? I've had enough! I am sure that if you all set yourselves to it with goodwill, in a day or two we'll hear no more of this tangled mess! And, as they say in the theatre at the end of plays: all's well that ends well between the sheets of a nice clean double bed! (*She laughs, much amused*)

Excited shouts outside the door . . . The sound of running footsteps.

VOICE FROM OUTSIDE: Raise the alarm! Raise the alarm! . . . There he is . . . Over there!

Knocking at the door.

ELIZABETH: (*To* MARTHA) What is it now? Go and see.

More knocking . . . more violent than before.

MARTHA: What's got into you? I'm coming! (*She opens the door a crack*) Just a moment . . .

GROSSLADY: It be the voce of thy Capitano of Guardi.

MARTHA: Yes, it's him. He says they've seen a man climbing up . . . Shall I let him in:

ELIZABETH: Let who in? Have we all gone mad? Let him into my bedroom first thing in the morning? The Chief of Police can deal with it . . . Egerton, search by all means, but do it outside my room.

EGERTON: (*Without raising his hat, sets off determinedly towards the audience*) With your permission . . . I will go immediately.

GROSSLADY: (*Blocking his way*) Stoppo! Here be a chasm! Dinna be previous into thy eternity box. (*She accompanies* EGERTON *to the door*) Your Impiousness, that snotto be verily, when it dicket 'When justizia be blind, pigs might fly . . .' Permetto the Guardi to entrare, Your Ladleship, there be grand perilsome.

MARTHA: She's right. If there really is an assassin around . . .

ELIZABETH: There is no assassin . . . it's all a charade to get the Palace into a state of panic so they can prevent Robert from coming to me. But I'm not falling for it.

She goes towards the bed.

MARTHA: Or maybe it's because you want to stop them before they can poke their noses between your sheets? Tell the truth, have you got someone in the bed?

ELIZABETH: Shut up, you witch! (*Opens the doors of the bed*) Thomas . . . hurry up, wake up!

A YOUNG MAN *appears, half naked.*

MARTHA: O, Father Christmas has come early this year! How are we going to hush this one up?

GROSSLADY: Hust tush! It be more splendido than a Royal Waddling. I can vidi the bedlines now: 'Midnight Gurgler in Suckingham Phallus' . . . Dost tha no ken what has chanced? A miracolo extraordinario! In the wee small hours o' the matin, and it was yet nearly darkmans . . . infatto, it was darkmans . . . previous to the bunrise . . . Elizabetta's lugs harkied a weeping blightingale . . . CHEEP CHEEP . . . in the gardino . . . She locomoted downio . . . and remark! there be a wee birdie . . . CHEEP CHEEP . . . tutto froze . . . she catched him up – poor wee sleekit frozen timorous birdie . . . CHEEP CHEEP . . . and she laid him on her breastie . . . and she – Good Samaritan that she be – retornaried to her virgin couch and she laid him down betwixt the linen sheets and she huffed on him, and puffed on him with gentle gree . . . and WHOOSH! . . . CHEEP CHEEP! . . . WHOOSH!! This young dimber damber upsprang! Incontinent the Queenly thumped herself down on her marybones . . . 'Santa Rosalia, the most bellissima santa of the lot . . . What should I facket with this young springer?' And the santa rispondida: 'Si. Si. Facket the springer and his dicky birdie!' And that be the truth the whole truth and nothing like the truth!

ELIZABETH: (*To the* YOUNG MAN) Thomas, wrap yourself up in this counterpane. (*To* MARTHA) Where shall I hide him?

MARTHA: Let him down from the window.

GROSSLADY: Bravo! Thus he'll be taken for the assassino . . . CHEEP CHEEP! He'll retornare back into a wee birdie!

ELIZABETH: (*To the* YOUNG MAN, *who is starting to get dressed*) Don't wait to get dressed, Thomas, there isn't time.

YOUNG MAN: Your Majesty, I can't go out like this . . . with the counterpane . . .

ELIZABETH: Go out? And let the guards discover that you've been with me?

MARTHA: Why don't you dress him up?

ELIZABETH: O be quiet!

GROSSLADY: Si, bravo! Drag him up bona in lady's togs. Bona idea.

ELIZABETH: As a woman?

GROSSLADY: Si.

ELIZABETH: (*To* MARTHA, *pointing to the clothes that are lying on the chair*) Give me those clothes. We'll pass him off as one of my maids in waiting. (*Gives him a pat on the backside*) You've got the pretty little bottom for it!

YOUNG MAN: It's not right for you to make a fool of me like this. Dressing me up in women's clothes!

ELIZABETH: Don't be difficult, Thomas!

YOUNG MAN: Don't make me, please! I'd rather throw myself out of the window just as I am!

ELIZABETH: That'll be good. That way everyone can go round telling each other how the Queen uses young men . . . She squeezes them dry and then throws them out of the window, stark naked! Get dressed. Go over there, come on. That's an order!

The YOUNG MAN *goes out, unwillingly.*

MARTHA: (*Referring to the* YOUNG MAN) Well, as Epicurus says, sleeping in the arms of young men does wonders for the complexion!

GROSSLADY: Thee be completo oversopra the toppo. Attenzione the noddle! Trouncy! Trouncy!

ELIZABETH: You are a hyena. I simply wanted to make an experiment. I wanted to see whether I was in a fit condition to bear the attentions of a man, in case Robert came.

GROSSLADY: The try-out springer! The titty tester!

ELIZABETH: What a disastrous night! A total failure! I couldn't bear to be touched anywhere. I hurt all over. You

have wrecked me, Dame Grosslady. I should have said:
'Stop that! It hurts!' But I didn't like to, so I went: 'O noooo
. . . Dearest . . . noooo.' The cretin thought I was doing it
out of passion and he jumped on me, he jumped on me! I
could have killed him! And then he had the nerve to ask me
'How was it for you, Your Majesty?'

GROSSLADY: (*Alarmed*) Your Margerine, there be a
rapscallion . . . undersotto in the gardino . . . in the maze
. . . the Guardies . . . be hollering and woofing after him
with the pooches.

MARTHA: Who is in the maze?

GROSSLADY: It must needs be that bastardo who was
essaying to climber-clamber dentro this chamber to mort the
Queenly. Oops, he be over forby.

ELIZABETH: Run down . . . order them to bring him to me
immediately, alive! (MARTHA *goes out of the main door of
the room*) I want to interrogate him myself!

GROSSLADY: Alive-alive-oh! Thus afterward we can
draggiamo him up as a femminile too! Ha ha!

ELIZABETH: Follow me, Dame Grosslady. We will go and
watch from the terrace.

She goes, using the door on the right.

GROSSLADY: Let us go, hugger-mugger! What spice! One
entire festivity here at court! A coup de theatre every
minuto! From the burnt cinder than canst vidi an
abscotchalator chased by hounds . . . a young dimber
damber starkers in the Queen four toaster . . . just like
Niente Sex Per Favore, We Be Inglesi!

She goes out, following the QUEEN.

Almost at the same moment, the YOUNG MAN *re-enters. He
comes from behind the bed, and is only half dressed as a
woman. He has the petticoat on, but his torso is naked.*

YOUNG MAN: Your Majesty, forgive me . . . I just don't
feel . . .

He looks round for the QUEEN. *A man appears from behind one of the hangings. It is the* ASSASSIN.

ASSASSIN: You imbecile, bloody little idiot. What the hell do you think you're up to?

YOUNG MAN: (*Amazed*) Who is that? O, it's you, father . . . The Queen can't be far away . . . and the whole place is swarming with guards.

ASSASSIN: Exactly. And you choose a moment like this, to make a fuss over a house dress and a woman's cap.

YOUNG MAN: But it's so humiliating!

ASSASSIN: Halfwit! What matters to you more: standing on your dignity or the success of our cause?

YOUNG MAN: Yes, but when they make you eat dirt . . . turn you into a drag act . . . degrade you . . .

ASSASSIN: Oh yes. Is that why you were cavorting in the bed of a murdering illegitimate bitch, letting her kiss and fondle you? She was slobbering all over you, you little gigolo . . .

YOUNG MAN: But you ordered me to let her take me to bed.

ASSASSIN: Yes but I didn't order you to enjoy it . . . ! Never forget, Thomas, it is she who murdered Mary!

From outside there is more shouting and a few shots.

YOUNG MAN: (*Indicating the window*) Who's the poor sod they're chasing?

ASSASSIN: Poor sod, you call him? If only you had his courage! He's been creating a diversion so I could get up here undetected. Now, get a move on, it's time for you to do your bit. You have to stay in this room for as long as you can to cover me. As soon as we've dealt with the Queen, you will give the alarm. And you make sure you send the guards upstairs to the attics . . . I'll make my escape down below.

YOUNG MAN: Are you sure we should do it? The place is going to be full of people soon . . . I heard them say Essex was on his way.

ASSASSIN: No, Essex won't come here . . . he might attack.

YOUNG MAN: Attack? But the Lord Chief Justice went to fetch him in person.

ASSASSIN: Listen to me carefully, Thomas: if Essex comes here, he will only come armed to the teeth and accompanied by all his men . . . And behind them, the whole city will be rising . . . They will finish off Cecil, Bacon and half the Lords . . . But they will save the Queen . . . and we cannot allow that to happen . . . So get a move on . . . Get on with it. You'll do everything she tells you without making a fuss, do you understand? Even if she asks you to walk on your hands with a lighted candle stuck up your arse.

YOUNG MAN: O no, not a lighted one!

ASSASSIN: Shut it! I'm going to get in here, in the horse.

He approaches the animal's stomach.

YOUNG MAN: How can you get in there?

ASSASSIN: There's a little door here. Come on, give me a hand.

He lifts the saddle cloth and opens the horse's back part like a door.

YOUNG MAN: O look, an arsehole that opens!

ASSASSIN: This horse belonged to Henry, Elizabeth's father . . . he used to hide his lovers in here . . . my mother among others. No one knows about this hidey-hole, not even Elizabeth. Come on, give me a leg up. No, stop. I don't fancy getting into the horse. Put it back. I prefer the chimney. At the right moment, when the coast is clear, give me the signal. Blow a few notes with this flute. (*He hands him a short flute*) come on, take it.

YOUNG MAN: All right, get a move on then!

ASSASSIN: Just be careful no one lights a fire.

He gets into the fireplace and up the chimney. More shots from offstage.

YOUNG MAN: Who'd want to light a fire. It's spring! Go on!

The QUEEN *and* DAME GROSSLADY *return.*
ELIZABETH *is wearing full ceremonial dress, wig, crown, jewels, etc.*

GROSSLADY: I desidero to savvy how that bloke confectionated to mort hissen.

MARTHA *re-enters from the gallery.*

ELIZABETH: Martha, who fired?

MARTHA: He did . . . he shot himself.

ELIZABETH: The shot that was supposed to be for me. So now we'll never know who sent him. (*She notices the* YOUNG MAN *who is looking uneasy*) And what do you think you're doing still in that state? I'll have to let the guards in in a minute . . . that thug is sure to have an accomplice. Do you want to compromise me?

YOUNG MAN: All right, Your Majesty . . . I'll put on the whole dress.

ELIZABETH: No, wait. Put on this dress instead.

She points to the dress on the dummy.

YOUNG MAN: But that's one of your dresses, Your Majesty.

ELIZABETH: Martha, help him. I want to see what it looks like on. I have never worn it.

YOUNG MAN: Wouldn't it be better to put it on your Maid of Honour?

MARTHA *and* DAME GROSSLADY *dress the* YOUNG MAN: *dress, pattens, wig and crown.*

ELIZABETH: No, it isn't her size. Anyway, I want you to really experience what it means to play the part of a Queen. All you young braggarts just flit around like dragonflies.

GROSSLADY: Elevate thyssen! Elevate!

ELIZABETH: That's where I want you. How do you feel?

YOUNG MAN: Squashed, squeezed . . . It's hell. I feel so embarrassed. Please don't ever tell anyone about this.

Smoke begins to come out of the fireplace.

GROSSLADY: Elevate thyssen sopra these bawdy shoon.

ELIZABETH: What's going on? What's that smoke coming out of the chimney?

GROSSLADY: Odds plut and her nails! The handleprick hath tumblied into the furplace.

ELIZABETH: (*Takes a jug of water and flings it into the fireplace*) Put that damn fire out!

GROSSLADY: O, mountaineers of fume!

We can hear muffled cries from the chimney.

GROSSLADY: Queenly, I can catch screech-howls from the chimbley: hark to the screams! AAAAAAARGH!

ELIZABETH: Who is screaming?

GROSSLADY: (*Imitating the sounds coming from the chimney*) AAAAAAARGH! It be the chimbley. It be the voce of the chimbley.

ELIZABETH: Don't talk rubbish. No one's screaming.

GROSSLADY: It must needs to be the Jenny Lind!

YOUNG MAN: Yes, yes. It's the wind.

GROSSLADY: Do they e'en torturare the Jenny Lind in Angleterror?

ELIZABETH: Be silent, all of you! (*Turning to the* YOUNG MAN) Adorable! Have you ever played girls' parts?

YOUNG MAN: No, never . . .

ELIZABETH: Do you know I maintain a company of boys?

YOUNG MAN: Yes, Your Majesty, the Children of the Queen's Chapel, I know them.

ELIZABETH: But not one of them makes such a believable girl as you do.

YOUNG MAN: Now you're making fun of me again . . .

ELIZABETH: No, not at all. I'm going to put *Hamlet* on here at the court . . . So I can find out what's behind it . . . and

you can play Ophelia, and Dame Grosslady can play the
Queen!

GROSSLADY: That thumping great blowsabella! Thanks but
no thanks.

The ASSASSIN *gets out of the chimney trying to stifle a
coughing fit and hides behind* ELIZABETH's *bed. More
shots are heard in the distance.*

MARTHA: What's going on now?

ELIZABETH: (*Looking towards the back of the auditorium*)
They're culverin shots . . . or . . . My God, they're coming
from Essex House. They've broken the truce! Give me the
telescope immediately! No, better still, I must talk to
Egerton. (*Towards the door on the right*) Egerton? Where
has he got himself to? (*To* MARTHA) Come along, we'll go
and find him.

They leave.

YOUNG MAN: (*He has picked up the telescope and he is now
looking out into the auditorium*) O how wonderful . . . !
Everything's so big!

GROSSLADY: (*She has discovered the flute left behind by the*
ASSASSIN) O vidi! A piccolo!

She blows into it; tries to get a few sounds out of it.

YOUNG MAN: Christ! What are you doing? No! That's the
signal! Give me that!

The YOUNG MAN *tries to snatch the flute out of her hand.
At this point an 'incident' occurs: sound of flute music begins.*
DAME GROSSLADY *makes signals to the sound operator.
The music does not stop.*

GROSSLADY: The Magic Flute! Tha canst sound it e'en if tha
doesna whuff in it! All tha needs do be dingle thy digits!

The music stops.

YOUNG MAN: Give me the pipe!

GROSSLADY: Give me a smacker in exchangio!

YOUNG MAN: No! Get away, you old hag!

GROSSLADY: Mio? Old hag? Tha kleps mio old hagslag? I would'st a bolt of blightning strike thee! CCRRRACHK!! (*She mimes a bolt of lightning reducing him to 30 cms*) As swart as that! Bawdy shoon and all! (*She goes off behind the bed*) Short-arse pygmy!

YOUNG MAN: (*Going to chimney*) Father? Not there. Let's hope he hasn't suffocated. (*Turns round to look through the telescope again*) This must be witchcraft! It's fantastic!

The ASSASSIN *comes out of hiding, and creeps up on the* YOUNG MAN *who has his back turned to him. Strikes him hard with the dagger.*

ASSASSIN: Got you this time, bitch! Die and rot in hell!

The YOUNG MAN *sinks to the floor almost without a sound. The* ASSASSIN *looks around.*

ASSASSIN: Thomas, where are you? Where's the little idiot hiding? Thomas!

YOUNG MAN: (*Weakly*) I'm here.

ASSASSIN: You?! Christ! What were you doing in the Queen's dress?

YOUNG MAN: What? But you . . . told me . . . woman's dress . . .

ASSASSIN: What a mess!

YOUNG MAN: . . . and then you go and butcher me! . . . Who's the biggest arsehole now?

GROSSLADY: (*Entering*) I be certoso I harked one screaming . . . Who wouldst thou be? Helpo! A bloke! A priesto assassino!

The ASSASSIN *moves towards* DAME GROSSLADY.

ELIZABETH: (*Offstage*) What is it, Dame Grosslady? Why are you screaming?

GROSSLADY: Dinna budge, Queenie! Shutty the Rory O'More! There be an assassino par here, and he be espying for thee, Queenie!

ASSASSIN: Damn bitch! Shut your trap or I'll kill you!

He threatens DAME GROSSLADY with the pistol. She runs off behind the bed and immediately re-enters from the left. She goes to her basket and gets out two jars, points them at the ASSASSIN as if they were pistols; while she's doing all this, she shouts.

GROSSLADY: The buzzies! Helpo! The buzzies!

The ASSASSIN fires at the DAME. She avoids the shot, and shakes the jars to get the wasps angry. The ASSASSIN starts twitching as if he's been attacked by a swarm of wasps. He drops the pistol and runs off behind the bed jumping and slapping himself like a madman.

GROSSLADY: Tha axed for this, swine! Duello with buzzies and pops!

ELIZABETH: (*Offstage*) Open the door, Dame Grosslady! That's an order!

GROSSLADY: Dinna entrare, Queenly. The chamber be buzzing with the stabbing buzzies!

The ASSASSIN, half hidden by the hanging, has opened the backside of the horse and mimes getting into it. He is so preoccupied by trying to do this and not be seen by the two women who are coming in, that he holds on to the hanging to help himself in and inadvertently pulls the whole thing down. We understand that he has hidden himself inside the horse.

GROSSLADY: Be artful! Draw a snot-rag o'er thy mush!

ELIZABETH enters, followed by MARTHA. They are wearing veils to cover their faces.

GROSSLADY: Guardies!

She shouts offstage. Two GUARDS come in. They try to protect themselves from the wasps by slapping themselves all over. Following DAME GROSSLADY's command, they run behind the bed looking for the ASSASSIN.

ELIZABETH: Where has he got to?

GROSSLADY: He was par ici ertwhile . . . I mind he must needs have ascended the chimbley.

ELIZABETH: Did you say he was disguised as a priest?

GROSSLADY: Nay. He must needs have been a veritable vicar . . . one of they fly-blown dunsters who hold thee the cross to canoodle wi' one mitt, and wi' t'other mitt they be tugging the string that'll drop thee, and with t'other mitt they be setting the fire undersotto thy trotters and benedicketting thee with t'other mitt . . . these vicars be possessed of a might of mitts!

ELIZABETH: Do something about these damn animals! Throw the window open!

GROSSLADY: Nay, attend. I have the Queenly buzzie here. T'others need pimply sniff her and they'll wing it dentro the pottle . . . Coo-ee! Mingle mangle cum buzzies! Your Queenie callios you! Guarda the buzzies winging it! Upsy daisy! Damndammit! The Queenie hath buzzed off . . . Where hath she fleed? O guarda! She hath winged it dentro the prancer's nosehole and tutti the buzzies be thripping after her. That be that then. Finito the perilsome.

The two women remove the handkerchiefs they had over their faces, and only now does ELIZABETH *notice the wounded* YOUNG MAN *who is lying on the floor.*

ELIZABETH: Thomas! O my God! They have stabbed you instead of me!

She kneels down and holds him.

YOUNG MAN: (*Speaks with great difficulty*) He mistook me . . .

ELIZABETH: Yes, yes . . . I understand . . . O my sweeting, you have saved my life!

YOUNG MAN: No . . . I meant to . . . I'm sorry!

ELIZABETH: What are you sorry for?

YOUNG MAN: That . . . dagger . . . was for . . . you . . .

ELIZABETH: O my God! Quick, Martha, get a doctor . . . so much blood!

YOUNG MAN: He couldn't even . . . look me in . . . the face . . . bastard priest . . . one slash with the knife . . . and off

. . . ! 'Play the woman . . .' he tells me . . . 'With a candle in your arse.'

GROSSLADY: O!

MARTHA: He's rambling, poor little soul . . . He's going . . .

GROSSLADY: He be bonkers . . . hark to him drumbling and mumping.

YOUNG MAN: 'Open the arse . . . I'll get in there . . .' he says . . . and then he says . . . 'No, in the chimney . . .' And he says to me . . . 'Play this pipe!' . . . I never blew it . . . but he . . . WHACK me . . . just the same!

GROSSLADY: He parleys mucho filth.

YOUNG MAN: And then he gets into . . . the horse's belly . . . like the Trojan horse . . . and now the wasps are eating him alive. (*He laughs*) Ha ha ha.

ELIZABETH: Don't laugh, Thomas. You've got a knife in your belly . . . It's not good for you . . . you'll see, you'll pull through . . .

THOMAS *dies in* ELIZABETH's *arms*.

GROSSLADY: Nay, nay. He be brown breaded. But he brown breaded contento . . . He was larking . . .

ELIZABETH: O God, O my God! It was me! It was my fault! (*She leaves* THOMAS *lying on the floor and gets up*) My life is full of corpses. I am a murderess.

She exits upstage.

MARTHA: (*Following* ELIZABETH) That's not true. It was just chance. An accident!

GROSSLADY: Si, a chanceo accidento! Guarda the brazen fortuna of these queenbees! They clapperclaw young dimberdambers into the four toaster to toast theyselves. and the dimberdambers – young groutheads – facket them the favore to take a stab in the stern as a thank you tip. And they facket theyselves to be cozied and mozied, tongued and grovelled . . . But mio . . . If I dicket to some young

dimberdamber, 'Gimme a smacker,' he respondies me . . .
'Hike off, trollop!'

EGERTON *enters, followed by the* GUARDS.

EGERTON: If I may . . . what has happened . . . ?

GROSSLADY: There hath been a vitriolic vicar and he hath
stabbed and morted her.

ELIZABETH *and* MARTHA *re-enter.*

EGERTON: Was she one of your waiting maids?

ELIZABETH: Yes . . . a male maid . . . I dressed him up for a
bit of a laugh.

MARTHA: (*Under her breath*) Don't talk nonsense. (*To*
EGERTON) It's shock, you see. (*To* ELIZABETH, *in a
low voice*) For pity's sake, there are guards here too!
(*Pointing to the corpse*) Take her away . . .

The GUARDS *carry* THOMAS *out;* EGERTON *follows
them.*

ELIZABETH: It's just rubbish. It's no use any more.

GROSSLADY: Guarda! The prancer hath the wibble wobbles!

MARTHA: So it has . . . And it seems to be neighing!

The groans of the ASSASSIN *inside, who is being eaten by
the wasps, sound like neighing.*

GROSSLADY: Sembra he be throwing a frenzy fit! Tutti the
buzzies dentro must be thumping a great battaglio

ELIZABETH: That's enough! I'm going mad! I'm having
nightmares again! Who is responsible for this sorcery?
(*Threatening*) It is you, Dame Grosslady . . . You are a
sorceress! It was you! You must be part of this plot . . .
They sent you here . . . (*Shouts offstage*) Egerton! Guards!
(*To* DAME GROSSLADY) Who sent you? Speak! (DAME
GROSSLADY *is paralysed with terror*) I'll have you hung
up by your feet from a butcher's hook until you confess!

GROSSLADY: Nay, nay tortura, nay!

ELIZABETH: Guards! Egerton! Seize her!

EGERTON *and the* GUARDS *run on and seize the* DAME.

GROSSLADY: Nay, Your Majestical . . . Pardonare me.

MARTHA: That's enough, Elizabeth! This woman saved your life just now . . . and look how you're treating her!

ELIZABETH: Let go of her . . . I'm sorry, Dame Grosslady . . . forgive me . . . I allowed myself to be carried away with fear.

GROSSLADY: Nay, Your Ladleship, dinna fash thyssen. It be comprehensive. It be normalo. When a Queenie doth take a frit, what can she confectionate to render hersen tranquillo? She pimply strings up a servitude by the trotters, and opla! Least said soonest blended. It be perfetto naturalo . . . Now I hath e'en besquittered my pettitose naturalo . . .

Lifting her skirt so she can go faster, she runs off.

ELIZABETH: (*Who has regained control of herself*) Egerton, a few hours ago, I asked you a question: why has there still been no sign of the delegation of Lords going to Essex House?

EGERTON: A great misfortune, Your Majesty . . .

ELIZABETH: What misfortune?

EGERTON: Essex and his followers have not kept their promises. No sooner had the Lords entered Essex House, than they were set upon and locked up.

ELIZABETH: But Essex has gone totally demented . . . I send the Lords to him so they can come to an agreement, and he locks them up?

EGERTON: That is, unfortunately, what took place.

ELIZABETH: When did this happen?

EGERTON: Late last night.

ELIZABETH: Last night? Just a moment . . . a few hours ago you told me that the meeting had been postponed.

EGERTON: I did not wish to distress you, ma'am. I was hoping to be able to put everything to rights today.

ELIZABETH: (*Ironic*) Your concern for me . . . is very touching, Egerton! (*Serious*) Were there any fatalities at the time of this offensive?

EGERTON: Yes, the entire escort . . . all of them cut to pieces.

ELIZABETH: All of them? And the Lords?

EGERTON: Safe.

ELIZABETH: Are you sure?

EGERTON: As soon as all four of them signed the letters . . .

ELIZABETH: (*Amazed*) What letters?

DAME GROSSLADY *returns.*

EGERTON: The letters written in the Lords' own handwriting in which they plead for the release of the twenty-four prisoners in exchange for their own freedom.

ELIZABETH: Twenty-four prisoners? I knew nothing about this!!

EGERTON: Your Majesty, they are those prisoners we took yesterday afternoon following the skirmish.

ELIZABETH: What skirmish??!!! Keep calm. Let me go over this again. So: I order you to send the Lords to Robert of Essex. Then, a few hours later, there is a skirmish, in the course of which twenty-four of the plotters are captured. Then the Lords go to Essex House, and he, justifiably furious because you have broken the truce, slaughters the entire escort and imprisons the Lords. Is that correct?

EGERTON: Yes. That is correct.

ELIZABETH: And why were there four of them? I ordered you to send two.

EGERTON: Secretary Cecil thought it would be better, he thought it would lend more prestige to the delegation to send the Earl of Worcester and the Lord Keeper of the Seal as well.

GROSSLADY: We facket tuttithing great and grandissimo here!

ELIZABETH: Splendid! You propose, you dispose . . . all without consulting me. You make me out to be a hallucinating halfwit . . . It was only a nightmare . . . The screams. The shots. Everyone in cahoots, starting with my Lady of the Chamber. And you too, Dame Grosslady.

Moment of embarrassment for DAME GROSSLADY, *who was attempting to disappear out of the left door.*

GROSSLADY: Ah, it be vino veritas, Your Ladleship . . . I harkened the shistol pots, but he dicket me . . . Sir Thomas, willst tha no helpo me out of this trappola?

EGERTON: Yes, Your Majesty, it was I who ordered them to keep silent. In order to avoid distressing you. We certainly never imagined things would turn round like this . . .

GROSSLADY: Desideri me to callo the gardies? I will preparare the hook of thee to string him up by his trotters.

She laughs.

ELIZABETH: You never imagined? Who are you trying to fool? You, Bacon, and Secretary Cecil imagined nothing else! It's crystal clear! You organised the trap yourself to get rid of Robert of Essex.

DAME GROSSLADY *has got a wooden stick and a metre of material out of her basket. She begins to measure* EGERTON *for a coffin.*

GROSSLADY: O che crafty rapscallion!

EGERTON: (*Aggressively to* DAME GROSSLADY) Will you stop meddling? Will you be silent?!

ELIZABETH: No, she speaks! You're always giving lectures about listening to the voice of the people, and as soon as the people opens its mouth, it's 'Silence!' Well actually, no. She speaks!

GROSSLADY: I parley, I measurey, I bury!

ELIZABETH: Of course, you want to go on proposing and disposing undisturbed. Why don't you put my crown on too . . .? Why don't you give me a good kick in the arse while you're about it?

MARTHA: Elizabeth, I'm sorry but . . .

ELIZABETH: And you can shut your mouth, trollop. You're an intriguer just like them . . . Go away!

MARTHA: No! How dare you treat me like this . . . I am not one of your Councillors, and I'm not one of your scullery maids either. Do you understand? Because I would like to remind you, in case you'd forgotten, how when that damned sister of yours threw you in the Tower, and all those featherbrained misses and court toadies dropped you like a hot brick – quicker than if you had the pox – I was the only one – daft cow that I am – (DAME GROSSLADY *comes and stands close behind* MARTHA) who went in there with you and kept your spirits up among the rats scrabbling around and the bats hanging on the walls!

ELIZABETH: Yes, I'm sorry . . .

MARTHA: No. No 'sorries'. You know where you can put your 'sorry'. Stuff it!

GROSSLADY: Ooops, the mopsqueezer be getting serioso . . .

MARTHA: Now you're going to listen to me . . . And as what I have to say isn't very pretty, ask your Chief of Police to step outside for a moment.

ELIZABETH: Your pardon, Egerton . . . We will call you back later . . .

GROSSLADY: Si, we can calliamo thee later for thy fitting . . .

EGERTON: Of course, Your Majesty . . . With your permission . . .

He exits.

MARTHA: Now then, first of all . . .

GROSSLADY: Attend till the questman intelligencer be departed. Ecco. Now parley.

MARTHA: Look at the state you're in: head over heels in love . . . desperate to look beautiful . . . heart going pitter patter at the very thought of meeting him . . . You are out of your mind, raving mad, fit for the nuthouse!

GROSSLADY: Martha, I mind thee hadst less perilsome to go tweak the hairs from a lion's cobblers . . . !

MARTHA: And you can shut your mouth as well! Piss off!

ELIZABETH: No, Dame Grosslady stays! All right, all right, I'm raving mad. I'm ready to be locked up . . . But you are responsible too, Martha. Who persuaded me to let myself be titivated at the hands of Dame Grosslady . . . ? The wasps on the breasts, the bloody worms in the ear even?

MARTHA: Yes, because you made me feel sorry for you . . . There you were, reduced to a snivelling heap. I put myself in your place, and I said to myself: I would do it too. But that's what's so bloody stupid. I'm not the Queen, am I?

ELIZABETH: Yes, and I'm not a human being, am I!? I'm not allowed to have feelings, passions . . . nothing!

MARTHA: O come off it. No one's forcing you to go on with it' . . . You want to lead the life of an ordinary woman? Well then, chuck it in: abdicate! All I know is that last year . . . if you could have seen yourself – the state you were in . . .

ELIZABETH: I would have been disgusted with myself . . . say it!

GROSSLADY: This carissimo amore of thine must needs have turned thee to a foolish grouthead. He doth paint himself forth so brave and bold, he be questionless capabilo of taking a whimsy to squat his bot on thy bonce, Queenie . . . assuring first to set thereon a round twilted cushion forby not to scratchle his arse on the pikes of thy diadem. (*To* MARTHA) Right?

MARTHA: Yes.

GROSSLADY: Preciso?

MARTHA: Exactly!

GROSSLADY: Soldio!

ELIZABETH: I can break him when and how I choose . . . if he goes too far.

MARTHA: (*To* DAME GROSSLADY) Did you hear that? If he goes too far!

GROSSLADY: Ah, amore, amore, it doth even drunk the Allblighty and set his halo tooralooring around his bonce! So. Thus: accordion to thee, he hath not gone o'er the top? He hath set on a revoluzione, he doth confectionate a sham-charade, making feint to come by thy palazzo to tip thee his respectuosos, he doth facket prisonerios of thy yes-mans, he hath massacreed the escorto . . .

MARTHA: And to cap it all he calls you 'Old hunchback'!

GROSSLADY: 'Old Crunchback'! Unpardonabilio. Let a ruffian call thee duncipated, let him call thee a bracket-faced slamkin, let him call thee 'stinking trollop' . . . 'Trollop' . . . I pardono thee, I amore thee for that . . . but let him call thee 'old' . . . Chop him to messes! Whack! Whack! Whack! Short arse thus! I should coco . . .

ELIZABETH: Yes, he shouldn't have called me that . . . that was naughty . . .

MARTHA: Elizabeth, stop this. It's high time you gave up all this cuddling and canoodling, the simpering and sweet nothings!

ELIZABETH: Why? Don't I have the right to make a fool of myself occasionally? To be empty-headed and giddy? Don't I have the right to titivate myself and wallow in the pains of love like every other woman in the world? Don't I!

MARTHA: No you don't! You are the ruler of this country and a woman just by accident.

A moment's silence. Then a complete change of tone.

ELIZABETH: All right then . . . thank you for the lecture. Be brave. Have Egerton come in. You see, Dame Grosslady, playtime is over. Look at the life I lead: until a few hours ago I was happy, I was getting myself ready for a night of love. (*She is moved*) I was waiting for my Robert to come. But instead, I'm getting ready for a trial whose outcome is a predetermined sentence of death!

GROSSLADY: (*Weeping*) That be forwhy I semper dicket I would ne'er be Queen! Never!

EGERTON *enters.*

ELIZABETH: Egerton, I ask you to forgive me for forcing you to witness one of my rather pitiful exhibitions just now.

EGERTON: But Your Majesty, what do you mean . . . ?

ELIZABETH: Allow me to continue. It will not occur again. First of all, please convey my congratulations to Cecil and Francis Bacon . . . They did well! It was an excellent idea to send the four Lords in order that they should be taken prisoner . . . And more excellent yet the provocation in the first place of the capture of the twenty-four conspirators, thus forcing Essex and his followers into retaliation. It was a truly exquisite notion. I wish I had thought of it myself. Well done!

EGERTON: Thank you, Your Majesty! I will convey them. It will give them the greatest pleasure, I feel sure.

ELIZABETH: You said that the Earl of Essex had persuaded the four Councillors to write some letters?

EGERTON: Yes, Your Majesty, I have copies of them here . . . These damn ruffians managed to get them read out in a dozen churches this morning, during the sermon . . . even in St Paul's Cathedral . . . If you would care to have a look at them . . .

He holds the letters out to her.

ELIZABETH: No no . . . I can already imagine what is written in them . . . The Lords say they are outraged by our trap . . . they declare that they too have been the victims of a plot.

EGERTON: Exactly.

DAME GROSSLADY *goes up to* EGERTON *and reads the letter silently.*

ELIZABETH: And then they themselves propose an exchange with the prisoners we are holding . . . they advise us that as they are faithful servants of the state, it is the duty of the state to save them.

EGERTON: This is amazing! One might say you had dictated these letters yourself.

ELIZABETH: And then they add: 'We are obliged to admit that there have been errors in the government of the country . . . and that if the conspirators have turned to rebellion, it must be because grave wrongs have forced them to it!'

EGERTON: Yes yes! That's it! Perfect!

GROSSLADY: Dicky bird for dicky bird!

ELIZABETH: What else did they write?

EGERTON: All four of them warn us that in the event of our deciding to sacrifice them . . . (*He reads*) 'That would be a sign of weakness and not strength on the part of the government and the state.'

GROSSLADY: O I hath harked that elsewhere . . . I chance not to mind me where . . . But I harked it . . .

EGERTON: (Still reading) 'And that their deaths would fall on the shoulders of the Queen and the whole of England.'

GROSSLADY: A diverso versione . . .

EGERTON: And they end with a threat. (*As before*) . . . 'Our deaths would signal the start of disaffection with your government and your credibility . . .'

GROSSLADY: Tutto copiato!

ELIZABETH: What arrogance.

MARTHA: You have to do something fast, Elizabeth.

ELIZABETH: Did you say that these bastards have made copies of these letters and that they're distributing them all round the city?

EGERTON: Yes. Someone, whom we have already identified, has even managed to print them . . . and they're being sold like ballad sheets.

ELIZABETH: What an excellent sense of propaganda!

EGERTON: I have already given the order for them to be seized and the printing presses to be closed down . . . and to prevent them from selling any more.

ELIZABETH: That's a mistake! That will simply arouse curiosity and they'll start going like hot cakes.

EGERTON: I hadn't thought of that . . . Very well, I will countermand the order immediately.

ELIZABETH: Organise sermons all over the city. Print your own pamphlets and distribute them . . .

EGERTON: It will be done . . .

Begins to leave.

ELIZABETH: Just a moment . . . What are you going to write in these pamphlets? It must be done with care . . . You must consult Bacon. Rule One, in war as in peace, if they take one of your men prisoner and demand a ransom, you must bring down the price of the goods that the enemy is holding . . . so devalue . . . devalue.

GROSSLADY: God, what a brainbox she hath! She sembras a bloke!

EGERTON: That will be difficult . . . The Lord Chief Justice and the Lord Keeper of the Seal are highly thought of by the people . . .

ELIZABETH: We will say that they are great statesmen, but now, poor souls, they are not to be trusted . . . Perhaps they have been tortured, or even drugged . . . They are no longer capable of rational thought . . . They are lost to us . . . perhaps they have been driven insane.

GROSSLADY: I hath harked that also, but I mind me not where . . .

MARTHA: Well done, Elizabeth, this is more like your old self . . .

EGERTON: The trouble is these damn plotters haven't left us much time. They demand a reply before this evening. At sunset they will start throwing the hostages off the walls, one by one.

GROSSLADY: Not frombye the walls!
AAAAAUUUUUOOORGH!!!

She mimes someone falling from a great height. The sound of a terrible crash – 'CRRRAAAASH!' – mimes that the person who has fallen has been made very small.

GROSSLADY: Those eternity boxes get tiddlier every minuto!

ELIZABETH: In that case there is no time to lose. Summon the two Chambers immediately. I will go and see them myself. If necessary I will speak in the Cathedral as well. I already have an idea of what I need to say. I will say that I am beside myself . . . that's logical . . . in despair . . . I will lower my voice . . . I will deliver a moving tribute to the four Councillors . . . and then I will burst out: 'But we cannot yield! This is the time to hold our ground! We cannot lower ourselves to make compromises with criminals!'

GROSSLADY: It doth smite our heart, it doth slice us to the nick, but we be obligato to sacrificiare these our dear brethren . . . A peck on the mush for the grieving trouble and strife, a peck for the orphelini dustbin lids, and a boot up the Khyber for the pooch! AAAARGH!

She mimes the kisses and the final kick at the dog which shits itself and runs off.

ELIZABETH: The state cannot yield!

EGERTON: So we leave them no way out?

ELIZABETH: No!

EGERTON: Like saying to the bastards: go on, kill them . . . in fact you'd be doing us a favour . . .

ELIZABETH: Precisely . . . with the situation as it stands now . . . with everything they've written and distributed . . . our eyes are brimming with tears . . . but . . .

GROSSLADY: They will haviamo a funeralo di stato!

ELIZABETH: Send for me as soon as the two Chambers have convened. Farewell, Egerton.

EGERTON: I will fly, Your Majesty . . . I will return shortly. *He exits.*

MARTHA: Well done!

GROSSLADY: Brava! Brava!

ELIZABETH: (*In despair, but controlling herself*) Leave me be. I am dying. With these other four corpses on his hands, Essex is well and truly done for now . . . he's dead already, and I am dying with him.

MARTHA: No. There may still be time for him to save himself.

ELIZABETH: No, Martha. He won't save himself . . . Give me a drink. A strong drink.

MARTHA: No, that's bad for you.

ELIZABETH: Give me my leaves.

MARTHA: No, dearest, you know they give you hallucinations.

ELIZABETH: The grand finale of the last act is beginning. Just like in *Hamlet*.

GROSSLADY: Back to this obfuscation with *Omelette*.

ELIZABETH: I am ill. Robert, don't leave your house . . . they will take you to the Tower . . . and I will have to seal your death warrant. O Robert . . . Robert . . . I am a madwoman . . . I am hysterical . . . I can't control myself. Help me. I am swelling up. I am having one of those attacks I had three years ago . . .

GROSSLADY: We must needs puttiamo her trotters dentro this basinetto of acqua.

ELIZABETH: I am swelling up.

GROSSLADY: Go to, we shall unpin thy laces bedietro.

ELIZABETH: My feet are exploding . . . quick, take my shoes off . . . and my stockings.

GROSSLADY: The stampers . . . away with the stampers.

ELIZABETH: Look, my legs are swelling up. My hands are swelling too. Take my rings off.

GROSSLADY: Acqua.

From this point onwards, DAME GROSSLADY's interventions must be calm and must not disturb ELIZABETH's dramatic monologue.

ELIZABETH: Goddamned rings, they're stuck to my fingers. Here's the smell of the blood still. I tell you yet again, they're buried, they cannot come out of their graves. Their little, little graves somewhere upon the Queen's high hands: here lies my mother; here a pretty dimpled boy I decked in rags of state; here's Leicester; here's a Lord still sweating on an errand for his Queen. Last ring of all that ends this strange eventful litany. Is Mary Stuart. Come, detested kite; not Afric owns a serpent I abhor more than thy fame and beauty. What, was it you that would be England's Queen? Rejoice! Rejoice and let thy severed head besport itself as 'twere a clodpole at a rustic feast. I fear no more the heat of your blood. And yet you were the captive I held hard for eighteen years. Alive! But how you struggled in the stone embrace of fortress walls as ever and anon your eyes turned to the sea, seeking the ships of Spain. They were the enemy without my gates, and you, pale Queen, the enemy within. More deadly than the adder fanged, and so . . . NOOOOO!!!! Give her another head. Bind up her neck. Have mercy, Jesu!

MARTHA: Wake up Elizabeth . . . wake up.

ELIZABETH: Soft, I did but dream; I prithee, hold my eyelids up. Suffer me not to sleep . . . What do I fear? Myself? There's none else by. Elizabeth loves Elizabeth. That is I am I. Is there a murderess here? No. Yes. I am. And I am bound upon a wheel of fire, but from this torment I will free myself, or hew my way out with a bloody axe. Yet why's my body weak and smooth but that my soft condition and my heart should well agree with my external parts?

Gunshots off.

GROSSLADY: Guarda. They be shootering. They have attrapped Roberto of Yes-Sex. He be prisonero.

ELIZABETH: The ships of Spain are here! The multitudinous seas encumbered quite. Sail upon sail, high sided forty cannoned whales of death. And on my side a clutch of pirates, earth's mere scum, enlisted but for drink . . . Turn my sweet hellhounds, turn and hear me speak! No, not the weighted words my Parliament will wag their beards at. Not the sceptred isles and stiffened sinews, precious jewel set in a silver sea, that never did nor never in the field of human conflict shall lie at the proud foot of a conqueror. Not all that crap. Hear me, you common cry of curs, now hear Elizabeth, you vagabonds and bastards . . . I am no taper of true virgin wax. I feed on fear like you; taste bile; need blood. My father was the first to name me bastard but so what? I live. I rule; howe'er I was begot.

Elizabeth expects each man this day will fight for booty and if you will not, I'll be up your arses with a fiery torch. I need no heroes – clowns who fight for honour. What makes a hero but the happy accident of time and place; a thief upon the winning side who writes his own deeds in the shifting sands of history. Strike your foe-men! I need to see the English Channel foaming with much blood. Now God stand up for bastards!

Cease your smiling, Mary, for we have in our hands a piece of paper the which will give us peace in our own time. Your death warrant. Who bears the palm of this most heavy deed? Davison . . . the Keeper of the Seal . . . convey him to the Tower. Burleigh, my Councillor? Him too . . . Now let them feel how wretched are those men that hang on monarchs' favours.

It is the only way. The general ear ne'er hearkens to a trial where Queen eats Queen in dainty banqueting. Mary, arise and walk. Love is Time's fool, sweet sister. Come, the bell invites you. Sing on, my choristers, sing on. Give her excess of it that surfeiting her appetite may sicken and so die . . . How fair you look, as pale as monumental alabaster, yet the brightness of your eye would shame the stars as daylight doth a lamp. Now bend up all your spirits to their full height. Tall. Regal. Then down you kneel, down, down, your hair like glistering Phaeton, tie it back. I pray you sir, undo that button. So farewell, a long farewell to all your revels now are ended in a sleep of death. And from this instant there's nothing serious in mortality, all is but wanton boys that cut me to the brains. I am Queen Elizabeth still. And as the poet says:

When the tiger and the panther kissed,
The smaller-mouthed soon lost her head I wist.

Look at your audience. Where be their smiles now Mary? You knot of mouth friends. Blood and a severed head are your perfection. This is Mary's last, who stuck and spangled with your flatteries now pays in Lethe spattered in your eyes.

Watch. I order you to watch.
And where the offence is let the great axe fall.
The hiss.
Useless imbecile!
Clumsy butcher!
She lives yet.
Strike again.
Again.
At last . . .
Cover her head: it's eyes accuse: she died slow.
Sound drums and trumpets; farewell sour annoy,
For here I hope begins our lasting joy.

It's a trap.

Here's hell. Here's darkness. Here is the sulphurous pit. Burning, scalding, stench, consumption.

That isn't Mary's head.
It is my head . . .
It is my head . . .
It is my head . . .

APPENDIX

In the Italian version of Elizabeth, *Dame Grosslady speaks in dialect. Where this translation departs from the original is indicated by a line in the margin, and a literal translation is given below.*

ACT ONE

Page 108

I wear it simply to cover up the ugly countenance that lies beneath it, Your Ladyship.

I hope you won't find it too frightening, Your Majesty. (*Takes mask off*) Well, this is the real me.

It's no use talking in French . . . as I understand it perfectly, Magnificent Lady. I know that I look like a man, an ogre . . . and not even very graceful. Don't make me feel more ashamed than I already do . . . and don't be afraid of me, my sweet queen. I am a good simple creature, and I am here to help you. (*She goes . . . etc*)

Page 109

We call this a walker . . . or a stroller . . . and we use it to teach you how to walk on whore's clogs without falling off.

These, look. (*Shows her two things . . . etc*) Pattens with soles three feet high.

The whores in Venice wear them to make themselves look taller.

But Milady, those whores earn a fortune!

Queen, if you prefer it, we can leave you the way you are.

Don't upset yourself, Magnificence. (*She slips*) Oooops! What have I slipped on . . . what's all this wet stuff! I might be wrong, but it seems to be . . .

Him? A wooden horse that pisses? That's good luck.

Page 110

O well then . . .

Come along, get up, Magnificence . . . Hurry up and get into the stroller . . . (*The help . . . etc*) Good, that's the way. Now we'll shut you snug inside . . . You can help me, Lady Martha.

O look at the queen . . . commanding over all . . . A miracle of height!

Would you like a dummy to suck, My Lady?

You don't want to compare yourself with that wooden pisser.

Walk, walk my sweet beanpole . . .

Page 111

Come along, come along dearie . . . settle your bum down here on the chair while I prepare the ointment I'm going to smear on you.

Ah Hamlet . . . I know him . . . I saw it at the Globe . . . played by that actor . . . when he came out with that terrible: 'Take yourself off to a nunnery Ophelia . . . Any husband of yours would be the greatest cuckold in the world! Take yourself off to a convent . . .' Ha, ha, ha, ha . . . (*She gets a jar . . . etc*)

Oh no . . . my voice is a bit off just now.

Flowers of alum.

Page 112

It's perfectly normal, my lady.

Beautiful . . . how does it go? 'The frog at the bottom of the well thought that the arse end of the bucket was the sun . . .' Splendid!

I've got it now! It's like seeing a reflection in a mirror! A reverse image!

Page 113

See? Biggedy show-off!

Hold your own tongue. Go and put the clogs away. (*To Elizabeth*) Really, I don't know where you get your servants from, Queen.

Take off your shift. Get undressed.

What are you ashamed of? We're all women. The only male here is the wooden pissing horse.

Don't be so naughty. You shouldn't put yourself down all the time. You're still a good-looking woman.

Page 114

He's playing a sort of drag dressing up game in the mirror.

Listen why don't you stop pulling her leg and taking the piss out of her.

You see how it balances out? Tit for tat . . .

What a muddle of families . . .

Page 115

The mirror image exactly! Exactly!

Shall I answer? But for the last time, mind you.

Well then. The Queen, Elizabeth of England, everyone knows, has one terrible weakness: when she sees curtains or tapestries moving . . . she always has a sword to hand . . . 'A ghost!' she cries . . . 'Thwack!' . . . and whoever's hiding behind it . . . never mind. (*She mimes . . . etc*)

Really, and she didn't stab you? Queen, you really should put in a bit more practice . . . You shouldn't have missed a cow like this one . . . Anyway, Hamlet has this weakness too . . . there's a scene where a tapestry moves and Polonius is behind it . . .

Oh what an allegory! Don't you see?! So, here we have this Polonius, who is the allegory for Cecil, and he's behind a curtain, and there's Hamlet talking to his mother, telling her the most terrible things . . . saying 'How could you marry that terrible man . . . slag!' That's how he talks to her . . . And then at a certain point the arras moves . . . AAARGH! A rat! WHACK!! You know over there in Denmark they have rats five and a half feet tall . . . five feet nine at the very least . . . SPLAT! The sword thrust! CLUNK! Polonius, the allegory, flat on the ground . . . (*To Martha*) And the next allegory is you . . .

Page 116

You don't agree with me? All right. I'll give you a second example. At the end of *Hamlet*, who arrives to sort out the shit heap?

Fortinbras of Norway. Good. And in this shitheap we call England, who, according to the Puritans, is the Fortinbras who's going to come from the north and sort it all out?

James of Scotland, who is perched on the border ready to come crashing down on your head, Queenie. (*She gives a violent tug . . . etc*)

It's just because I'm keen.

Mongol indeed! You look wonderful . . . Look here, I've completely got rid of your double chin.

You're right. You had a double nape!

Page 117

I got it! Shall I explain?

No. I will tell her. The thing is, the actor who plays Hamlet is called Richard Burbage. I know him well. He's a man of forty-two . . . on a good day he doesn't look a day over sixty-two . . . sixty-four . . . He's got a little bit of a pot-belly . . . and unbelievably short of breath . . . every time he performs, after a bit he gets asthma . . . and during the duel, when he's with Laertes – Laertes is young, he jumps, he takes great leaps . . . Look what Richard Burbage does in the duel . . . he knits . . . (*She mimes knitting*) . . . So at a certain point . . . although he's not actually moving, he goes 'Arh, arh, arh'. (*Panting sound*) And the Queen says to him . . . 'O Hamlet, you're not a boy any more, you're breathing through your arsehole!' Shakespeare, eh? Then they censored it . . . but that's what he wrote . . . Well then, this Burbage is covered in sweat . . .

Yes that's true . . . he walks all crooked, with his feet turned out. But when he's acting . . . he has such power, he intoxicates the whole audience . . . (*She acts out in nonsense talk . . . etc*)

And you understand everything he says. He's a force of nature . . . even if he is a bit camp.

It shows. It shows . . . all he needs is the feathers growing out of his arse . . . And why did they give the part to this numbskull? There must be at least five other actors in the company who would have made a better job of it: younger, thinner, better actors . . . why did they pick this woofta?

Page 118

Well, you can't say that any more. Not about your face

anyway. Feel how firm it is! (*She gets Elizabeth out of the chair . . . etc*)

We've got to get rid of belly, haven't we?

Slugs. (*Shows her . . . etc*)

No. Leeches suck your blood. These sluggies only suck fat . . . Oooh . . . They suck like . . . Look how lovely they are. And their little blue eyes . . . perky little thingies . . .

Yes. And on your hips and thighs too.

Page 119

On the shoulders, the arms. And on the widow's hump at the back of your neck.

And on your back, and your bottom . . . They'll slim you beyond belief. Look at the beasties! Look how greedy this one is! Attila! Caligula!

O how vulgar. The F-word from a queen. And in front of these shy little worms as well. Look at this one, he's gone quite pale. Suck away dearie.

And now I've got the key to this whole mirror image business of his . . . So, for example, when he says 'Denmark is a prison' . . . he means 'England is a prison' . . .

O yes . . . at the end there are dead bodies all over the place. Laertes run through over here; the poisoned queen gasping over there . . . the king vomiting here . . . and Hamlet breathing his last there . . .

Page 120

Hamlet's. Everyone knows it's Hamlet's fault because he can never make up his mind, he dithers around . . . He could have resolved everything long before: he stabbed his treacherous uncle right there, when he was praying. 'Now I'll stab him . . . No. Hang on a minute' . . . he said to himself . . . 'I'd be doing him a favour, because he'd die purified of all his sins, and he'd go straight to heaven. My father, on the contrary, died full of sin, and Boom!, he went to hell. I'll wait till my uncle goes into the bedroom with my mother and they start doing dirty things together . . .' And then he gets out the knife . . . 'No. I won't do it now . . . tomorrow . . . we'll see . . . the day after tomorrow . . . I don't know . . . maybe next week . . .' O God, he could have resolved the whole thing in the first scene, when the ghost of Hamlet's father came on, came to him and said: 'Ha-a-amlet . . . ' – The Ghost father had an echo, like all self-respecting ghosts – 'Ha-a-amlet, it's your u-u-u-cle, he's the assass-ass-ass-i-i-in . . . stab hi-i-im . . .'

I couldn't give a damn about five acts . . . and then there's Ophelia dying, and that other one who goes off his head . . . goes to England, comes back . . . then the duel. Phew! I like things to be clear. Only one act, but clear. The father's ghost comes on and says: 'Hamlet, he's the murderer!' 'O, is he? Right you are then!' Out with the knife. 'Assassin' . . . But no, we get: 'Now I come to think of it, I'll wait and see, I'll put it off, I'll hold on . . .'

Page 121

Noooo!

O no, silly woman . . . the slugs are all squashed. O what a disaster. It's just like the end of *Hamlet*. You've even squashed the queen.

Squashed slugs? They're right.

It's because you're too good to them, and you let them go on prattling . . . if I was you . . . whack!!

It's not my finger. It's one of the little wormies that's crawled into the hole . . .

It's not my fault if worms like greasy holes, is it?

I can't hang on to him . . . O there he is . . . Ooop-la! . . . I've got him! Look how fat he is! What lovely little eyes!

Page 122

. . . And these new worms on the floor . . . Just look . . . (*Elizabeth goes off, followed by Martha, to get dressed*) Look what a feast this one's had. He's so plump! OOOH, my goodness these slugs have got fat . . . They're so full of fat it makes you sick . . . now I'm going to go straight home to my husband, he's a fisherman. And when I give him these fattened worms, he'll go crazy . . . he'll go straight out fishing . . . he'll stick these worms on his hooks and throw them right to the bottom of the river. And the minute they see these worms, the fish will appear: 'The slugs!' EOUGH! And tonight we'll have a huge fish to eat. Ha ha ha . . . Now I come to think of it, we won't be eating a fish, because these worms have eaten the queen, and the fish eat the worms . . . so really what we'll be eating is the queen! What about that for a clever idea, eh! What about that for an allegory! To tell you the truth, I didn't make up that little parable . . . it wasn't me who made it up . . . It was Shakespeare . . . actually it was his idea. When he makes Hamlet say: 'A king will sit down at a banquet. Not to eat, but to be eaten . . . because he is dead and the worms will eat his corpse . . . A fisherman will walk by . . . and he'll take a handful of worms from the king . . . and he will go fishing. He catches a big fish! And a poor man, the lowest of the low, finds this fish and eats it. At the end of it all, the beggar eats the king!' It's enough to give you the shivers! What a brain, that Shakespeare! You can't have a single idea that he hasn't copied already!

Page 123

O no, it's certainly not your imagination, queen . . . you must be thinner. You only have to see how swollen these beasties are from sucking at you . . . They look pregnant.

You call that a little miracle! If you give me time I can even resurrect the breasts for you too . . . I'll give you two titties so big that when you try to cross your arms, it'll be like resting them on a shelf . . . you'll be able to put a vase of flowers on them and water them every morning . . . O how beautiful! What a dress!

Yes, he'll be reeling. Almost as much as I am now with this story of you being Hamlet's double.

I'm sorry, queen, but I don't agree. Come on now! A rebellion organised by theatre people? Can you see them, all the thespians with their wooden swords and their cannons loaded with talc and face powder? 'Ready for the rebellion! Load the cannons! Fire!' BOOM BOOOM! (*She mimes the explosion . . . etc*) End of the rebellion!

Page 124

(*Under her breath . . . etc*) She's playing the part of Hamlet. He's a sort of pansified transvestite, with feathers in his arse, and he's taking the piss out of the queen . . .

(*She explains – 'mimes' – the plot . . . etc*) . . . and that's the end of Act One! (*To Elizabeth*) My Lady, I have to explain this to him because he doesn't know anything about Hamlet. He must be a policeman . . . (*She continues to explain . .*) . . . end of Act Four!!

Page 125

I've nearly finished Act Five!

You'd see that *Hamlet* is a sort of drag act, making fun of the queen . . . and he's stuck at the bottom of a well, disguised as a frog, looking up at the arse end of a bucket saying: 'O what a beautiful sun!'

Page 126

And it can piss too!

No, milady, he doesn't understand.

But look at the expression on his face. He doesn't understand.
There's no light in his eyes . . .

I'm not interrupting, but he doesn't understand.

Page 127

That's not surprising!

I am here checking it word for word to make sure you're not
making anything up.

Page 128

He'll really finish us off!

This is terrible! Now I understand his terrible machinations!
This Shakespeare is saying to people: 'What are you up to?
Why don't you move yourselves? You consent to being treated
like slaves, put upon like beasts of burden, just because you're
afraid that if you die you'll burn in hell . . . Arseholes! Hell is
here, here on earth! Not down below. Don't be afraid, get on
with it, rise up! Kick this shitty government to kingdom come!'
(*She begins to sing a revolutionary protest song*)

Keep calm! Your brain will explode. It's too much to take in
all at one go like that! Take it step by step.

(*She mocks . . . etc*) PLOP! The egg of harmony! With a
miniature Jesuit inside!

And then you can burn it . . . A gust of wind and some
wandering sparks . . .

Page 129

Beautiful! Beautiful line . . . what a metaphor! . . .
Shakespeare? Shakespeare, Shakespeare . . .

But it was Shakespeare's style!

Page 130

Ha ha, very good! Shakespeare!

But what does this Shakespeare ever write that's his own, eh? What? Thief!

Don't you understand, dear queen . . . these ruffians have the nerve to come here and kill you.

Page 131

After I've done you the shelf with the vase of flowers for you to water . . .

Ah! Terrible queen!

Page 132

O Jesus . . . I must be seeing double. I can't believe my eyes.

Down there, at the end of the street . . . It looks like your beloved, the Earl of Essex . . . isn't he handsome . . . with all his men . . . . O isn't he handsome? They're coming in a procession . . . some men and women are clapping them.

(*Gets another telescope . . . etc*) . . . Have a look, queen, have a look . . . I'm really afraid we've had it this time . . .

Page 133

It's mine. I brought it back from Venice. They sell them on stalls in the Piazza . . . with every ten wooden gondolas you buy, they give you one free . . . Military secret!

I'll go to the door with you.

Well said queen! Then at the first whiff of cannon fire they'll piss themselves worse than your horse!

(*She has taken a pen . . . etc*) I'm ready to take notes . . . I'll do the writing, your Ladyship . . .

Wait a minute, I've got to write down the address: 'To the Earl of Essex, Essex House . . .'

My Lady, if the Lords get lost on the way . . . then the message would get lost . . . It doesn't take long to write the address.

Page 134

'To the Earl of Essex, to be put into his own hands . . .'

(*She repeats . . . etc*) 'We come . . .'

'. . . the Queen . . .'

(*As before*) '. . . to understand . . . French.'

'To understand the cause.' Full stop! Well, that's clear enough!

It was the end of the sentence.

Well then, comma!

Semi-colon!

Exclamation mark!

But now I'll have to turn this full stop into something else, won't I? Shall I draw a flower over it? A dragon? Saint George on his horse?

Comma.

'. . . why certain tickles i'faith . . .'

Page 135

Tickles . . .

(*As one . . . etc*) 'Ah! Tickles!' . . . I see the irony now . . . (*She begins to write . . . etc*) . . . Ah. Ah. 'Tickles!' Ah. Ah.

Another queen?

The same queen as before! (*She writes*) 'The queen, the same one as before . . .'

Are they supposed to guess?

'A tissue of lies . . .'

(*As if to say . . . etc*) Of lies.

Bless you!

Or not to be, that is the question . . .

'Dressed . . .'

'Ah! Dressed!'

'Undressed . . .'

Ah! You shall have more. Ah! More tickles! (*Elizabeth looks . . . etc*) 'Shall . . .'

Page 136

Just as before. More tickles, just as before . . . (*She has got to the bottom . . . etc*)

'Just a . . . just a . . .' (*Turns the . . . etc*)

There's no room left for justice! (*She goes . . . etc*)

Yes, I've got that! 'Fucking cow!'

Stepnitalian! It is understood everywhere!

Ah queen, did you see how pale Sir Thomas turned when you told him about the graffiti against him? I bet Cecil and Bacon have got the shits!

Page 137

I learned to talk smutty by hanging around queens . . . fucking cow!

I can do it, but I must warn you it might sting a bit.

Yes. From these. (*She holds up . . . etc*)

Buzzies.

First of all, Martha, you take this little piece of sandalwood. That's to make some smoke. I place the open jar, with the bees inside, on the breast itself . . . then I let a bit of smoke inside . . . and the bee gets cross and FATANG! He stings you! Then in a little while you'll see how beautifully the breast will swell up! Plump! Firm! Taut!

(*Referring to . . . etc*) O you'd need a hornet for her . . .

Page 138

Yes, you can do it with cotton but it doesn't produce the same result, cotton. There's an old proverb that says 'Cotton is cotton. It isn't satisfying!' And suppose Robert wants to stroke you. Anyway a bee sting doesn't hurt very much . . . because I'll smear a little honey and myrrh on the breast to lessen the pain.

Well they won't be like balloons, but I can promise you they'll be beautiful.

Good. Just wait while I smear on the honey and myrrh. Help me. (*Hands Martha . . . etc*)

Oh . . . three days . . . maybe five . . . it depends how long we leave the sting in.

No, no. Half an hour is too long. You'd grow a breast like a water melon – like this!

Sweet queenliness, take a deep breath.

Go on, Martha. Do the smoke round it. (*She puts . . . etc*)

Page 139

Wonderful! That's marvellous! It stung her straight away! Hurrah!

Don't give in, don't give in . . . Majesty, I'm going to put a little camphor on it. (*We see her . . . etc*)

No, just a little while longer . . . wait, my sweetie, don't give in . . . Look, look, it's swelling up already!

O he's lost his sting now. He's dead. Wait till I get another jar ready . . . with a new bee . . .

No, the titties have to swell at the same time . . . So you can keep an eye on them . . . You don't want one of them to grow and grow, and the other one to stay as flat as a pancake . . .

That's normal. Bees' stings always have that effect. Pee as much as you like, we'll blame the wooden pissing horse. Now then, let's go with the second one! (*She applies the second . . . etc*) Is he stinging?

Page 140

(*To Martha*) Make some smoke . . . smoke . . . (*Turns back . . . etc*) Stinging now?

O you naughty bee! Don't want to sting eh? Well I'll teach you a lesson! (*She shakes . . . etc*)

No no . . . Here we are, I've got the avenger! (*Gets another jar . . . etc*)

An Irish hornet.

Don't be afraid, sweet splendiforousness . . . It has a more delicate puncture than the bee's. Come along now, don't get agitated. (*Without realising . . . etc*) Hold her, Martha!

Page 141

Fool, burning the queen's bum. (*She takes . . . etc*) Sit down here dear . . . sit in this basin, the water will cool you down.

No, this time you sat on the jar of bees . . . naughty bee! He didn't want to bite you on the breast, but he bit you on the arse! Catholic! Republican!

ACT TWO

Page 145

Here I am, duckie . . . How splendiforous! Up on your wooden pissing horse, so early in the morning!

New waspies, dearie.

Good. We call those Venus's love bumps dearie. Hold on tight to the horsie, we're going to go backwards. (*She pushes the horse . . . etc*)

O that's wonderful dearie. It's an erotic game! The men go potty for it! . . . Now we'll take all the hairpins out for you.

Page 146

No, my lady, there was no battle. I was out and about too. I crossed the whole of London looking for wasps and I didn't hear so much as a dog barking. It was so quiet you could have heard the flies buzzing . . . the flies that were buzzing in London last night!

No?!

No!?

Alive? The head was alive? Like Saint John the Decapitated! Well that would be useful, wouldn't it? Because without turning your head, you could look . . . (*Mimes holding a head . . . etc*) . . . look over here . . . look over there . . .

O no!

A raspberry from the chopped off head.

Page 147

Bouncing?

Then what?

Goddammit, it was right! Where is the woman's head? O yes! She was holding it. All right. Dammit, I understand what it all means. Now I understand. This dream means that the Earl of Essex has lost his head.

He's lost his head from love . . . of you.

(*To Martha*) While we're on the subject of good news, why don't you tell her who's on his way!

Robert of Essex has decided to come and pay his respects to you. Happy?

You just be careful you don't go out of your head for real . . . you know what happens to those sort of people . . . (*Mimes heads . . . etc*) Bouncies!!

Page 148

Yes your ladyship. (*Martha helps . . . etc*)

(*Going to the door*) There's no point in knocking. The Queen can't see anyone because she's all undone and looks like she's been dragged through a hedge backwards! (*She peeps . . . etc*) Your ladyship, it's the chief of police. The bloodhound.

Let him in, my lady, to see what a mess you're in?

Blindfold the chief of police? That would give him a turn!

That's an idea! Come in, Sir Thomas! (*Pulls his hat . . . etc*) It's the Queen's order that I have to pull your hat well down over your eyes because . . . O dammit, what a head . . . Your Ladyship, his head is so big it won't go into the hat . . . It's so big that if it fell into a headsman's hands he'd jump for joy . . . there we are . . . that's got it. Off you go dearie.

Page 149

There's plenty more where he came from.

Answer her, milord.

Smooth tongued bastard! (*Pushes horse . . . etc*)

Conspirators. Shakespeare is a rebel? Well that's a turn up for the book!

Page 150

(*Gobsmacked*) No! My Lady! Theatricals taking to politics! Unheard of! Whatever next!

She's gone. (*She lifts . . . etc*) I'll lift your hat. Get a breath of air.

You were lucky you didn't see the look that came into her eyes . . . wicked, terrifying . . . just like her sister, Bloody Mary, when she set up the courts of inquisition . . . There's nothing to be done about it . . . She's a redhead . . . she too, just like her father, Henry the Redhead . . . terrible. A whole family of redheads. All wicked!

Page 151

There's a proverb in my country that goes: 'Red head at night, Henry's delight. Red head in the morn, prepare to be shorn.'

THWACK! The poet's head in the basket too! Do you know, Sir Thomas, why English coffins are shorter than those anywhere else?

Because in England nearly everyone is buried holding their head in their hands.

(*Swiftly pushing . . . etc*) Don't laugh so loudly, here's the queen. (*To the queen*) How are you feeling? Better?

Page 152

It's the voice of your Captain of the Guard.

(*Blocking . . . etc*) Stop! There's a chasm there! It isn't time for the short coffin yet. (*She accompanies Egerton to the door*) Your Ladyship, it is true what the proverb says: 'When justice is blind, the police force is at least squinty and cross-eyed!' . . .

Let the guards come in, your Ladyshipness, there is great danger.

Page 153

Don't pass remarks! Busybody, you have no idea what's happened. An extraordinary miracle! Very early this morning, when it was almost still night, well in fact it was still night, before morning . . . Elizabeth heard a goldfinch crying CHEEP CHEEP in the garden. She went down. And there was the little birdie . . . CHEEP CHEEP . . . all frozen cold. She picked him up, the poor little frozen birdie, CHEEP CHEEP, and she pùt him between her breasts. And she, good Samaritan that she is, came back here to bed, and she put him between the sheets and she blew a little warm air on him, and WHOOSH! CHEEP CHEEP! WHOOSH! This young man sprang out. Straightaway the Queen got down on her knees: 'Saint Rosalie, the most beautiful saint of all, what should I do with this young man?' And the saint answered her: 'CHEEP CHEEP, unite the young man with his little bird!' And that's how it went!

Well done! That way he'll be mistaken for an assassin . . . CHEEP CHEEP! He'll turn back into a little bird!

Page 154

Yes, well done. Dress him up as a woman, that's a good idea.

Yes.

You are too much. Just mind your head! Bounce!

The try-out boy. The titty tester!

Page 155

(*Alarmed*) Your Majesty, there is a man . . . down there in the garden . . . in the maze . . . the guards . . . are chasing him with the dogs.

It must be that bastard who was trying to climb up into this room to kill the Queen. Now he's gone over there.

Alive! So that afterwards we can dress him up as a woman as well. Ha ha!

Let's go! God what fun! It's just one long party here at court. A coup de théâtre every minute. From the window you can watch a fugitive being chased by dogs. A half naked young man inside the bed . . . Just like being at a play!

Page 158

I'd like to know how that man managed to kill himself.

Get up! Get up!

Page 159

Get up on these platform clogs!

O Goddammit! The candlestick's fallen into the fireplace!

Oh, what a lot of smoke! (*We can hear . . . etc*) Queen, I can hear screams coming from the chimney. Listen to the screams! AAAAAARGH!

(*Imitating . . . etc*) AAAAAAARGH! It's the chimney. It's the voice of the chimney.

It must be the wind!

Do they torture the wind in England too?

Page 160

That great slag! O no thank you, dearie.

(*She has discovered . . . etc*) O look! A pipe!

The Magic Flute! You can play it even if you don't blow in it! All you have to do is move your fingers!

Give me a kiss in exchange!

Page 161

Me, old hag? You called me an old hag? I hope lightning strikes you: CCRRRACHK! (*She mimes . . . etc*) As short as that, clogs and all. (*She goes off . . .*) A short dwarf!

(*Entering*) I'm sure I heard someone screaming. Who are you . . . ? Help! A man! A killer priest!

Don't move, Queen! Close the door, because there's an assassin in here and he's looking for you!

Page 162

The wasps! Help! The wasps!

You asked for it, you swine! Duel with wasps and pistols!

Don't come in here, Queen, the room is full of the stinging wasps!

Be careful . . . cover your face with a handkerchief.

Guards! (*Shouts off*)

He was here just now . . . I think he must have got up the chimney.

Page 163

No. He must have been a real priest, one of those madmen who give you the cross to kiss with one hand while they're holding the rope that's going to hang you in the other hand; and with the other hand they're lighting the fire under your feet, and blessing you with the other hand . . . These priests have got so many hands!

No, wait. I've got the queen wasp here. The others only have to get a sniff of her, and they'll all fly into the jar . . . Coo-ee, come on waspies, your Queen's calling you! Look at them coming! They're falling in! Dammit! The Queen's flown out . . . where is she? O look . . . she's got into the horse's nostril

and all the wasps are following her. That's it then. Danger
over.

Page 164

Oh!

He's beside himself . . . Listen to the way he's talking . . .

Everything he says has a dirty double meaning.

He didn't. He's dead. But he died happy . . . he was laughing!

Yes, a chance accident! Look what brazen luck these queens
have. They haul young lads into bed to warm themselves up,
and then these fools do them the favour of taking a blade
between the shoulders as a tip as well! And they get themselves
cuddled and stroked, licked and nuzzled . . . But me . . . If I
say to a young man: 'Give me a kiss,' he says to me, 'Shut your
face, tart!'

Page 165

There was a killer priest in here and he stabbed her and killed
her.

Look, the horse looks as though he's got the shakes.

It looks as though he's having a fit. All the wasps inside him
must be having a fight.

No, not torture, no!

Page 166

No, Your Majesty, forgive me.

No, no milady, don't worry about it. It's understandable, it's
normal: when a queen gets a fright, what does she do to relieve
her mind? All she has to do is hang a servant on a hook and
everything's fine again. That's only natural. I just shat myself
of course . . .

Page 167

We do things on the grand scale.

Page 168

Yes it's true . . . I heard the shots . . . But he told me . . . Sir Thomas, won't you help me out of this trap?

Your Ladyship, shall I call the guards? I'll get the hook ready so you can hang him up by his feet a bit. (*She laughs*)

O what a fine cunning fellow.

I speak, I measure, and I bury.

Page 169

Ooops, the woman's getting heavy . . .

Yes we'll call you back later and we'll measure you properly.

Wait till the spymaster's gone. There. Now you can speak.

Page 170

Martha I'd say you'd be in less danger if you went and tried to pull the hairs out of a lion's bollocks.

This dear love of yours, his Lordship, must surely have turned you into a mental deficient; he's got so above himself he's capable of taking a fancy to sitting on your head, Queenie, making sure to put a cushion on it first so's not to scratch his arse on the spikes of your crown. (*To Martha*) Right?

Precisely?

Sold!

Page 171

Ah, love that inebriates even God and sends his halo whirling round his head! So according to you, he hasn't gone too far yet? He's started a rebellion; he makes a charade of coming to

pay homage to you; he takes your councillors prisoner; he
slaughters the escort . . .

'Old hunchback'! That's unforgiveable. Let a man call you a
fool, a gibbering idiot, let him call you 'Whore' . . . 'Whore'! –
'I forgive you, I love you for that.' But if he calls you old . . .
Chop him down! Whack, whack, whack . . . down to that.
Come off it dearie . . .

Page 172

(*Weeping*) That's why I always said I'd never be Queen! Never!

Page 173

Word for word!

Oh I've heard that somewhere before . . . I can't remember
where . . . but I've heard it . . .

. . . a slightly different version . . .

All copied!

Page 174

God, what a brain she's got. She's like a man!

I've heard that too, but I can't remember where . . .

Page 175

Not off the walls! AAAAUUUUOOORGH! (*She mimes etc*)
The coffins get shorter all the time!

It breaks our heart, it cuts us to the quick, but we are obliged
to sacrifice these dear brothers of ours! A kiss for the widow, a
kiss for the orphans and a kick for the dog! AAAAARGH!
(*She mimes etc*)

They'll have state funerals!

Page 176

Brava! Brava!

Back to the obsession with *Hamlet*.

We'll put her feet in this basin of boiling water.

Come on, we'll unlace you at the back.

The shoes, off with the shoes.

Page 177

Water.

Page 178

Look, they're shooting. They've taken Robert of Essex
prisoner!

The Open Couple

written with Franca Rame
translated by Stuart Hood

The Open Couple was first performed at the Teatro Communale di Monfalcone, Trieste, on 30 November 1983. Franca Rame and Nicola de Buono were the performers and Dario Fo directed.

Interior of an apartment. A MAN in his forties is knocking on the door of the bathroom. His face is lit by a spotlight.

MAN: Don't be silly, Antonia. Come out – say something. What are you doing? Listen – maybe you're right, it's my fault – but please come out. Open the door. We'll talk things over – OK? Christ, why do you have to turn everything into a tragedy? Can't we work things out like rational people? (*He looks through the keyhole*) What are you up to? You're mad and you simply don't care – that's what's wrong with you.

A WOMAN appears at the side of the stage. She is also lit. The rest of the stage is in darkness.

WOMAN: The uncaring madwoman in there – actually it's the bathroom – is me. That other person – the guy who's yelling at me and begging me not to do anything foolish – is my husband –

MAN: (*goes on talking as if the WOMAN were in the bathroom*) Antonia, come out, please!

WOMAN: I'm taking a cocktail of pills. Mogadon, Optalidon, Femidol, Veronal, Cibalgina, four Nisidinetritate suppositories – all orally.

MAN: Say something, Antonia.

WOMAN: My husband's already called an ambulance. They'll break down the door.

MAN: The first-aid squad's on its way. They'll knock the door down. Christ – this is the third time.

WOMAN: The thing I can't stand about emergency treatment is having your stomach pumped. That damned tube down your throat – and then the dazed state you're in for days and the embarrassed looks everyone gives you. Making these vague idiotic comments – just to say something. And then, of course, they make me see the psychologist – pardon, the analyst. A prick who sits there looking at you in silence for two hours with his pipe in his mouth and then suddenly says: 'Do cry, please, do cry!'

MAN: Antonia, say something. Give a moan at least. Then at least I'll have an idea of what stage you're at. I'm going now and you won't see me again. (*He bends down to squint through the keyhole*)

WOMAN: Actually it's not the first time I've wanted to die.

MAN: Antonia! Don't swallow the yellow pills. They're for my asthma!

WOMAN: Another time I tried jumping out of the window. He grabbed me just when I was taking off. (*The* WOMAN *jumps onto the window-sill which has been brought onto the stage. The* MAN *grabs her ankle. The lights come on full*)

MAN: Please come down. Yes, you're right – I am a bastard but I promise you, it's the last time I'll put you in a situation like this.

WOMAN: Do you think I give a damn? Can't you understand I'm simply not interested in you – in your affairs – in your stupid women?

MAN: You mean – if they'd been intelligent you wouldn't have minded so much? Let's talk it over – on the floor. Come down.

WOMAN: No, I don't give a damn – I'm going to jump.

MAN: No!

WOMAN: Yes!

MAN: I'll break your ankle first.

WOMAN: Ow! (*She steps down from the window. Her husband hands her a crutch*)

WOMAN: (*to the audience*) And he really did break it, the idiot. A month with my leg in plaster! And everyone asking me: 'Have you been skiing?' God, was I angry. (*Limping, she puts down the crutch and from the drawer of the table or some other piece of furniture, takes out a gun*)

WOMAN: Another time I tried to shoot myself –

MAN: No, damn it, stop! (*The MAN makes a move to stop the WOMAN*) I haven't got a licence for it. Do you want to get me arrested?

WOMAN: (*Talks to the audience as if not involved in the action*) The reason I wanted to die was always the same. He didn't want me any more. He didn't love me any more. And the tragedy erupted every time I found out about my husband's latest affair.

MAN: (*Trying to take the gun away from the woman*) Try to be reasonable. With the others it's only a sexual thing – that's all.

WOMAN: Oh yes? and with me it isn't even sex any more.

MAN: But with you it's different. I've a tremendous respect for you.

WOMAN: Well you know what you can do with your respect! (*To the audience*) Yes, in this sort of situation I always get a tiny bit petty. But it was my husband's thoughtlessness that drove me up the wall. It couldn't go on like that. He hadn't made love to me for ages.

MAN: I don't know why you get a kick out of dragging everything out in public –

WOMAN: Oh, it pisses you off, eh? (*To the audience*) At first I thought maybe he was – overtired. (*She is about to cross in front of the window. Her husband who is looking out of the window stops her*)

MAN: Watch! You'll fall out!

WOMAN: No, I won't. There's the stage.

MAN: Yes, but the set ends here.

WOMAN: Right – but I'm a character in a play. I'm telling a story so I step out of character and I can step out of the set. (*To the audience*) I was saying – I thought maybe he was overtired and then I found out he had an extremely active sex-life with other people – naturally. And when I asked him to explain what had happened to him – 'Why don't you want me any more?' – he would find excuses. (*During the last part of her speech the* MAN *sits on the window-sill with his legs dangling*)

MAN: I would find excuses?

WOMAN: Yes, you. Once you even tried to lay the blame on politics.

MAN: Me?

WOMAN: Watch out, you'll fall!

MAN: I'm a character in a play, too!

WOMAN: No, you're not. You're on the fourth floor. (*To the audience*) I was saying that he tried to lay the blame on politics. He trotted out the bits about the political backlash. 'You've got to understand. How can I make love with all that's going on in this country? The unions –'

MAN: I didn't make it up about the backlash. It's a fact. Isn't it true that after the failure of all those struggles we went through we felt a bit frustrated – teetering on the brink. Look about you – what do you see? Cynicism.

WOMAN: Great! Some people get fed up with politics, dump their families and join the Hare Krishna lot – or else they chuck the office and open up a macrobiotic restaurant – and some of them set up whorehouses for their own personal use. And it's all the fault of politics!

MAN: I admit it's a silly kind of hobby – trying to set up as a sexual athlete – But I swear it's different with you. You're the only woman I can't do without. You're the person I love most in all the world – I feel really safe with you – like my mother.

WOMAN: I knew it! Your mother! Thank you very much! You've promoted me. Wives are like civil servants. When they're no use any more they kick them upstairs – make them director of some useless public corporation. Well, I'd rather be demoted to a one-night stand. Thrown on the bed and desired. I'm damn well not interested in being a warm blanket for you. Your huggy! Your mother! But don't you see what a bore you are? How you humiliate me? What am I supposed to be? An old boot you throw into the rubbish heap? Your mother! You'll see I can find men how and when I like.

MAN *reacts.*

WOMAN: It's no use putting on that ridiculous self-satisfied smile. I'll set up a brothel for you – yes, a brothel opposite where you work. I'll walk up and down on the pavement with a billboard. It'll have on it: 'Now available – the wife of Mr X – special offer – washed and scented. Handsome discounts.' Passed by the Board of Advertisers.

MAN: That's what I like about you – the way you always shit on my moments of honesty – of sincere feeling. I try to open up – to talk –

WOMAN: Then why don't you talk? Talk! Explain yourself. Explain to me what's got into you? All these stories – about bed – bed – bed. As if I didn't have a properly furnished house. (*While she is speaking the* MAN *tries to take the gun away*) And let go of this gun! I swear I won't shoot myself.

MAN: Word of honour?

WOMAN: Word of honour – I won't shoot myself. I don't feel like it any more. (*The* MAN *lets go*) I've changed my mind. It's you I'm going to shoot. (*She points the gun at him*)

MAN: Don't play silly tricks.

WOMAN: I'm not. (*She fires a shot that just misses him*)

MAN: Have you gone mad? You fired. You just missed me. Look, we're only re-enacting things.

WOMAN: And I'm getting furious all over again just thinking about it.

MAN: Aren't I ever allowed to be a character in a play?

WOMAN: Shut up! Hands up! Face the wall. Stay like that. I'm going to have a word with them – then I'll kill you. (*She turns to the public still pointing the gun at her husband*) Then one day he counter attacked.

MAN: And what did you do to stop things from falling apart? And when I did something about it and looked for some affection elsewhere – some sort of stimulus – a bit of passion – something different – did you try to understand me?

WOMAN: Something different! (*To the public*) One day I discovered him – I was there in the house – washed and perfumed – I discovered him in the loo masturbating like a fifteen-year-old – out of hours. That was something different too!

MAN: That's mean! What sort of a kick do you get out of shitting all over me like this? OK, every so often I get into self-gratification. It's healthy. It relaxes me – especially when I'm tense and depressed. Like taking a sauna.

WOMAN: Yes – sauna my – Don't make me say rude things.

MAN: That's right, try not to. There are a lot of men –

WOMAN: (*Threatens him with the gun*) Shut up! (*To the audience*) As I was saying, my husband counter-attacked – the things he came up with! 'We must talk, you and me – we can only save our relationship if we change our cultural attitudes.' He trotted out all the hypocrisy that goes with bourgeois after-dinner talk – the most disgusting moralizing.

MAN: Of course! Faithfulness is a disgusting idea. Uncivilised! The idea of the married couple, of the family, is tied up with the defence of the immense economic benefits the patriarchy gets out of it. What you aren't able to understand is that I'm perfectly capable of having a relationship with another woman and at the same time of being friends with you –

WOMAN: Did you think this all out yourself or did you have an old boy's reunion? I understand. Adultery's out. Nowadays we behave like modern people – civilised – politically aware. No! No! I can see myself and I won't stand for it. The bell rings. I go to the door. Who is it? Oh, it's my husband. 'Hello – and who is the nice young lady?' 'May I introduce you – this is my wife – my girl-friend.' 'How nice to meet you. Do come in. She's charming. How old are you? Only twenty-five years younger than my husband! That's marvellous. Do feel at home. Supper is ready. I hope you like our house. This is your bedroom. I mean our bedroom – but you're welcome to it. I'll sleep in my son's room. Or maybe it would be better if I went out. You'll feel freer then. I'll go to my sister's. No, don't worry – it's no trouble – somebody will keep me company. There's Norman – he's free too this evening because his wife's going out with – Have a nice supper and good night. Good luck and I hope it's a boy. No, not that – we have two boys already.' (*To the public*) And him – he can't believe his luck – sees himself in a kind of harem with his ladies getting along together all sweetness and light. There are only two so far – but later who knows? Everyone happy and without a care in the world. (*To her husband*) Is that what you'd like? But it's not like that! There are attacks of nerves, bouts of anxiety – then they start popping pills and they're off to the analyst and the looney bin. It's no go. Lots have tried and failed.

MAN: Who gives a damn? When others fail and fall flat on their faces that's when we have a real go at it, start from the beginning again.

WOMAN: Invent open marriage from scratch! Get out! (*To the public*) But in the end he convinced me. To defend our marriage, our friendship, our privacy, our bed has to go public. There's the problem of the children. Oh, the children will understand, said he. To be able to talk, to discuss, argue, give advice to each other we had to make love 'elsewhere'. Incredible as it may seem it was my son, Robert, who gave me the courage to try. (*When she plays the part of the son she takes on the blasé attitude of youth today – when she plays herself she takes on the mannerism of an embarrassed mother*) 'Mum, that's enough. You two can't go on like this. You've got to come up with something else. To begin with you can't go on living like some sort of extension of Dad's. You've got to have your own life. Dad goes after women and you – not for revenge but because it's right, healthy and human – you should find yourself another man.' 'What are you saying, Robert?' I don't know why but I put on a funny accent. 'Mum, don't go on like that. Get yourself a nice man – maybe younger than Dad. Just watch – I'll help you.' 'But Robert, what sort of a way is this to talk to your mother? Look, I'm terribly upset – all of a sweat. How on earth am I supposed – at my age – to start looking for men?' 'No,' he says, 'all you have to do is let it be known you're available. Live your own life, Mum. At least try, Mum!' I couldn't resist that 'Mum' so I tried. First of all I went off to live by myself, here. I took all the clothes I got since I was married and threw them away. Then I rushed off to get a new wardrobe. I bought way-out pants and ridiculous skirts.

MAN: I see. You turned yourself into a typical modern idiot.

WOMAN: That's right! My husband's idea of elegance is a woman who gets her clothes at Laura Ashley's. She may be very elegant but she doesn't have to find herself a boy-friend – but I do darling! I changed my way of dressing – then my make-up – purple! I looked horrible. Then my hair – a crazy cut. Punk! All my hair standing on end. I looked like an ad for . . . And the way I walked! Because you all know what a state we get into when our husbands cheat us – when they don't want us any more. SAD! Ugly! We cry. We get round-shouldered. Take me for example – before it happened I had completely forgotten that I had thighs. Abandoned yes – but I had thighs didn't I? I walked without the slightest wiggle. Stiff like a board. I clumped along. (*She takes a few steps*) Like this. Like an arthritic camel. I kept looking at the ground – I don't know why – all I ever found was dog-shit. What a time that was. The incredible thing is that the moment I forced myself to loosen up a little, to pay some attention to myself, to return friendly glances – well, I found what I wanted. They fell into my arms – after a while I had quite a crisis. First of all because they were almost all younger than me. What were they looking for? A second mother for an oedipal relationship! I fell for it once. There was this chap – but handsome – so handsome – eyes? – he seemed to have more than two – blue they were – and hundreds of teeth! Madly in love. He wept. He rang me up. I lifted the receiver. All I could hear were sobs. I'm – I'm only a mother. One day I said to him: 'OK darling' and made a date – right out in the suburbs – frightened I'd be seen. I actually thought of putting on a false nose. I arrived all churned up – like an idiot. With my heart going TOM TOM. We sit down. Along comes the waiter. 'What will madam have? And your son?' That was it. 'A double whiskey, please – he'll have a lemonade with a straw.' Yes. there were men of my age too – maybe it's my luck – but the ones that came my way were so sad, so beaten, deserted, betrayed by wives and lovers, by their children and grandchidren.

MAN: You mean – you had a terrific time.

WOMAN: Instead – this husband of mine – the moment I gave him the OK – 'Off you go – we're an open couple – make love as much as you like' – You should have seen him!

MAN: Well, yes. It was the effect of that 'open couple'. I didn't feel got at any more by a guilt complex. I was free!

WOMAN: I had a terrific attack of paranoia but he was walking on air. He took off! When we met he used to tell me how he was getting on.

MAN: But, love, forgive me but it was you who always asked me to tell you things – so I told you.

WOMAN: Yes, I'm a masochist. This was when he was having

a relation with a woman – a girl of about thirty but terribly intelligent and liberated – left-wing intellectual – you know the type.

MAN: Yes, she was an intellectual – but why do you say it with that contemptuous voice?

WOMAN: Me? Contemptuous of an intellectual? On the contrary, I was honoured to have one in the house. There was only one week that was a bit heavy-going. She had been in New York. Suddenly she didn't speak her own language any more. 'Say, can I have some cawfee,' 'Have a nice day,' 'You're welcome'. It wasn't as if he fell in love with women of 80. Then it would have been understandable. 'Poor boy, he had an unhappy childhood. He needs his granny. Sit her down there with her knitting.' But this girl – he said to me: 'She's not very pretty but she has a lot of charm. When she's sitting down she exudes sexuality – from her ears!'

MAN: That's mean.

WOMAN: She loved him in quite a different way from – not possessively. In fact she had another man and he had a relationship with another woman and she was married to another man who – a daisy-chain of open couples. But what a job. They needed a computer. X has a date with Y on Monday, Y had a date with Z on Tuesday. Such a business! Then of course – he was very active – he was always away from home. He was only ever there to eat. And at the same time he was carrying on with a very pretty young girl – very nice – always eating something. Ice-creams – even in winter. It was a kind of joke for him. She was still at school and he helped her with her homework.

MAN: Yes, it was a kind of game. I really played with that girl.

WOMAN: Oh yes, they played – hide-and-seek under the sheets. He told me.

MAN: I like her because she's crazy, unpredictable, has tantrums, laughs, throws up ice-cream in lumps. She makes me feel young too – and fatherly at the same time.

WOMAN: A boy-father!

MAN: That's cheap!

WOMAN: 'Watch out that she doesn't get pregnant' I told him. 'Of course', he says, 'watch out but I can't be there to keep an eye on her when she goes out with other boys. She doesn't like that.' Isn't that right?

MAN: Yes, but it was only a joke. It's obvious.

WOMAN: (*To the audience*) One day my husband comes to me all embarrassed and says:

MAN: Listen, this is women's stuff – why don't you go with Paula –

WOMAN: That was the ice-cream girl.

MAN: To the gynaecologist and get her fitted with a coil. Maybe you can convince her – she'll go with you – that's for sure.

WOMAN: Yes, of course I'll be mummy to little Paula – of course I'll take her to the gynaecologist. 'Doctor, please fit my husband's girl-friend with a coil.' Let's hope he's got as good a sense of humour as we have. I'll fit you with a coil. In your foreskin!

MAN: (*To the audience*) You see how she reacted. And that's nothing. (*To his wife*) Go on – tell them what you did!

WOMAN: Yes, I admit I did react. I'd just finished opening a tin of peeled tomatoes – a 5 kilo one. I poured it over his head and pushed the tin down till it came to his chin – like that. He looked like Sir Lancelot ready for the tournament – sponsored by Buitoni. Then I took advantage of his momentary embarrassment and pushed his hand into the toaster. (*She laughs*) It was on.

MAN: Look – I've still got the marks. I looked like a toasted sandwich. I walked about with lettuce leaves between my fingers so that people wouldn't notice. (*To the audience*) Then the shouts, the insults – a fine open couple – a democratic one.

WOMAN: Well, what did you expect? I had taken huge steps towards centrifugal sexual freedom – but what a nerve! to want me to play nanny to his baby dolls. I don't know what came over him. He didn't use to be like that. A man possessed. He leapt from one woman to another at the speed of light. I've talked to other women, friends of mine – I did a bit of research. Their husbands are always randy too. It must be a virus – the randicoccus. Even our porter's wife – he's randy – always looking for it. But the fact is that my husband doesn't only look for it, he finds it. He's got a mania. Like those people who look for mushrooms – only one thing on their minds – always going to the woods and collecting masses of them. And then they pickle them! Or dry them. Only he collects – birds, chicks, pussies. I swear – it's got to be an obsession with me. I've gone mad. I kept seeing the house full of female sex organs – used and thrown away! I go into the bathroom and instead of a cake of soap – 'It's a pussy!' I put on my shoes. 'Help – there's a mouse!' No, it's a pussy. There are young ones, intelligent ones, stupid ones, good and bad ones, huge ones, thin ones and fat ones. How do I keep them alive? I water them. I get the right stuff to keep them alive from the sperm bank where my husband is an honorary member.

MAN: This is too much. I'm not putting up with any more. Just to please a handful of hardline fanatical anti-male feminist friends of yours you're lynching me!

WOMAN: OK, maybe I've exaggerated for effect. A bit.

MAN: A bit! Here I am reduced to a caricature of a guy who collects mushrooms. The classical example of the penis-dominated sex-maniac and absolutely incapable of any feelings – bang-bang, thank you ma'am! But you took good care not to mention that, for example, I go out with a lot of these women just to talk and not necessarily to go to bed.

WOMAN: But it was you that was always talking to me about sex!

MAN: Yes, of course, because I know for sure that if I tell you that between you and me it's mostly a feeling of closeness you'll get even crosser.

WOMAN: Yes. Maybe. I have to admit that every time I told him about my idiotic moralistic block – about how impossible it was to have a relationship with other men – he gave me a push – like a real comrade, a really understanding friend.

MAN: Now you've discovered I'm not the right man for you, make yourself a new life. You must find a nice man – you deserve it! You're an extraordinary woman – intelligent, generous, fascinating.

WOMAN: (*To the audience*) Dynasty! (*To her husband*) No – please! I can't. I'm all right like this. If you don't want to stay with me, I'd rather be alone – I'm quite calm – believe me. I'm OK here in my own house. I feel good.

MAN: (*To the audience*) And then she would burst out crying and threaten to kill herself.

The WOMAN *jumps up onto the window-sill again clutching the gun.*

Stop! What's got into you now? Be reasonable – don't be an idiot! (*He tries to stop her by catching her skirt which he pulls down to her feet*)

WOMAN: Don't make me die without a skirt on! I want to die! I can't go on. I'm sorry I keep involving you and putting you through all this. But this time I'm really going to finish things. I'm going to jump and while I'm falling I'll shoot myself.

MAN: No, Antonia! Why don't you try to look at things with a little detachment – behave like a normal person.

WOMAN: (*Gets down from the window and turns to the audience*) So the day came when I finally behaved like a normal person. I got a job. I was fed up with being a domestic martyr. Out! I said. So I went out and found a job – an important one. In the morning you leave the house and take your nice bus. You've no idea how many people you know on a bus. No one! But just to see all these people – squashed together. They pick your pocket. You don't feel alone any more. Whereas at home I was as lonely as a dog. Me and the telly. The commercials. (*TV jingle needed here*) . . . So I went out in the evenings too – to a drug-addiction centre. Meanwhile he – by the way he hadn't stopped coming round my place even with all those great loves of his – noticed that I was getting more relaxed from day to day.

MAN: Well, what surprised me most of all was that you weren't interested any more in the stories of my adventures.

WOMAN: So to make up for it you kept asking me – (*To the audience*) There was a hail of questions – he wanted to know if I'd made anyone –

MAN: And she always denied it –

WOMAN: I didn't deny it so much as avoid the question as you did to begin with – remember? It was natural reticence. Your husband is your husband after all! (*To the audience*) But one day I made up my mind – told him everything. (*To her husband*) You know, darling, maybe I've found 'Mr Right'.

MAN: Oh yes! Who is he?

WOMAN: Said he and stopped breathing just like that.

MAN: (*Annoyed*) Naturally – you caught me on the wrong foot. I felt a pang in the stomach and my belly swelled up –

WOMAN: (*To the audience*) Of course – I'd forgotten. My husband has a terrible ailment. Aerofagia nervosa. When he has a strong emotion – I was even worried on our wedding day – his stomach swells up and – prot – prot – prot! That's with me. Prit – prit. With the others he sings.

MAN: Shut up, will you? When you're at it why don't you let them hear it in stereo. PROT PROT PROT. But I swear – deep down I was very happy for you.

WOMAN: Very deep down. So deep there was no sign of it.

MAN: First of all I gave you a hug right away – you've got to admit it – and with passion.

WOMAN: Too much – but let's play the scene for them.

MAN: Yes, we were playing cards. I was banker. (*They sit at the table to play rummy*)

WOMAN: It's my cue and I say: You know, darling, maybe I've found Mr Right!

MAN: Delighted to hear it. I'm really terribly pleased for you. (*He mixes the cards and ends up by letting them fall*)

WOMAN: That was the first time he dropped them.

MAN: Mr Right? At last! Who is he, then? What does he do? (*He picks up the cards*)

WOMAN: I bet you can't guess. To begin with, he's not anyone you know.

MAN: Really? Well, I prefer it that way.

WOMAN: He's a professor – of physics.

MAN: A don! You know, you mustn't be carried away by appearances.

WOMAN: Hold on! He has a chair in the university.

MAN: With tenure! Wow!

WOMAN: And he's doing research on nuclear energy – for the Atomic Energy Commission.

MAN: Nuclear energy! (*He lets the cards fall again*)

WOMAN: That was the second time.

MAN: Very interesting. So you'll have learned all there is to know about the safety and social advantages of our nuclear power stations. He'll have convinced you the safest place to install a new megawatt nuclear station is up there – at Dounreay.

WOMAN: (*Ironically*) I'm sorry to disappoint you but he is opposed to all those nuclear power stations they're putting up. He says they're out of date – built with stuff the Americans discarded – really dangerous junk – and that our rulers are real villains because they've let themselves be corrupted – but above all they're dangerous because they're idiots. Who is this man? One of his colleagues tells me he's indispensable – otherwise they'd have got rid of him long ago.

MAN: Indispensable? He must be very brainy.

WOMAN: Yes, he's a member of Mensa – but he doesn't give himself airs. He's sensitive and intelligent. The things he says – they ought to be preserved for posterity. When he comes out with one of them he sort of looks away and I take out a notebook and write it all down. The other evening he said: 'There's no doubt that the lowest level of intelligence is that of the politicians – but we scientists are close seconds – that was how we thought up Hiroshima together!'

MAN: He certainly sticks his neck out!

WOMAN: He's got guts – nuclear guts – he's politicised – witty – he makes me lose my head – we spend some wonderful days together. Then I found he's been nominated for a Nobel prize. (*She lays her hand on the table*) Rummy!

MAN: Just imagine – my wife's lover almost a Nobel prizewinner! It's great to find you have a genius in the family. I'm very honoured.

WOMAN: Yes, but last time you weren't so laid back about it. You said it out of the side of your mouth, 'I'm very honoured.'

MAN: I hope you won't mind an indiscreet question – have you ever been together – I mean, have you made love yet?

WOMAN: And when he asked this question this laid-back, liberated husband – the male half of the open couple – had another attack of his ailment. Prot Prot.

MAN: Cut out the details. I got short of breath. But answer my question.

WOMAN: I'd like to be able to say Yes – but it's No!

MAN: (*With ill-concealed satisfaction*) No love-making. Is there something wrong?

WOMAN: No, nothing. I like him a lot – I'd like to very much. But I don't feel like it yet. He was amazing – he understood at once –

MAN: Understood? What did he understand?

WOMAN: That I didn't feel comfortable about it. 'Urania,' he said . . .

MAN: Why 'Urania'? Aren't you called Antonia any more?

WOMAN: Yes, but he calls me Urania which is the core element of Plutonium. He's a physicist – do you want him to call me 'darling'? 'Urania,' he said, 'this thing of ours is too important to rush it. We need a breathing-space.' 'Yes,' I added, 'if not there's the risk it will just be a quick fuck and that's all. It happened to me once before – and I felt like an old rag afterwards.'

MAN: When was this quick fuck? You didn't tell me about it.

WOMAN: Well, it was an unimportant relationship – believe me – just a sexual thing that's all.

MAN: Are you sending me up? That's one of my lines.

WOMAN: It's certainly not one of mine – you know that if there's no love I feel empty – sad.

MAN: And who was it made you empty and sad?

WOMAN: Does it matter?

MAN: Yes, it does. I've always told you all about me.

WOMAN: Well, I don't. I'm reserved. Even with the professor I had problems talking about it.

MAN: Ah, so you told him!

WOMAN: Yes, I did. I feel it's right and honest not to hide anything from him. To show him myself as I am.

MAN: While with me you can show yourself as you aren't. (*Changing tone*) So it's serious with the atomic expert?

WOMAN: Yes, I think so. Why? Would you rather it was a big joke?

MAN: But why? It was me that advised you – told you how to behave. I'm a civilised person too – democratic and understanding. (*He gives a shriek*) Aaaaah! I'm an idiot.

Look at this – I'm sweating all over. I feel like the original example of the male shit.

WOMAN: Ah you see, one has to admit – the open couple has its disadvantages. Rule Number 1: For the open couple to work properly only one part of it has to be open. Because if it's open on both sides then there are terrible draughts.

MAN: You're right. I feel fine so long as I can chuck you over. I use you, discard you, but if anyone dares pick you up – watch out! If some bastard notices that your wife is still attractive – even if she's been abandoned – and wants her and appreciates her – then it gnaws away at you till you go mad. And into the bargain you discover that the bastard who picks her up is more intelligent, has any number of degrees, is witty – democratic!

WOMAN: Don't put yourself down like that.

MAN: Damn it – all that's missing is for him to play the guitar and sing rock.

WOMAN: You know him then?

MAN: Know who?

WOMAN: The professor. You've had me followed.

MAN: Followed! What are you saying?

WOMAN: Then how do you know that he plays the guitar and sings rock music?

MAN: He really does?

WOMAN: Who told you?

MAN: No one. I just came out with it – I guessed. God damn it! a singing atomic scientist! And I've no ear for music. In any case a man his age who tries to sing like X . . .

WOMAN: What do you mean, of his age? He is thirty-eight. Eight years younger than you. And he doesn't copy X – he has a style of his own. He plays the guitar – the piano – the trumpet – can do American slang . . .

MAN: Ah, so he can do American slang. He's a don at

Cambridge and an adviser to the Atomic Energy
Corporation. I expect he's a Vegan as well.

WOMAN: And he writes music too –

MAN: I was just saying to myself: 'I wonder if he writes
music?'

WOMAN: Yes, words and music. He's had a couple of hits.
You know the one that goes – 'a woman without a man is
like a fish without a bicycle' – the one that what's her name
sings.

MAN: He wrote that!

WOMAN: Yes!

MAN: He writes feminist songs. I never could stand male
feminists. Specially when they're thirty-eight.

WOMAN: But it's an ironical song – he's sending up trendy
feminism. He wrote one and dedicated it to me. I'm a bit
shy about it – but you and I – we're very close – if you like
I'll try to sing it.

MAN: Why don't you go on being shy?

WOMAN: I'm glad you didn't insist. I'd have felt terribly
embarrassed singing a song to my husband that my new man
wrote for me. Wait – I've taped it. (*She turns on the tape-
machine*)

and you were there
you still hadn't dialled the number
to put you through to my love
and you were there – so beautiful
On the monitor of my thoughts
you appeared
with the speed of a telex –
marvellous interference –
so lovely
you blew all my circuits
you blew all my circuits – oh yeah!

MAN: That's great. But you'd think it had been written by the
speaking clock and not an atomic physicist.

WOMAN: You're right. I had not thought about it. I'll tell him the moment I see him.

MAN: When are you seeing him?

WOMAN: In a minute – at lunch.

MAN: At lunch – already?

WOMAN: Yes, we're spending the weekend together. Do you mind? I've only an hour to get ready.

MAN: But damn it, if he's so important to you – if you get on together – why don't you go and live with him?

WOMAN: Not on your life! I'm not going to be an idiot again and set up with a man. I've had enough of that!

MAN: Not even if – it's just a suggestion – I was to propose it myself?

WOMAN: Never! I'm sorry but I've gone through too much. What's up with you? Don't you feel well? You've been biting your nails for the last hour. You're almost down to the knuckles, my darling. Why don't you have a drop of vodka?

MAN: It's disgusting.

WOMAN: Vodka?

MAN: No – vodka's all right. I'm disgusted with myself. But I asked for it – there's nothing I can do about it. It was me that suggested being an open couple and I can't expect you to go back on it just because I'm fed up with the whole thing. You have an absolute right to organise your own life. God, what balls I'm talking. But, tell me, doesn't rock make you want to throw up? You used to say it was stuff for mental defects and psychopaths. The moment you heard that bam-bam-batapang you got a pain in the stomach.

WOMAN: Yes, that's true. It was a classical case of the total rejection of anything new – anything you can't understand.

MAN: I suppose you like it now because it's in. Because you're carrying on like a teenager – and the professor plays it. All this post-modernist stuff. The truth is – he put you on the right path.

WOMAN: Of course – if a woman improves her mind, transforms herself, there has always to be a man behind it – the latest Pygmalion. What an idiotic idea! (*The telephone rings*)

MAN: If it's one of my girl-friends say I'm not in, I've gone out.

WOMAN: Why?

MAN: Never mind – I just don't feel like talking –

WOMAN: He's holding out on the harem. (*She takes the phone. She is excited*) Hi, it's you. Why on earth? Am I late? You gave me such a fright. (*To her husband*) It's him.

MAN: Who?

WOMAN: Oh piss off. (*To the phone*) Yes, I'm almost ready. You're coming over? Half-an-hour. (*Embarrassed*) No, of course I'm alone. Absolutely. I'll be waiting. Yes, I do. Yes, so much. All right I'll spell it out. I love you so much. Bye-bye. (*She slams down the receiver. Furiously*) You could at least not stand there looking at me with these eyes. You made me terribly embarrassed.

MAN: Why did you say you were alone? Was it too much for you to say I was there?

WOMAN: No. Yes! you're right – it was too much.

MAN: I see. So the Brain is jealous.

WOMAN: Jealous? Don't talk bilge. Drink up your vodka and get out.

MAN: Why?

WOMAN: Didn't you hear? He's coming any minute.

MAN: What is this? Are we swopping roles now? The husband who has to clear out so that the lover doesn't find him there! So it's true. He's jealous of me!

WOMAN: He's not jealous. I just don't want you to meet.

MAN: I see – you're afraid I'll sus out that he's not what you've cracked him up to be. That I won't like him: 'Is that all there is to him? What a let-down!'

WOMAN: What I'm really afraid of is that he won't like you – that you'll be the let-down.

MAN: What do you mean?

WOMAN: Well, you see I painted a very flattering portrait of you – I said you were an extraordinarily intelligent man, witty, open-minded, generous –

MAN: I suppose you mean I'm not –

WOMAN: No, for goodness' sake, you have your points – even you have some. But you see – well – I exaggerated a little. It wasn't exactly a true likeness. Of course everyone has their weaknesses. I like you with all your shortcomings. We've known each other for ages. You were my first big love – but now I'm so totally changed people who know me now can't imagine how I lived with you for so long.

MAN: I didn't notice anything. Do you realise how nasty you are being to me? Who do you think you are?

WOMAN: A different woman, darling.

MAN: Yes – but that means you've gone round the bend. You've blown your mind going alone – with these Brains, these intellectual snobs that write rock lyrics. But I don't give a damn for you or for your stupid friends with brains coming out of their ears.

WOMAN: Great! But I thought you'd make a scene. Now please go away. In any case I can't stand that thing you've got round your neck. You look like something out of a Thirties film.

MAN: Shut up! shut up! I can't take it any more! (*He comes up behind the* WOMAN *and putting his scarf round her neck tries to strangle her*)

WOMAN: What the hell are you doing? Are you out of your mind? Bastard! Coming to my house to make me commit suicide.

MAN: It's your own fault. You keep on provoking me. Don't you see – I felt like killing you.

WOMAN: It did cross my mind. But calm down. Look at your stomach – it's swelling. If you're ashamed to go into the bathroom just get rid of it here. It's only hot air after all. Anyway I'm just like your mother. I'll put on a nice record, then you can relax.

MAN: Stop it! You're a bitch.

WOMAN: So I'm a bitch! I try to laugh things off – to cool it so that you don't feel guilty. OK – do you want to hear the truth? I am dying with fright. You should have seen the eyes you made. You looked like the Pope when people talk about contraceptives.

MAN: Sure – I can imagine. But I felt so got at. The idea that you wanted to leave me for good. I felt so desperate. Antonia – I love you. (*He tries to embrace her*)

WOMAN: Stop! I'm suffocating.

MAN: Take your clothes off – please. Give me a kiss.

WOMAN: Yes, I'll give you a kiss – but wait a minute. You're splitting my dress – and breaking my ribs.

MAN: Let's make love. (*He takes off her skirt and boots*)

WOMAN: Here? Now? But I was going out, darling. I have a date.

MAN: Yes – now – this minute. Let's make love. I'll help you to get your clothes off. (*He makes her lie on the table*)

WOMAN: The telephone! (*He takes the telephone out from under her back*)

MAN: Hello? There's no one there. I need you to prove to me –

WOMAN: Prove what?

MAN: That I still mean something to you. (*He unzips his trousers and begins to take them off*)

WOMAN: You're right. It's a question of pride for you. Yes, I love you. I've been longing for this moment. I love you . . . You're the only one. You're the greatest bastard on earth!

MAN: You really have gone out of your mind!

WOMAN: Just look at yourself. With your pants – you're a sight! Who do you think you are?

MAN: But I love you. After all what have I done? I only wanted to make love to you.

WOMAN: So that's all he wanted! For years now you didn't even know I existed. You didn't even see me. And now that there's this atomic scientist . . . the atomic peril – we have to make love right away on the small table. With the telephone sticking into my back! And then he talks about an open couple! No – all you want is to get possession of what is yours by law. You can lend me out if the conditions are spelled-out clearly but never let go of me. If you could you'd brand me on the bottom with a red-hot iron – like a cow.

MAN: Now you're exaggerating – on the wrist would do. You're talking like one of those old-hat feminists. What are you doing – getting dressed? So you really don't want to? But that means it's really finished. Curtains! May I know what's got into you?

WOMAN: Who knows what's got into me.

MAN: You seem to me to have shot off at a tangent. You seem to have become – I don't know what to call it – I know! – a complete stranger – something from another world. I love you just as much as before. Try to come to yourself again. The person who insults me – who swears at me – who tries to throw herself out of the window – who shoots at me and misses. That's the Antonia I like best. Come to yourself.

WOMAN: Come to myself? Poor desperate Antonia? Throw yourself out of the window on Thursday – hang yourself on Friday – rest on Sunday. Find your ego. How banal you are! All that stupid rational crap! 'No I can't come out today – I'm looking for my real self.' My ego. Who's got at my ego?

It was here – next to the telephone. I can't find it any more. Who's taken it? Excuse, but didn't you see my real self going past? Yes – my real self – it was on a bicycle with its oedipus complex on the crossbar.

MAN: Listen to her – just listen. What irony – what language – what a vocabulary! And then she gets pissed off if I say she's learned it all from that professor. Do you mind telling me one thing – how did you get to know him?

WOMAN: Through his daughter.

MAN: So the Brain has a daughter.

WOMAN: Yes – she's fifteen. I knew her already from the committee on drug addicts.

MAN: You mean one of the girls that works along with you.

WOMAN: No, she's the drug addict.

MAN: She's hooked?

WOMAN: Yes, we're trying to get her off with Methadone. But it's difficult. I got to know her father through her.

MAN: (*With ill-concealed pleasure*) The professor has a fifteen-year-old daughter who takes drugs?

WOMAN: Did you hear how you said that?

MAN: How?

WOMAN: Look – I know you. You almost sounded pleased.

MAN: What at?

WOMAN: At finding out the professor has a drug addict for a daughter.

MAN: You're mad – as if I –

WOMAN: Look me in the eyes!

MAN: OK then – it's true. Spit in my face if you like – you're right – I am a worm. This prof. was beginning to get on my tits – too good to be true – young, witty, bang up-to-date with everything – everything about him the tops. Oh but at last he's fallen down over something.

WOMAN: No, it's you that has fallen down. Do you know what you are?

MAN: Don't tell me. I know it all. I know that today to manage to bring up a child without its being warped by violence – or getting mixed up with drugs – it's like winning the pools – and just as possible.

WOMAN: Well then?

MAN: I'm disgusted with myself – I have to admit it. But still I was pleased. The rich sweet pleasure of the reactionary!

WOMAN: You should be ashamed of yourself. Who was this I married? If you'd got to know him the way I did! He was an empty shell, grey – he seemed done in.

MAN: Really! I'm beginning to like him.

WOMAN: He was desperate. 'I haven't given this child of mine anything – never – a few hugs, silly things – but real affection – I never even tried. I always thought about myself – only myself – and about my career.'

MAN: And you said to him: 'No – don't say that, professor! It's not your fault – it's society's fault.'

WOMAN: Listen – don't start sending me up.

MAN: Didn't you console him, then?

WOMAN: If anyone needed to be consoled then it was me.

MAN: So you kept each other company?

WOMAN: More or less. Then one day I said: 'Listen – don't let's go on weeping and wringing our hands.' We were talking about missiles – about Molesworth and disarmament and we were saying how little people care. 'What about us,' I said, 'it's not as if we do much!' 'Let's go on the next demo.'

MAN: When was this?

WOMAN: A month ago.

MAN: I'm sorry – but didn't you go to Cheltenham to see that cousin of yours who got herself pregnant and had to have an abortion?

WOMAN: That was the story for the husband.

MAN: OK. Apart from the fact that you really disappoint me –
you two intellectual snobs – caught up in protest politics and
out to Molesworth along with a bunch of left-over hippies.
And a dozen lunatic masochists who want to get beaten up
by the police.

WOMAN: You really are reactionary!

MAN: What do you mean reactionary? No one believes in
demos like that any more, the real Left keeps clear of them.

WOMAN: What do you mean keeps clear of them! What about
the last CND demo in Trafalgar Square?

MAN: Another big cosy get-together – sort of carnival – that's
OK in London but who's going to go to Molesworth? A
couple of MPs from the Labour Left – some Euro
communists and a load of feminists.

WOMAN: That's just what we thought. 'Let's go along
anyway.'

MAN: So how did you go?

WOMAN: Motorbike.

MAN: You must have been keen!

WOMAN: Why keen? Motorcycling's a hobby like any other.

MAN: Maybe I can see you – with all the gear – boots, leather
jacket, helmet, on a roaring Suzuki.

WOMAN: You're wrong. It was a Guzzi.

MAN: So he's mad about Italy. With you huddled up at the
back. Go on, tell me the rest.

WOMAN: We stopped off at Lincoln.

MAN: Lincoln! That was a bit out of your way.

WOMAN: We sort of didn't feel like the demo any more. It's
not as if the danger of atomic war has really got to the
masses. And Lincoln is lovely. Remember we went there
once.

MAN: I remember.

WOMAN: This was different. So lovely. We walked about. Looked at the cathedral. Had a meal at that restaurant – it's in the Good Food Guide –

MAN: Board and lodging. But even then you didn't manage to make love.

WOMAN: Why? How do you know?

MAN: You told me a while ago. How you felt inhibited.

WOMAN: But only as far as York.

MAN: A tour of the cathedral towns! So you lost your inhibitions in York.

WOMAN: It was marvellous. In a bed and breakfast. The professor wanted to buy the bed – but the landlady wouldn't sell it. Good heavens – what's the time? It's more than half an hour since he called. Damn it – it's your fault, making me chatter on like an idiot. Come on – on your way. No, not that way – go out by the back door. I don't want you to risk meeting him on the stairs.

MAN: So you're going to throw me out by the back door. I used to be your husband – now I'm the milkman.

WOMAN: All right – if you're so easily hurt go out any way you like but put a move on!

MAN: No.

WOMAN: What do you mean No?

MAN: I'm not moving from here. I've had second thoughts. I'm going to wait for him. I want to see him face to face.

WOMAN: Please – don't spoil everything. Get out.

MAN: No!

WOMAN: Are you out of your mind? You promised.

MAN: I didn't promise any damn thing. It is my inalienable right to meet the lover of my wife. I want to look him in the eyes and if, when he looks at me, he so much as moves a muscle of his face – contemptuous like – and does the rock-musician bit I'll smash his guitar over his head.

WOMAN: You're a bastard. I mean to say – first you do everything to make me go along with this disgusting idea of the open couple – so as to be modern and civilised. It makes me want to throw up but – I go along with it to make you happy. I feel bad about it but you go on and on at me and I get round to the idea of looking for a man. I find one. I like him. I fall in love and now, you bastard, you have to wreck everything for me and let him see you as you are – a miserable disgusting creep. And then you want to break his electric guitar as well. Why don't you say you wish I was dead. All right – you know what? This time I'll really do it. The gas – I'll turn on the gas. (*She runs to the kitchen*)

MAN: (*Stopping her*) Stop! Don't waste gas. I'm going – but by the window so you won't have to go through with having to introduce me – if that's what's worrying you. But this time it's for good! (*He climbs onto the window-sill*)

WOMAN: Don't be an idiot! Get down from there. You're simply ridiculous.

MAN: What do you mean – when you get up on the window-sill it's tragic – it's high drama. I get up and it's ridiculous and embarrassing.

WOMAN: That's right – it's a question of style. Come on – get down!

MAN: What else can I do? If you don't play along there's no drama in it. I always gave you a hand – caught you by the ankle – begged you –

WOMAN: But how am I holding you back – how? Because if you jump you're so overweight you'll take me with you. And just now I don't want to die for real. Come on – get down. Think of your funeral. It'd be like a demo. All your women behind the hearse. Think how unpleasant it would be – all pushing and shoving to show how cut up they were. A couple jump into the grave – the one with the ice-cream weeping all over the coffin.

MAN: OK, go on taking the piss! (*He gets down from the window*) All right – now you'll see (*He seizes the gun*) when you made your scene it was almost empty – but this time I've put the bullets in – now it's loaded. (*He fills the magazine*)

WOMAN: But why waste them all? One will do. Give over – was I as silly-looking as that? Hand it over – don't be a lunatic. You really might let one off. (*Tries to get the gun from him*)

MAN: Let go – I'm going to shoot myself. (*A shot goes off*)

WOMAN: Idiot. You fired.

MAN: OK – no harm done. It missed.

WOMAN: What do you mean missed? It hit me right in the foot.

MAN: Oh I'm sorry. (*Passes her the crutch*)

WOMAN: The great thing about this house is that everything's laid on. There's always a crutch handy. You're a disaster. You're useless. You can't even commit suicide without dragging your wife into it.

MAN: You're right. I'm a washout.

WOMAN: Listen, washout. Since I'm bleeding and, apart from anything else making a mess of the carpet, would you mind going to the bathroom and getting me a towel – a bandage – anything.

MAN: Sure – right away. Just as well – can only be a graze. (*He goes to the bathroom. There's a sound of running water. He comes back with a towel, a bandage, disinfectant etc*)

WOMAN: Yes, it's just a scratch – just like in a film – the heroine is never badly wounded – otherwise – I'm pleased because the treatment for this sort of wound is very slimming! Did I hear you turn on the bath?

MAN: Yes, I did.

WOMAN: Why? If you feel like having a bath then go home.

MAN: At home I don't have a bath and the shower doesn't work.

WOMAN: What doesn't work? That's enough – I've had it. Get out. Can't you understand I don't want him to find you here?

MAN: But I won't be in the way – you see. When the Brain of Britain arrives he can help you to pull me out of the bath.

WOMAN: Look – I've got other things to do with the Brain of Britain – as you call him – in any case why should the two of us pull you out of the bath?

MAN: Because you wouldn't manage alone. Corpses are heavy.

WOMAN: That's great – my husband drowns himself in my bath. With my plastic flowered cap on his head to stop getting his hair wet! Listen – to drown in my bath you need a superhuman effort. Just think – to lie down under the water with your nose plugged and suffocate yourself – that takes guts. You wouldn't manage, being you!

MAN: Don't worry. I've had another idea. Once I'm in the bath with the hair-dryer in my hand all I have to do is to press that button there and Boom! There's a tremendous flash and that's that. Electrocuted.

WOMAN: So you saw *Goldfinger* the other evening on Channel Four.

MAN: I don't need a film or a professor of physics to give me ideas – I get them on my own!

WOMAN: Shitty ideas!

MAN: All right. Excuse me a minute, I have to get ready. (*He goes into the bathroom*) I have to undress.

WOMAN: You're going to commit suicide in the nude.

MAN: Certainly – I have a certain style. I don't suppose you want me to get into the bath with jacket and trousers on . . . (*He shuts the bathroom door*)

WOMAN: (*Knocking on the door*) Stop playing the silly ass and come out of there. All right – maybe I did make mistakes, I went a bit far humiliating you like that. Come out. Talk it over. Let's discuss things like civilised people. Come out. (*She squints through the keyhole*)

MAN: It's too late, love. And don't peep. Aren't you ashamed?

WOMAN: He's mad. He really has plugged in the hair-dryer. Stop!

MAN: Sure. That way you'll learn not to humiliate me. I want to die. God, the water's cold. Doesn't the boiler work in this house?

WOMAN: Stop. It's not true – any of it. I made it all up. The professor doesn't exist.

MAN: (*Puts his head round the door*) So you made up the Brain of Britain. And when the telephone rang a little while ago you did it all by ventriloquism, is that it? (*He comes in wrapped up more or less in a towel. He has the dryer in his hand and points it at his wife*)

WOMAN: But there was someone on the line – only they had got the wrong number and rang off. I went on pretending it was him.

MAN: My compliments on your acting. But it doesn't hold water. You're trying to distract me and make me lose time – so the professor will arrive shortly and the two of you will jump on me and stop me. (*He backs away pointing the dryer like a gun*) Stop. Don't come any closer or I'll jump.

WOMAN: For goodness' sakes don't do it with a hair-dryer. I know – let's call the Atomic Energy Commission. I'm going to ring Enquiries and get the number. (*She does so*) I'll have a good laugh when you say: 'Excuse me but have you a head of department who writes rock numbers?' (*On the phone*) Hello – can you give me the number of the Atomic Energy Commission? (*The* MAN *cuts off the phone*) Aren't you going to speak?

MAN: So I fell for it like an idiot. You really did invent the lot.

WOMAN: Phew – the fright you gave me. Are you feeling a bit calmer now? Relax. It would have been such a tragedy! OK,

I made it all up but I did it to make you see how much a person suffers. Yes, you fell for it but –

MAN: No – you fell for it.

WOMAN: How?

MAN: All that stuff about suicide!

WOMAN: So it was all –

MAN: Look at it – it's burnt out. I just did it to make a scene. I'd no intention of taking a risk and ending up flambé – like some sort of zombie. Darling, I see daylight ahead!

WOMAN: You made it all up?

MAN: Yes – it was a joke. (*Laughs*) Anyway I should say thank you – it was a gas. How does that song go? 'You came up on the telephone . . .'

WOMAN: You're a despicable bastard.

MAN: Stop it, Urania. (*The bell rings*)

MAN: You go. I'm enjoying myself. (*He goes on singing and sending the song up*) 'And you appeared on my screen you blew my circuits.' (*The* WOMAN *goes to the door. There's a man in his forties. It's the* PROFESSOR)

PROFESSOR: Sorry I'm a little late. (*He kisses her*)

MAN: Who's he?

PROFESSOR: Is this your husband? Am I wrong or was he humming my song?

MAN: Who is he, please?

WOMAN: But, love, who should it be – the rock professor.

MAN: Him. No. The Brain exists. He really does exist! (*He grabs the dryer and rushes into the bathroom. There is an explosion and a huge flash*)

WOMAN: Oh no!

An Ordinary Day

written with Franca Rame
translated by Joe Farrell

An Ordinary Day was first performed at the Teatro Nuovo, Milan, on 9 October 1986.

An Ordinary Day was first performed in this translation by Borderline Theatre Company, who toured the play in May/June 1988 with the following cast:

JULIA	Juliet Cadzow
TOM	Bill McElhaney
JIMMY	Laurie Ventry
FEMALE CALLERS	Barbara Rafferty
	Elizabeth Philips Scot
POLICEMAN	Lawrie McNichol

Directed by Morag Fullerton

A one room studio-flat, with cooker and bed-settee. Photographer's lamps with spotlight and reflector.

A woman is fiddling about with a video-cassette recorder. She checks the monitor and big screen situated at the far edge of the stage to ensure that they are in working order. She moves, poses, observes herself but is plainly unhappy with the result. She claps her hands and immediately one of the arc lights goes on. She shifts the reflector. She changes her dress. She inserts a shade and a coloured gel into one of the lamps. Now she is apparently more or less satisfied.

JULIA: Perhaps I am too far back . . . it's too big that way . . . just look at the bags under those eyes. I'll need to open out the light. (*She claps her hands again and the light attached to the reflector goes on*) Let's try the automatic follow-shot. (*She switches it on*) Come on – over here. (*She moves left and right, followed by the camera on a tripod on wheels*) Good boy! The only thing that follows me now is the tripod. (*The phone rings*) No, I've no time. The answering machine's turned on, so just you talk to it quietly and don't bother me. (*She goes over to a coat-hanger where an enormous assortment of clothes are hanging*) How about this little number? An ankle-length dress. (*She puts it on, stands in front of the camera and has a look at herself in the monitor*) Good God! See how overweight it makes me. Obese. Maybe I am fat! If I come on like that, he'll take me for Cyril Smith. I can just see him ordering up two tins of

some fancy sea-weed for slimmers. For a time like this a
wedding gown would be just the thing. Yeah, but with a
spare tyre like mine, I could hardly get a leg in. Anyway,
God knows where the wedding dress ended up. Probably I
made a tent out of it.

*She continues to change the dress at top speed, in a kind of
quick-change routine. It might be helpful if she went behind a
screen where two stage hands could help with the costumes.*

No, this one's better – nice and simple, in tune with what's
going on. No, this might be just the ticket, loose fitting and
serious . . . I've got it, I've got it. A party frock. (*She looks
at herself for a moment*) All I need is a bunch of bananas on
my head and I'd look like Joan Rivers on an off day. No,
no! – No strong colours – a Social Democratic outfit –
(*Putting on a dress picked at random*) – afternoon tea in
foggy London town. Here we are . . . all systems go . . .
(*She presses a button on the video-cassette recorder*) Action!
(*She runs and places herself in front of the camera. A
moment of confusion and embarrassed silence*) Bloody hell!
With all these things I was just bursting to say . . . now look
at me, struck dumb . . . Ah yes, the hands – let's kick off
with the hands. (*She runs over, turns back the tape, and
starts again*) Action! (*She takes a deep breath and holds her
hands out towards the camera*)

Look at my hands . . . go on, have a good look . . . do you
see them? They are right in front of your nose . . . do you
recognise them? Big . . . fleshy . . . do you recognise them?
You have held them in yours . . . you have kissed them.
And the thing behind them is my face . . . do you recognise
me? It's me, I'm your wife! (*She stops. She goes over and
runs back the tape*)

I must be out of my mind. What way is that to begin? It
sounds like a horror film . . . Zombies On The Prowl. I
don't want to scare him stiff with those two monstrous
hands. And what made me say 'Right in front of your nose'?
Who's he supposed to be anyway? Pinocchio? In front of
your very eyes sounds better. And then that 'It's me, your

wife.' It comes over like the voice of God. (*Shouts*) It's me, me, your wife . . . come back from the dead to throttle you. Poor thing.

No, that's not going to do. We need a new opening, something completely different. (*Switches on the tape recorder which produces a love song*) What made me launch with the hands? Maybe I should draw up a plan of what I'm going to say. Got it. I know how to get going: with the letter. (*Sets up the video, gets her pose right. Silence for a few minutes, then, with the music still playing in the background*)

Hi! It's me, Julia, I've just got to talk to you. Are you sitting comfortably? Then I'll begin. I know . . . for one thing this is not the ordinary way of communicating. I wrote you a letter . . . but I didn't post it. I'd rather read it to you. Anyway, I'd rather you were able to watch me when I'm talking to you. You see, the fact that afterwards . . . I mean, right now for you . . . the fact that you will be there watching me . . . it gives me encouragement . . . gives me strength . . . and I really need that. When you receive this video-letter. (*The soft music ends. A piece of rock music explodes from the tape-recorder*)

My God, what a fright! Just a minute till I turn this thing down . . . (*Adjusts the sound*) I'm sorry, but rock music brings me out in spots. As I was saying. Thanks to the mediation of this electronic instrument . . . (*The phone rings*) Dear God, not now. I should have pulled out the plug. Oh how stupid I am. I have put on the ansaphone. I bet you do not remember what day it is tomorrow. It is our anniversary. It's exactly one year since we separated. During this year, I thought about you a lot . . . then less and less . . . and now . . . I hardly think about you at all. I still have some feelings for you. To me, you are like a relative . . . an older cousin . . . one of the family, a nice sort, somebody that you like to see every so often . . . at funerals, weddings, christenings . . . So it seems quite natural to turn to you for . . . (*She is suddenly interrupted*) Excuse me. Somebody's on

the phone. I can't make out who. I've lost my concentration.
I'll go and unplug the machine, then we'll start again.

*She switches off the video-recorder, switches off the arc lights
with a clap of her hands and moves to the telephone
answering machine. She presses a button and listens.*

JEAN'S VOICE: Hello. Forgive me for disturbing you at this
hour, Doctor. This is Jean Alred, do you remember me? I
am the one with the burn on the buttocks because of the
brick. I have to talk to you – no, not because of my
buttocks. Oh, Doctor, I'm very low. I hope I'll be able to
contact you in a couple of hours. If you do go out, would
you leave a message on your answering machine, so that I'll
be able to trace you. I'm desparate. I'll phone back.

JULIA: (*Puzzled*) Doctor? She's got a burn on the buttocks
and she's feeling down. She must have got my number
mixed up with some analyst. Funny analyst all the same,
who goes around burning her clients' bums.

*She claps her hands and the lights which she has dimmed
come back up. She puts the video-recorder back on and goes
round in front of the camera.*

Sorry about that, but a funny thing has just happened.
Someone got the wrong number and took me for a
psychiatrist. She was looking for help . . . from me! She has
stumbled onto the right woman and no mistake. A right
nutcase. Yes, that's not just a manner of speaking. I am
quite, completely crazy, mad, ready for the strait-jacket . . .
but lucid. You have no idea how many times, at the dead of
night, I got up, intending to come round to your place and
do you in. I mean it! I even bought a gun. That's right, with
a proper gun user's licence. Once I even thought of
shadowing you while you were going to the station to pick
up your new woman, and then just as the train was drawing
in, I was going to give you a little push under the wheels.
Scared? Well, relax, take it easy. Have a drop of whisky and
wipe your brows with an ice cube. All this happened at the
very beginning, when my metabolism was altering, for my

metabolism was totally, one hundred per cent dependent on you. And I thought I was a liberated woman! I have really made an effort, you know. I have even done some dreadful exercises. Look at this. You see what I mean. You have to get yourself into a position like this. Come on. Have a go. Don't get embarrassed, now. You have to raise one leg, slowly, very, very slowly, until you reach knee level, and then you swing one across the other. Gently does it. Much more gently. It should take you about two hours to get it up, two hours to let it back down, that's four hours a leg, eight hours all in all. And so the day goes by. Then you go to bed and after all that . . . you still can't get a wink of sleep!

That's the idea. On you go. It'll do you the world of good.

I've been through one hell of a time. But here I am, I've made it. Or maybe I am just kidding myself that I have made it. Paranoia? Could be. But I am not well. The problem is that I have no interests. I do not give a damn about anyone. Not even about my job . . . advertising! Hour after hour, racking my brains to think up some way to make people buy things they could do perfectly well without. It's hell with other people, it's hell on my own. For some time I've been wondering what I'm doing here in this world. If you want a laugh, I could recite 'To be or not to be that is the question'. Don't worry. It was a joke.

Nevertheless, I would like to talk to you about my existential problem. Do you know, I have discovered that living in this world is all a question of keeping up with the play . . . adapting and accepting the ritual . . . if you don't, you just throw in your hand. You know, like, when you're playing poker and you get one of those dud hands and there is no way you can do anything with it. So what do you do? You just throw it in. You sit it out. Well then, here's me, with a hand that would make you vomit . . . but it's not a matter of bad luck. I've been cheated. Yes, yes, I know, I could shrug my shoulders . . . wait for a good hand . . . then I could do the cheating. It is just that . . . that kind of game doesn't interest me any more. Everything is so savage, barbaric, improbable or downright vulgar. It's all over in about twenty minutes, just like those soap operas on the TV.

I know what you are going to say. 'Well, what do you expect? We are living in a TV culture. You've got to make the best of it, put up with it . . . don't aim too high, be like the rest.' I had worked out a programme for myself, with stacks of wonderful ideas, padded out with dreams . . . and, with beautiful Utopias into the bargain. And why not? I threw myself into it, and I found myself flying headfirst into a swimming pool, a moment after they had drained out all the water.

I could hear them guffawing all around me. 'Get a load of this one. She still believes in fairy tales, in togetherness, in changing the world. You'll need to be a bit more down to earth, a bit more realistic, Julia.' It makes me sick, this 'realistic'. No, no, I am not going to comply. Arse-lickers, opportunists, hypocrites, people who would trample over other people's faces . . . you see them hawking their own self-respect, offering you their bums. No, I don't want to put up with it . . . I won't comply . . . I'll throw in my hand . . . I'll sit this one out. What is it they call it, the dead hand, the dummy hand? What difference does it make? What's all the fuss? What is this death, anyway? It is merely the moment the machine stops churning . . . breaks down . . . is ready to be thrown out . . . and so somebody comes and tosses it on the heap. In my case the whole central system has seized up. Yes, I still move, talk, even tell jokes, but it's a trick. It's really just the inertia force. I'm a cog that is worn out, waiting to be thrown away. I've got to give the final touch, switch off the power. No, don't you get agitated. In any case, when you get the video-tape, it will be all over.

(*Phone rings*) Damnation, the phone at a time like this! I'm sorry, but this time I've switched off the answering machine. I'll have to answer. (*Goes to the phone*) Hello?

JEAN'S VOICE: Good evening, Doctor, at last I've got you.

JULIA: Again? Wait a minute till I turn off the camera and put out the lights. (*Goes to switch them off*)

JEAN'S VOICE: What were you saying?

JULIA: I was saying that you've got the wrong number.

JEAN'S VOICE: What do you mean? What number is that? Just a minute, is that not 611 3002?

JULIA: Yes, certainly.

JEAN'S VOICE: Then it's the right number.

JULIA: It might be the right number, but it's not the right person, at least not the person you're looking for. Excuse me, where did you get this number?

JEAN'S VOICE: In the magazine . . . there, what's it called, wait a minute . . . here it is, it's called *Health*, and on page 38 there's an article all about you.

JULIA: Who? You?

JEAN'S VOICE: You, you! It says 'Famous Analyst Completes Specialist Research in Japan.'

JULIA: I've never been to Japan.

JEAN'S VOICE: Ah no. Well, you know how it is, you can never trust what you read in the papers, but the important thing is that the method is the right one and that it works, don't you agree?

JULIA: What method?

JEAN'S VOICE: Yours. The one that is described here: The psycho-respiratory technique with the emission of appropriate vocalisations.

JULIA: And what happens . . .

JEAN'S VOICE: You attain diapason. Diapason employed by the holy men of Indonesia who thus manage to levitate. Isn't that right, Doctor, that they manage to rise?

JULIA: But, I don't know . . . but why, instead of rising . . . do you really want to rise . . . what are you, some kind of home-made bread?

JEAN'S VOICE: No, I don't want to rise at all. The very idea! My husband can't stand me when I'm just normal, standing on the floor. I'd hate to think what he'd do if I went floating around the house, banging my head against the ceiling. He'd be only too glad to get his gun and bring me down with a bang! All I want is to get rid of this neurosis of mine, just like you say in your article.

JULIA: What did you say this magazine was called? *Health*. I get it sent to me. (*Goes to search in a paper rack*) If it's the last issue . . . just a minute, I must have put it . . . here we are, page 38 you say.

JEAN'S VOICE: Yes, if you look at the bottom of the page, you'll see the phone number as well.

JULIA: You're quite right, they've got my number here. What kind of joke is this? Obviously there's been a mistake.

JEAN'S VOICE: No doubt, a private number. They've got no sense of manners, you just don't go handing out a private number. It's been a bit of good luck for me, because I can ask your advice personally. What do you think I should do, Doctor? I might be pregnant. I'm waiting to check the blue window.

JULIA: Now look here, I've already told you. I am not the doctor you are looking for.

JEAN'S VOICE: I can quite believe it. You are not an obstetrician, you're an analyst. The only thing that interests me is to know whether these exercises with the brick would be ill-advised in the event of the tests telling me . . . 'Yes, you are pregnant.'

JULIA: Look, please, quite apart from the fact that you have caught me at a somewhat, shall we say, delicate moment, listen to me, whatever the blue window says, I cannot give you any advice, because I have no medical qualifications.

JEAN'S VOICE: Ah, you're one of these fly-by-night people! Doesn't matter to me, though, I had all my teeth done by a very fine dental mechanic, and he was one of those cowboy operators. It cost me half of what I would have paid on the NHS, though.

JULIA: I'm not a dentist either. I work in advertising.

JEAN'S VOICE: Medical advertising?

JULIA: No, travel and holiday advertising, films, videos, that sort of thing.

JEAN'S VOICE: So what are you doing in the house of a medical analyst? Are you a relative?

JULIA: What do you mean relative? This is my house!

JEAN'S VOICE: I get it, the analyst is staying with you. Let me speak to her, if you don't mind.

JULIA: (*Exasperated*) No, I won't let you speak to her. I cannot let you speak to her!

JEAN'S VOICE: That's lovely that is! And why not?

JULIA: Because she's not here . . . she's away checking for blue windows.

JEAN'S VOICE: For blue windows?

JULIA: (*As though insane*) That's right, for blue windows. Then she gives them to hysterical women who find relief from tension by getting pregnant.

JEAN'S VOICE: (*Puzzled*) Pregnant?

JULIA: Yes with a cowboy or a dental mechanic, a fly-by-night operator . . . Is that clear?

JEAN'S VOICE: (*Terrified*) No, but I think I've got the wrong number, I'm sorry. (*She hangs up.* JULIA *does the same*)

JULIA: At long bloody last. It would drive you nuts, all this. God help any analyst who ends up having to treat her! (*Picks up the magazine and reads it*) There's one born every day . . . do people really believe this garbage? (*Reads aloud*) 'Stretch yourself full length on a table, placing a brick beneath your buttocks, move your knees apart while keeping your heels closely together. Let your head hang over the edge of the table. Take deep breaths and hum the sounds A-u-o-i-e-u-o, on the Do-Ray notes until you reach Fa. Then come back to Do.'

Did you ever hear the like? (*She sings out the notes making the whole thing ridiculous*) AU OO EU OOO, IAUU! There are people who actually believe this! Some folk have done time for less . . . they should put this one up against a wall! (*She tries again*) AU OH OOO UIOAA. (*Switches on the video-recorder, goes back in front of the camera. The lights go up again*)

Here I am again. I was saying that I have decided to end it all. You'll be asking yourself why I'm telling you all this. Perhaps you don't believe what I was saying a few moments ago. Maybe you think I'm out for revenge because you were so keen to reduce me to despair, or maybe you imagine that I'm trying to make you shoulder the blame for this insane act I'm going to commit. It's not that. You can put your mind at rest. This last little chat has as its overriding objective . . . is that not good, eh? Quite a turn of phrase . . . Has the overriding objective of removing ambiguities, misunderstandings, and . . . and arrogance. I mean the greatest arrogance of all, that of believing yourself the cause of my suicide. I will not grant you that satisfaction. You would have quite liked that, wouldn't you? I can just see you, preening yourself. The man whose face is lined with the tragic memory of the woman who slew herself for love of him. Who could resist such a man? And when they put up a monument to your wild love affairs, am I supposed to be the little female crouched at your feet? Andromeda bleeding to death before the great Perseus! Not on your life! It has nothing to do with you! Divest yourself of the laurels of Perseus. (*Interrupting herself*) Perseus! What the hell has Perseus got to do with it? (*She claps her hands, the lights go down, she switches off the camera and turns on the video-recorder. The picture of JULIA, playing the part just recorded, appears on the screen*)

The first bit is OK, then I started to waffle. (*Goes and lies down*) Take it easy . . . let's just calm down . . . I mean, it is not as though it is one of the commercial breaks that you dream up on the spur of the moment. This is the last break of my life, so it had better be good. This is one for the archives. I can just see the whole family gathering for the festive season, Christmas, New Year . . . all sitting round the table and somebody saying: 'Let's have a look at Julia's video . . . let's listen to what she said before she did herself in. It's always good for a laugh.'

Calm down . . . there's still plenty of time before night . . . you've got it in you . . . first I'll make myself something to eat . . . the last supper! All by myself; not even Judas to keep me company. I never thought I'd have been able to do all this with such detachment. Is this the catharsis of the return to the warm womb, as Seneca put it, while he was slashing his wrists, in the bath? In fact God knows how many times I've read about people hanging themselves, shooting themselves or slashing their wrists and all the time nobody had the slightest idea that they were getting ready for the great deed. All calm, all normal, as if it were an ordinary day. That's just how I intend going about it. An ordinary day. I'll even stick to my diet today. So, today is Thursday, what's on the menu today? (*Looks up a kind of list*) Chicken, boiled chicken, a whole chicken is permissible! An orgy! Carrot juice. These jockeys' diets are just the job.

Switches on the television, where a soap opera is being shown. JULIA takes the chicken from the fridge and places it on the table with evident disgust. While watching the pictures from the soap opera, JULIA cleans the vegetables and puts them into the pot along with the chicken. Once she has completed this operation, she sets the table with meticulous care. At the tear-jerking climax of the programme, she goes and flops onto a settee.

MALE: (*On TV*) Cast your eye on this photo. What does it tell you?

FEMALE: (*On TV*) It's him, my husband! But who is that little whore with her arm around his waist?

MALE: That's no little whore. That's the daughter of his best friend and business associate.

FEMALE: Who? Tom?

MALE: Yes, him. You can bet that if Tom finds out that his daughter is rolling about on his best friend's bed every afternoon, he'll tear him apart, limb from limb.

FEMALE: Where did you get this photograph?

MALE: Someone from the Argo Agency took it.

FEMALE: A private investigation agency? You mean you set one of these infamous dicks on the heels of my husband?

MALE: No, I set the private dick on the heels of her, Elsa, Tom's daughter. No one was more amazed than me to find your husband mixed up in this business.

FEMALE: You see what a bastard he is! But what gave you the idea of shadowing that Elsa in the first place?

MALE: I told you that before you and I fell in love, I had an affair with a girl . . . well, that girl was her, Elsa. But later I began to harbour the suspicion that, although she was still seeing me, she was two-timing me with someone else, and that someone else was none other than your husband.

FEMALE: Antony, you rat! However, I'm glad it was him who lured that simpering little bitch away from you.

MALE: Excellent. Then you'll be happy to know that his affair with Elsa is only a cover-up.

FEMALE: A cover-up for what?

MALE: The investigator also shadowed your husband's business associate, and stumbled on the fact that Tom and your Antony are lovers.

FEMALE: Oh no . . . I'll kill myself. (*Bursts out laughing*) Ha, ha! What did you expect? Did you really think I was going to kill myself? Ha! Ha! Well, I'm sorry to disappoint you. I knew all along! Ha! Ha!

MALE: Then I hope you'll be able to laugh as heartily at this. Tom's got Aids.

FEMALE: No, that's a lie. It's all an invention.

MALE: Yes, and was it an invention to have him observed in the very hospital where they were carrying out the tests? But it was worthwhile, because in that way I found out that your husband has got Aids too.

FEMALE: I knew this all along as well. It was me that passed it on to him.

MALE: What?

FEMALE: Yes, my dear, I've got Aids – so I have passed it on to you too.

MALE: How can you be sure? Perhaps I didn't catch it.

FEMALE: Just go and have a little look in the mirror. You've got so many spots all over your skin that you look like a giraffe without the neck.

MALE: It's true. I hoped against hope that it was only leprosy. How is it that there are no marks on you?

FEMALE: I am a healthy carrier of the disease.

MALE: What about Tom and Antony?

FEMALE: They are clean carriers as well. You, dear John, are the only one who has gone bad. Goodbye, John!

MALE: But I love you. Don't leave me! Don't leave me! I love you.

FEMALE: I love you too, John . . . but I'm not leaving you. You are leaving us all.

MALE: What do you mean I'm leaving you all?

FEMALE: You see, you're leaving me, you're leaving the world. You are dying, John. Farewell, forever.

JULIA *switches off the TV. Switches on the record player and light, sentimental music fills the room. She absent-mindedly reaches for a bottle on the drinks trolley; immediately a siren begins to screech and a light on top of the fridge – of the same kind as seen on police cars – starts flashing. A loud deep voice rings out.*

VOICE: It is established by sociological research that the social vacuum in the life of the average housewife often leads to alcoholism.

JULIA angrily replaces the glass and the bottle. Once she does so, the flashing stops and the voice falls silent.

JULIA: For God's sake, I haven't touched a drop. Alcohol is bad for the liver, the liver swells up, you catch hepatic cirrhosis, your belly gets bloated, bloated, till one day BANG! it blows up and the neighbours phone the council.

Switches on the TV again, to find pictures of a policeman, shots, car chases, explosions. The phone rings and JULIA automatically picks up the receiver. At the same moment the POLICEMAN on the TV screen picks up the receiver of his own phone. JULIA does not notice the confusion.

Hello, who's speaking, please?

POLICEMAN: (*On TV*) Yes, madam, what can I do for you?

JULIA: I beg your pardon, it was you who called.

POLICEMAN: Take it easy, don't get excited.

JULIA: I'm perfectly calm, thank you very much. Well then, what are you after?

POLICEMAN: When did all this take place? Let's have a bit of order around here.

JULIA: Whose order, may I ask? It's all perfectly clear. Are you all mad today?

POLICEMAN: Now look here. If you imagine for one minute that the entire city police force is waiting here for the first streetwalker to phone us with a load of old cock . . . I'll come right round and knock some sense into you.

JULIA: How dare . . . (*Realised what has been happening*) Away and chase yourself. (*Hangs up*)

POLICEMAN: Hello! Hello! She's hung up, the lousy whore.

JULIA *once again stretches out on the settee. Quite mechanically, she lifts the lid of a cigarette case and picks out a cigarette. She lifts a heavy lighter from the table, and as she does so the pictures on the wall open out to reveal a series of posters with anti-smoking slogans. There is one with the picture of a smoker with a sickly green face, strangled by an enormous cigarette. Another shows a skeleton puffing away with evident delight, while underneath there are legends like . . . 'Your bronchial passages are putrid sponges, sodden with black tar', or 'nicotine equals cancer', or 'smoking ruins your sex life, slows your reflexes and dulls the brain'.*

JULIA: Bloody hell! I set up all those little traps by myself and then I go and forget all about them. No way is it going to be allowed. I am determined to die the very picture of health. No smoking!

She stubs out the cigarette she had just lit in the ash-tray, puts the lighter back on the table and everything goes back to its previous position. Meantime on the television screen, violence, punch-ups, tough interrogations follow one another in quick succession. The telephone rings once again. JULIA makes the mechanical gesture of reaching out for the receiver but stops herself in time.

Eh no, not this time. I'm not falling for it again. (*The telephone continues to ring*)

POLICEMAN: Would someone out there be good enough to pick up the phone. (*Pointing his finger directly at JULIA*) Hey, you! Wakey, wakey! I'm talking to you.

JULIA: (*Amazed*) Oh, is it my phone? Oh, I am sorry. (*Lifts the receiver*) Hello!

WOMAN'S VOICE: Good evening, Doctor. How are you? Forgive me if . . .

JULIA: Here we go again. Back to this 'Good evening, Doctor' business.

WOMAN'S VOICE: Did you get my message on your answering machine?

JULIA: Yeah, I got it all right, but I have to say that you are . . .

WOMAN'S VOICE: I know, you're right, Doctor, and I swear that I tried it out but the only result was that, once I lay down on that hot brick, I burned my bum.

JULIA: Listen, will you stop going on about that hot brick and pay attention.

WOMAN'S VOICE: Don't ask me to give up my brick, because, to tell you the truth, madam doctor, the first day it gave me a bit of . . . em . . . pleasure but thereafter . . . the thing is, I have not got a note in my head and I cannot get the harmonies right, especially in the rising scale. Listen . . . AOOUOOAAAUIOUIA . . . AOOUOOAAAUIUOUIAA.

JULIA: (*Trying to interrupt*) Ooooah. Stop!

WOMAN'S VOICE: You see what I mean about not having a note in my head. So that must be why the treatment is having no effect. Listen, how would it be if instead of trying to make the sounds in a singing voice, I had a go at whistling? I am much better at that. I'll try it out. See what you think. (*Whistles*)

JULIA: Look, if you don't listen to me, I'm putting the phone down.

WOMAN'S VOICE: All right! Don't get mad, please, I'm listening.

JULIA: It's all a mistake. I am not the analyst you take me for –

WOMAN'S VOICE: But the number . . .

JULIA: The number is the right one . . . but it's also the wrong one, and I am somebody else.

WOMAN'S VOICE: Ah, you're somebody else. So you're another one who's suffering from split personality. (*Laughs*) Come off it, Doctor . . . I recognise you. That's your voice, the same as before.

JULIA: It's not my fault if the voice is the same. The other one fell into the trap as well.

WOMAN'S VOICE: A trap! Are you having me on, Doctor? I get it. I'm annoying you. I'm annoying you with my problems and so to scare me off, you pretend to be somebody else. You make out you are some hysterical pregnant wife. But it is not going to work, you know. I really am unwell and you are going to have to listen to me.

JULIA: Now that's where you are wrong! This time you have really done it. (*Makes to hang up*)

WOMAN'S VOICE: Hold it, Doctor. Don't try to hang up on me or I'll come round there and smash up the house.

JULIA: (*To herself*) She can see me!!! (*Into the telephone*) Now listen here. You don't scare me. Quite apart from the fact that I would really like to know how you would manage to find out where I live, because the magazine only gives the phone number, isn't that so?

WOMAN'S VOICE: Aha! But I phoned up the exchange. I've got a friend who works on the computer section and he gave me the address . . . 138 Bentinck Street, fourth floor, second door on the right, so there.

JULIA: Oh God. Now I'm done for.

WOMAN'S VOICE: Here's me going through this terrible time . . . just you try to give me the shove and I'll be right round there . . . it's only ten minutes you know . . . I'll set fire to your place and I'll shoot you between the eyes. I've got a revolver here, you know. Property of a friend of mine. Understand?

JULIA: I've already told you that you don't frighten me. For your information, I've got a gun as well, so you bring yours round and we can have a shoot-out, like *High Noon* . . . a flight to the death. Anyway, if you get me, so much the better.

WOMAN'S VOICE: I understand. As hard as nails, you are. But I don't mind. Because, my dear doctor, you must admit it is not on to write certain articles in magazines, bringing a glimmer of hope to a poor woman driven to despair by her neurodelirium – and then to create a fuss over a phone call.

JULIA: (*To herself*) Oh God in heaven, is everybody out to get me . . . You can't even kick the bucket in peace. (*Speaking into the phone*) All right, all right. I'm listening. What can I do for you?

Meantime the action of the detective story continues on the screen. JULIA, who had been fiddling with the remote control, unintentionally turns up the volume.

POLICEMAN: (*On TV*) Let go of that hysterical bitch . . . can't you see that she's just a schizophrenic whore.

JULIA: (*Quickly switching off the TV*) I'm sorry. I didn't mean that.

WOMAN'S VOICE: Did that refer to me? A hysterical bitch! You tell your husband that I . . .

JULIA: No, it wasn't my husband. It was the TV detective.

WOMAN'S VOICE: You mean to tell me there's a TV detective in your house?

JULIA: No, no, I'm not living . . . inside the TV set, if you see what I mean. I just happened to turn up the sound on the . . .

WOMAN'S VOICE: Pull the other one! How did your TV detective know I'm on the game?

JULIA: On the game!

WOMAN'S VOICE: I'm a call-girl, a street-walker, anything you like, Doctor. And don't sound so dumbfounded because I told you all about it the other day in your surgery. You and your husband were the only ones who knew about my schizophrenia. You told me yourself. And tell that bastard of a husband of yours to lay off or I'll blow his brains out as well.

JULIA: Great! So who am I making this video for? Listen here. You keep your hands off my husband. Let him live, so that he dies of despair!

WOMAN'S VOICE: Hello. What have I said? I don't understand.

JULIA: It doesn't matter. Well, hurry up. Tell me what you want.

WOMAN'S VOICE: I don't know. It's just that I've done all the exercises, like you said, but apart from the burns on my bum, nothing has happened. I'm no further forward . . . in fact it's going from bad to worse, because I had a crisis at work . . . bloody awful it was . . . I nearly ended up in the clink for assault.

JULIA: Why? What did you do?

WOMAN'S VOICE: Well, there I was, going about my lawful business, as I was telling you. I was getting him ready.

JULIA: You were getting him ready? Who were you getting ready?

WOMAN'S VOICE: A client. I was practising . . . what do you call it . . . the oral thing that that wanker Reagan in America doesn't like.

JULIA: Ah, I see. Then what happened?

WOMAN'S VOICE: Well, all of a sudden, a fit of rage came over me and I sank my teeth right in.

JULIA: You did what?

WOMAN'S VOICE: Snap . . . just like that. Got the old fangs right round it. Talk about the Hound of the Baskervilles. I didn't let go. He was howling as though it had been chopped off, and he gave me a thump on the head. That wasn't a good idea, because it was like bringing a hammer down on a nutcracker. Snap! You know what I mean. Zak! It jumped right up in the air.

JULIA: His what do you call it!

WOMAN'S VOICE: Just one of his balls. Fortunately it rolled under a cupboard and I managed to pick it up. I put it neatly in a plastic bag with some blocks of ice and rushed at top speed to the nearest casualty ward. You know how in the hospital nowadays they do grafts and things. Anything that falls off they can put back on. It's wonderful.

JULIA: Miracle workers, eh.

WOMAN'S VOICE: I must say he was quite good about it. He didn't even report me. He told the cop on duty that it was a ravenous ape at the zoo who took a swipe at him while he was giving it sweeties. No gratitude, these apes. However, you'll understand that in my line of business I cannot live on with the risk of these crises. Once you have chewed off four or five testicles, the word gets around, and the punters cross the road when they see you coming. So, you tell me, Doctor, what am I going to do?

JULIA: Well, for a start . . . you know those rubber gum shields that boxers put in their mouths to stop their teeth getting knocked out . . . I'd put one over my teeth if I were you . . . and then I'd give the exercises a miss.

WOMAN'S VOICE: Even the humming vowels?

JULIA: Even them. In fact keep your mouth tightly shut, especially when you find it in the vicinity of male genitals, and breathe gently through your nose.

WOMAN'S VOICE: Is that all?

JULIA: There's only one other thing that you should do but it's very important. (*To herself*) What's going on here? How did I get myself into this? Here am I playing the agony auntie. I feel like a life-guard . . . a testicle-guard, more like. (*Picks up the phone again*) Now listen carefully.

WOMAN'S VOICE: I promise, I promise.

JULIA: Tomorrow, take the first train and go back home. You're from Forfar, right?

WOMAN'S VOICE: Not exactly, I'm from Brechin.

JULIA: It's all the same . . . does your mother still live there?

WOMAN'S VOICE: Yes, poor old thing.

JULIA: There you are then. You go back there for a wee while, at least a month, and you'll see you'll get better. Get bags of fresh air, do a wee bit of work in the country but nothing too strenuous. You'll feel a new woman.

WOMAN'S VOICE: Are you sure it works?

JULIA: Couldn't be surer. I've tried it hundreds of times myself and if you could see me now . . . full of oomph, up-and-at-'em, you know what I mean? There aren't enough hours in the day!

WOMAN'S VOICE: God bless you, Doctor. I'll do what you say. I'll set off right away. You're a saint. I feel better already. (*She hangs up.* JULIA *does likewise*)

JULIA: It would drive you mad, this trying to cure madmen and madwomen. I nearly spoiled everything. If she really had come round to fight a duel and burn down the house, I'd have had to postpone the whole thing. And then when would I have got myself psyched up again to do myself in? Talk, talk . . . I'm just wasting time . . . I must get my video done. (*Lights up a cigarette with a worried look. Immediately, the pictures open out, the siren goes off and the light begins flashing*) Oh you're really getting on my nerves. One cigarette, after all this carry on, that's not too much to ask. And then, I must concentrate, do you understand? (JULIA *has the lighter in her hand, and throws it violently against the wall. A scream is heard.* JULIA *stops in dismay. The scream comes from the next door flat*)

FEMALE VOICE: (*From next door*) You're a bastard.

JULIA: Oh God! The wall is talking.

FEMALE VOICE: You batter me because I can't defend myself.

JULIA: Ah! The next door neighbours.

MALE VOICE: You're pretty good with your hands yourself – you bastard you.

FEMALE VOICE: You're the bastard. Always at it with that whore of yours.

JULIA: They always quarrel and then they make love.

FEMALE VOICE: I'll kill you. (*A crash, caused by something being thrown, is heard*)

MALE VOICE: You're mad. You nearly got me on the head . . . put that thing down . . . Jesus Christ, it's bronze.

FEMALE VOICE: I'll break it over your head!

MALE VOICE: I swear to you that there is nothing between me and that woman. Put that thing down.

FEMALE VOICE: No, Maxie. (*A slap is heard*) Ow, that was sore. (*Voices of the two begin to drop*)

JULIA: (*Draws close to the wall and shouts*) Louder! I can't hear a thing. Come on, you can't start a story and then switch off the sound right in the middle. But I have, right here, my microphonic, amplifier stethoscope.

Takes out two acoustic implements, sticks them to the wall, pulls the wires across to the amplifier and inserts the pins into the machine. Instantly the voices of the two neighbours, still squabbling, can be heard clearly.

FEMALE VOICE: I know, Maxie . . . it's just that when I see you near another woman . . . I start thinking that you might be . . . you know what I mean . . . might be saying or doing to her what you say to me . . . oh, Maxie, I go out of my mind . . . I feel my legs shaking.

MALE VOICE: Come on, how could you imagine that I could ever prefer that hag to you . . . her bum hangs down round her ankles . . . Have you ever seen yourself next to her. In comparison to her, your bum looks as though it were tucked under your arms!

JULIA: A flamingo!

FEMALE VOICE: Ah, so it's just a question of bums?

MALE VOICE: No, no . . . eyes as well.

FEMALE VOICE: You mean my eyes are tucked under my arms?

MALE VOICE: Don't talk stupid . . . apart from the fact that I've always believed that a high bum means high emotions . . . there's no one on your level . . . I love you.

FEMALE VOICE: Yes, no one, no one . . . Go on, say it, Maxie.

MALE VOICE: No one can come up to you . . . not even in high heels. (*Little groans and kissing sounds*)

JULIA: Better than *Dallas* any day!

MALE VOICE: I'm mad about you.

FEMALE VOICE: Again, again . . . say it again. Oh Maxie, you're wonderful. You're great . . . I'd die for love of you . . .

MALE VOICE: But you must promise that there will be no more of these scenes.

FEMALE VOICE: I promise. I promise.

MALE VOICE: And that you'll stop throwing these bronze book ends at my head.

FEMALE VOICE: No, never again at your head. No, darling, not like that. You're ripping my blouse. Let me.

MALE VOICE: No, let me. I enjoy it. God, what a lot of buttons.

FEMALE VOICE: I sewed on some extra ones just to tease you. Let me take your clothes off.

JULIA: Off! Off! Off!

MALE VOICE: You're a pet. Ahh . . . Ohh . . . like that. You take them off. Oww!

FEMALE VOICE: What's wrong, what have I done?

MALE VOICE: The zip, the zip in my trousers . . . it's caught the, the whatdyecallit . . . AAAh . . . it's sunk right in.

FEMALE VOICE: Oh, poor darling . . . wait and I'll fix it . . . oh my God, right on the tender spot. I can't move it.

MALE VOICE: Easy, easy. You're making it worse . . . Aaah help.

FEMALE VOICE: I'll have to cut off the trousers.

MALE VOICE: You'll do bugger all of the kind. They're brand new. Maybe we should go to the hospital. Aaaaah . . .

FEMALE VOICE: There you are. It's all done. Poor thing, I've cut a wee bit off.

MALE VOICE: You've what?

FEMALE VOICE: Come here and I'll look after you . . . a teensy weensy bandage . . .

ENGINEER'S VOICE: Bloody marvellous. You need the bandage yourself and you know where you can stick it. Use a whole roll. For God's sake! Are you going to give over with that wailing like a cat on heat. We're all needing a bit of sleep.

JULIA: That must be the engineer in Flat 3A.

PIANIST'S VOICE: Shut up, you dirty old bastard, you! Leave these two young people who love each other alone. They're so sweet.

JULIA: The pianist woman in 3B! (*The two lovers fall silent*) There, I knew it, complete silence. So I'll never know if love is stronger than the bandage. (*The chicken is cooked. JULIA removes it from the pot, places it on a serving dish, garnishes it with olives, a slice of orange, and lettuce leaves. Looks at her handiwork and says*) Lovely, but just the same you make me sick. You're nothing but a clapped-out battery hen. Every day stuck in there with thousands of others, and a pair of green glasses over your beak to make you believe that the garbage you were gobbling up was top quality lettuce and fresh peas! Bloody idiot! And am I supposed to munch my way through a corpse like that? The last meal of the condemned prisoner? Not bloody likely. I'd rather die with an empty stomach. You sleep the eternal sleep more peacefully that way. No fear of nightmares. (*Goes to sit down, looks around her, heaves a sigh*)

I'll need to find a way of finishing this commercial. I could make him watch the last preparations. Slowly, slowly, take out the bottle, the syringe, do the injection and then, slowly, the death mask. (*Makes a sickly grin*) No, poor boy, he'd never get to sleep again.

For a few seconds she gazes around her silently, not sure what to do next. Her eyes fall on the magazine Health. *She picks it up, and reads, section by section, the article in question.*

'A warm brick under your back level with your kidneys . . . the head hanging over the side . . . humming vowel sounds.' I must have a go. Why not? I've tried everything else. Right then, first thing, the brick. How about the lid of the chicken pot. (*Picks up the lid*) Still hot. Prepare the table. (*Removes the tablecloth and plates. Places the lid on the table. Lies down on top*) Please God don't let me levitate too high. (*Lies down. Begins to wail*) Ahaa . . . Ooooh I see where the sounds come from. (*Lets her head hang over the edge of the table, starts the humming effect*) AUoooo . . . Aiiooo . . . it's all in the mind, but I do feel relaxed. Aooeee . . . Auooiieeuuoooh.

ENGINEER'S VOICE: At it again are we? Back to the cat on the tiles routine, eh?

PIANIST'S VOICE: On you go, groan away. Pay no heed to that decrepit old so and so. (*The* PIANIST *encourages them by playing the piano. The two lovers in the next room start breathing heavily once again*)

FEMALE VOICE: Yes, yes . . . oh Maxie . . . I could die . . .

MALE VOICE: Easy now . . . Ouch. You're knocking off the bandage.

FEMALE VOICE: Oh, how lovely. Aah . . . I'll put it back on in a minute. I'll put on a whole roll of gauze. Oh God! Oh God!

MALE VOICE: Oh God, you're killing me.

JULIA: I always wonder why when people are making love, God always gets mixed with it. Oh God, how lovely! Oh God, I could die!

FEMALE VOICE: More, more! Oh Mother of God, I can't take any more.

JULIA: Every so often, you get God's Holy Mother as well.

PIANIST'S VOICE: Oh yes, more . . . go on, more, more.

ENGINEER'S VOICE: For God's sake, stop.

From outside the sound of a baby crying.

JULIA: Already! A bouncing baby boy! The child of the bandage! (*Comes down from the table, saying*) I'm starving. (*Looks at the chicken*) I'm not touching you. Right into the bin with you. What can I have? (*Clapping her hands*) Spaghetti, the first recorded case of spaghetti suicide. Let's really go to town, one quarter, a half pound, three quarters of a pound of spaghetti . . . an overdose of pasta. Fill up the pot with water (*Putting in the water*) and I'll swallow one of these little pills to reduce animal fat. (*Places the pot on a gas ring*) Spaghetti . . . spaghetti. (*The phone rings and JULIA lifts the receiver*) Hello!

KATIE'S VOICE: (*On telephone*) Doctor, please, please don't start shouting at me. I really must talk to you . . . hello, can you hear me?

JULIA: Hello. Yes, I'm listening.

KATIE'S VOICE: It is you, right. You are the doctor. I haven't got the wrong number.

JULIA: (*With resignation*) No, you haven't. It's me, the analyst. (*To herself*) Why not?

KATIE'S VOICE: Perhaps I've chosen an awkward time to call.

JULIA: Well, in fact, it is just a bit inconvenient.

KATIE'S VOICE: I could ring you back later, if you're still up.

JULIA: That's just it. Later on I won't be . . . up.

KATIE'S VOICE: Is there something wrong, Doctor? From your voice, you sound a bit down.

JULIA: No, no, I'm fine . . . just a bit tired, you know how it is. Unfortunately, not all of my patients who call me at

home are civil and understanding, like you. There's one who
has the little problem of waiting for the blue window . . .
then there's one who bites the balls off a client . . . and . . .

KATIE'S VOICE: They chewed the balls off one of your
clients, in one go!

JULIA: No, the client wasn't mine. Anyway it's a long story,
too long for the moment. Let's forget it. Tell me all about
yourself. Hang on a minute till I change the receiver. (*Pulls
out the plug from the wall and puts it into a machine linked to
a headset of the type used by exchange-operators*) Sorry, but I
was just sitting down to eat.

KATIE'S VOICE: Forgive me. I know I am being a nuisance.

JULIA: Don't worry, with this headset I can move about quite
freely.

KATIE'S VOICE: A headset?

JULIA: I had to get one a while back for when my mother
phones up. She goes on and on for hours. I used to be stuck
there listening to her. This way I can listen to her and go
about my business. So, you were saying.

KATIE'S VOICE: (*Aggressively*) Yes, well, I have tried out
your method and pardon me if I'm quite frank with you, but
the only result was that while I was warbling away, the
firemen and the police came storming up.

JULIA: (*Laughs*) Ha! Ha! . . . Really.

KATIE'S VOICE: (*Annoyed*) I am glad you find it so funny.

JULIA: I didn't mean to laugh at you . . . you've got a good
sense of humour yourself . . . So you mean to say you got no
benefit at all from the . . . course of treatment.

KATIE'S VOICE: Quite the reverse. I could have kicked
myself.

JULIA: Why?

KATIE'S VOICE: Oh, come on. A woman of my age, with a
brick under her bum and her head see-sawing back and

forward . . . it's not real. I don't know how I could have
fallen for such gibberish.

JULIA: (*Amused but making an effort to appear offended*)
Gibberish! A method tried and tested in Japan.

KATIE'S VOICE: That's just it. You had to go to Japan to try
it out, because if you had done your experiments here,
they'd have knocked you black and blue and tossed you in
the clink for a bloody fraud.

JULIA: Oh so that's it! Black and blue, eh. You come on to
my phone, in my home, just to insult me, right at the very
moment . . . you have no idea how delicate this moment is
for me . . . and all this to tell me I should be knocked
black and blue and tossed into the slammer. There's no
end of people who want to see you drown in the shit. I
was better off with my street-walker. All she wanted to do
was to burn down my house and bite off my husband's
whatnots . . .

KATIE'S VOICE: Take it easy . . . I'm sorry, you're quite
right. I'm an aggressive, loud-mouthed, ill-tempered cow.

JULIA: (*During this conversation she is setting the table and
putting the spaghetti in the pot*) Now hold on . . .

KATIE'S VOICE: Self-centred and feeble-minded.

JULIA: Don't overdo it.

KATIE'S VOICE: A right bitch.

JULIA: Oh well, if you insist.

KATIE'S VOICE: It's just that I'm going through a bad patch.
If only you knew, Doctor.

JULIA: You don't need to tell me.

KATIE'S VOICE: I cannot stand anything or anybody. Look, I
wasn't always so gloomy and aggressive.

JULIA: Yes, but, these are the classic symptoms of paranoia,
the very ones I've got myself, by the way . . . You spend all
day observing your own navel as though it was the centre of

the world. You let a little tear splash into your navel every so often till it forms a tiny pool, and then you dip in your finger and shout . . . 'Look, the ocean'.

KATIE'S VOICE: You dip in your finger and say that it is the ocean!

JULIA: Metaphorically. It was a literary paradox.

KATIE'S VOICE: Thank God for that!

JULIA: (*Puts her hand over the microphone receiver, says to herself*) Here, it's not bad this business of being an analyst. I have found a vocation. A pity it's too late.

KATIE'S VOICE: Anyway I wanted to let you know that you have got the wrong person. If you wanted somebody to make a fool of themselves, I am myself the number one. If you came to my house, you could have a look at the posters hanging on my walls.

JULIA: You've got posters on your walls. What do they say?

KATIE'S VOICE: Well, for instance, I am trying to kick smoking and to lose weight.

JULIA: Not another one.

KATIE'S VOICE: Why? Are you reducing or are you worried about smoking?

JULIA: Who isn't? Women doctors get fat as well, you know.

KATIE'S VOICE: Yes, of course. And to think that just today I was going to get stuck into a whole chicken. It nearly made me spew.

JULIA: Don't tell me. So you chucked it out.

KATIE'S VOICE: No, I wrapped it up in a nice little package and posted it off to my landlady. She wants to evict me. With a bit of luck, and with the way the post works nowadays, it'll be stinking to high heaven when she gets it.

JULIA: (*Laughing*) Ha! Ha! Very naughty of you, but I like your style.

KATIE'S VOICE: Style . . . Yeah . . . enough style to make you sick. I have one hell of a neurosis that I just cannot get over. My body is scarcely in working order, I eat raw grain and I stick garlic suppositories up my bum so I end up with breath like a dragon in a zoo.

JULIA: Listen, I must tell you something, and I am not speaking as a psychiatrist. In fact, I may as well tell you that I am an ordinary woman, somebody that you got on the phone by mistake. And the incredible thing is that you seem to be a photocopy of me. It is as though I was looking at myself in a huge mirror. You see, I feel empty and desperate, just the same as you, and perhaps even more. I go around hanging up posters and I eat the right food and what's more I believe I am an emancipated, modern woman just because I have electrical and electronic gadgets, even in the toilet.

KATIE'S VOICE: Stop right there, Doctor. I know where you are heading. I am not one of your half-witted ravers that you lead by the nose with this guff about mirror games or by yelling 'Same here! Same here!'

JULIA: So you don't believe me. You think I'm a phoney.

KATIE'S VOICE: Quite the reverse. I think that you are one of the best. Thank God that you are neither a psychiatrist nor one of these trendy analysts.

JULIA: What do you mean I'm not an anal . . .

KATIE'S VOICE: (*Interrupting*) I understood after we had been talking for five seconds. Your language is too human and intelligent for you to belong to my profession.

JULIA: Your profession? You mean you are . . . ?

KATIE'S VOICE: Yes, I am a doctor.

JULIA: Why didn't you tell me to shut up earlier?

KATIE'S VOICE: Because I really needed someone like you . . . someone to talk about ordinary, everyday things . . . before I kick the bucket.

JULIA: Kick the bucket! What are you up to?

KATIE'S VOICE: I am going quietly. Can you still hear me? I am finding it hard to get the words out.

JULIA: What have you done, Doctor? Speak. Have you taken something?

KATIE'S VOICE: No, I've switched on the gas . . . very slightly . . . so that I can go almost without noticing. You know, it is quite a pleasing feeling.

JULIA: Listen, this time you have got to believe me. This is not a trick. I had decided to finish myself off as well. I have already got a solution of paraquat all ready, you know that weedkiller stuff. I was going to take it in a wee while.

KATIE'S VOICE: No kidding! What a coincidence.

JULIA: Do you not believe me?

KATIE'S VOICE: Yeah, I believe you. Oh well, then, all the best.

JULIA: No, wait a minute. I had my mind made up until a few minutes ago, then this carry on of acting the analyst, of listening to other people's despair, of hearing the very words that I think and say but speak with a different voice . . . Well, it all seemed so absurd! First it was all so logical, and now it just seems madness.

KATIE'S VOICE: Well, you know what they say, madness and logic are so near.

JULIA: Come on now, tell me where you live. Give me your address and I'll come round, we can talk . . .

KATIE'S VOICE: We've done enough talking, don't you think, and it was really nice. I really needed to hear a kindly voice like yours to keep me company as I slip away.

JULIA: Please, I beg you. Give me this chance. Tell me where you live.

KATIE'S VOICE: I really am so grateful for your concern, but it is no use. Quite apart from the fact that it would be dangerous for you, because I have been fixing up the wires of the doorbell so that the first person who presses the button sets off a spark and BOOM, the whole place'll be up in the air. I don't want those bastards of my relatives to find even the teeniest piece of furniture or the slightest rag of my clothes to divide among themselves. And I'd give anything to see the face of the landlady who threw me out. 'Go on, let's see you renting out this heap now!' Anyway enough of this. I have been intruding on your courtesy too long.

JULIA: Hold on, don't hang up. Try and be reasonable!

KATIE'S VOICE: Reasonable? Now that's rich. Listen to who's talking. You have decided to do away with yourself with paraquat weedkiller, and you tell me to be reasonable. (*A ring from the buzzer*)

JULIA: Just a minute, don't go away. There's somebody at the door. I'll be right back.

KATIE'S VOICE: OK, I'll hold on, but not for long.

JULIA: (*Runs over to the intercom*) Hello.

DOORKEEPER'S VOICE: It's the doorkeeper. There are two delivery men with flowers for you. I'll just send them up.

JULIA: No, wait, hello. Hold them there and I'll . . . hello. She's hung up. (*Re-adjusts the headset*) Hello, Doctor. Still there. Can you hear me?

KATIE'S VOICE: Yes . . . I can hear you . . . Your voice has gone funny . . . it's starting to work.

JULIA: Pay attention to this. Throw the windows wide open. Switch off the gas. At least tell me your name.

KATIE'S VOICE: What's the point? Anyway, if you really must . . . I'm called Katie.

JULIA: Listen to me, Katie, if you have decided to kill yourself, nobody is going to pay any heed.

KATIE'S VOICE: Maybe not . . . but right now I have the guts it takes . . . I can do it . . . afterwards who knows?

JULIA: But don't you have a voice telling you that perhaps it is not guts at all, but cowardice. I'm saying this to you because . . . (*A ring at the door.* JULIA, *still talking, goes towards the outside door*) it might be the fear of facing up to . . . (*Loudly towards the door*) I'm coming . . . (*Talking into the telephone again*) the terror of (*Opens the door. A huge bouquet of flowers is literally hurled into her face*) . . . My God! (*The telephone headset is knocked off. Two men, one young, the other older, appear from behind the flowers. They have guns pointed at* JULIA)

OLDER MAN: Freeze! If you move or scream, you're dead.

YOUNG MAN: It's a hold-up. And blowing you to smithereens won't bother us.

JULIA: Pity. If you had got here a wee while ago, you would have done me a good turn.

OLDER MAN: What are you on about? Don't get scared. We are not staying, but we want your cash, the lot.

JULIA: Bad luck, lads. I was just setting off, shall we say, on my travels.

YOUNG MAN: Fine. Hand over your travelling money.

JULIA: It was a free trip . . . One way.

OLDER MAN: Listen here, no more messing about, understand? Fish out all that you've got, otherwise . . .

JULIA: Cool it, now, take it easy. No problem. You can have the lot, OK? (*Goes for her handbag*)

YOUNG MAN: (*Grabs the bag*) Not so fast!

JULIA: There's only seven pounds.

YOUNG MAN: Bloody hell. She's right. One fiver and two singles.

OLDER MAN: You wouldn't like to get us all wound up, now would you? Get the dough out, like I said.

He lifts the cigarette lighter to threaten JULIA. *Sets off the mechanism, the pictures open out, the siren goes off and the light starts flashing.*

YOUNG MAN: Oh Christ. The alarm. (*Rushes towards the exit*)

OLDER MAN: Stop there. It's just posters and pictures arsing about.

JULIA: Yes, it's just my little game. It's a trap I invented for myself to force me to stop smoking.

YOUNG MAN: Bitch! You've got me all trembling. (*Gives her a slap. The lights go out*) What's going on now?

JULIA: When you hit me, you made the transformer blow.

YOUNG MAN: When I hit you!

JULIA: That's right. You see that box on the wall? It's a sensor which goes on and off every time it hears a smack. Allow me. (*Gives him an almighty slap. The light goes back on*)

YOUNG MAN: Hey! What are you at?

JULIA: There you see. It works.

YOUNG MAN: Yes but, you bastard. I'll blow your head off. (*Points the gun*)

OLDER MAN: (*Stops him with a blow. Lights go off*) Cut it out, you idiot. (*Another slap to bring the lights back*) If you kill her, who's going to tell us where the loot is, eh? (*Another punch*)

YOUNG MAN: Don't you go punching me . . . and don't call me an idiot, OK? (*Gives him a punch. Light effect. They hit each other, with the lights going on and off*)

JULIA: Have you finished? Don't overdo this one potato, two potato act, boys, you'll break the switch. Why don't you get on with this hold-up? Take what you fancy and get on your way because I've got some important business to attend to. (*Picks up the telephone headset*)

OLDER MAN: Just what is that?

JULIA: It is a telephonist's headset. When you came in with the flowers I was chatting to a friend.

OLDER MAN: A friend. So this woman must have heard everything. Give here. (*Puts the ear piece to his ear*) She's hung up.

JULIA: Oh God!

YOUNG MAN: She must have phoned the police.

JULIA: Not at all. The way she was feeling.

YOUNG MAN: Do you see her game now? The bitch! That's why she was clowning about . . . to gain time. Let's get out of here. (*Goes towards door but is stopped by his companion*)

OLDER MAN: Not so fast!

YOUNG MAN: The police'll be here any minute. (*Tries to pull himself free, but receives a punch. Lights off*)

OLDER MAN: We're not leaving empty-handed, do you understand?

Deals the younger man a blow, at which he grabs a bottle from the trolley intending to smash it over the head of his companion. The mechanism snaps into action. The written message comes up. The recorded voice booms out. Terrified, the younger man drops the bottle.

PEREMPTORY VOICE: It's no good kidding yourself on! There's no way out!

OLDER MAN: What the hell's that?

YOUNG MAN: They've got us. (*Makes to run for it*)

PEREMPTORY VOICE: Alcohol kills slowly but inexorably.

JULIA: (*Grabs the bottle, puts it back on the trolley. Silence falls, everything goes back into its place. Slowly*) Another of my little tricks to make me cut down on alcohol.

OLDER MAN: If you don't quit buggering us about . . .

Aims another blow, but this time JULIA *bends down and the blow lands on the* YOUNG MAN's *face. Lights off.*

JULIA: No more violence against women! (*Throws a tremendous punch and the robber falls to the ground. Lights on*)

YOUNG MAN: Get a move on. The police are on the way.

OLDER MAN: The dough, fast.

JULIA: But I have no more, I swear it. I wasn't expecting you.

YOUNG MAN: The jewels will do, starting with these ones. (*Seizes the necklace* JULIA *has round her neck. All the pearls clatter to the ground*)

OLDER MAN: You bloody idiot! (*Blow. Lights off*) When did you ever see anyone in the pictures grabbing necklaces like that? Put on the light. (*The* YOUNG MAN *slaps himself on the face and the lights come back on*) It'll take at least half an hour to pick them up one by one.

JULIA: If I were you, I wouldn't waste my time . . . I picked it up at a jumble sale, it is not worth much. (*The younger robber, fiddling about with the video-tape, has switched on the camera*) Please, don't touch. These are very sensitive machines. If you are desperate to tape your partner, allow me. Wouldn't you like to come on screen too. Big smile. 'Real life hold-up of a woman on her own with punch-up and special lighting effects.'

OLDER MAN: Hey, cut that out. (*To the younger man*) You've been high on drugs so long, your brain's clapped out. What do you think you're doing? Why don't you run along with your cassette to your nearest police station? (*To* JULIA) Turn off this trap and rub out the tape.

YOUNG MAN: It's you that's off your head. And quit calling me crazy or I'll go mad. You think this machine is a trap . . . You're still after jewellery . . . How much do you think this little baby is worth, eh? At least £5000. (*To* JULIA) Isn't that right? Come on, how much did it cost you? Speak, you bitch.

JULIA: Now, come on, fair's fair . . . You're not really . . . I need this for my work. If you take it away, how am I going to live?

OLDER MAN: What do you care? You're going off on your travels, aren't you? (*The two start loading the camera and the video-recorder on their backs*)

JULIA: At least leave me that one cassette, because I have recorded . . .

YOUNG MAN: We'll not be long in rubbing it off. Don't you worry.

OLDER MAN: Get a hold of that radio.

JULIA: Nooo! Not the radio.

OLDER MAN: (*To* JULIA, *brandishing his gun*) You stay nice and quiet. I'm warning you, if you call anybody, I'll be right back to blow your brains out.

JULIA: No, no, cool it. (*The two struggle out with their burden*) Let me get the door . . . good-bye, I mean good evening. (*The two go out.* JULIA *closes the door behind them and puts the headset back on*) Hello, Katie. Damn, she really has hung up. (*Takes off the headset*) What do I do now? God, that bastard really hit me. (*Pulls herself together*) The police! Must call right away. What's the number? What a fool, 999, just as well I know it off by heart. (*Dials the number*) It's ringing. Hurry up. There they are. Hello.

POLICEMAN'S VOICE: (*On telephone*) Hello, police station here.

JULIA: Sorry I am finding it hard to get the words out. He gave me such a thump that he left me reeling.

POLICEMAN'S VOICE: Who did, madam?

JULIA: A burglar, two burglars in fact.

POLICEMAN'S VOICE: You've been burgled madam? When was this?

JULIA: Yes, just two minutes ago . . . at my house . . . they came in with flowers . . . but this is not why I am phoning . . . it's that . . .

POLICEMAN'S VOICE: Where do you live?

JULIA: 138 Bentinck Street, fourth floor, second door right . . . but it is urgent that you go to . . .

POLICEMAN'S VOICE: 138 Bentinck Street, fourth floor, second on right, telephone number 611 3002.

JULIA: How did you know?

POLICEMAN'S VOICE: A woman phoned up a short time ago to report a burglary at that address.

JULIA: Good. That's the woman you've got to trace at once. Did she leave her address?

POLICEMAN'S VOICE: That's the problem. We asked her but she refused. We thought we were dealing with a hoaxer. Her voice sounded unnatural, as though she were drunk.

JULIA: No, she's not drunk. She's on gas.

POLICEMAN'S VOICE: Grass?

JULIA: Not grass, she's not on drugs. She's switched on the gas. Now you'll need to be very careful when you ring the bell . . . that is under no circumstances ring the bell, because she has criss-crossed the wires, so that the whole place will blow up.

POLICEMAN'S VOICE: What will blow up?

JULIA: The flat, with the furniture and everything . . . because she does not want to leave even the teeniest stick to those bastards of relatives of hers . . . and the landlady will be left trying to rent out the rubble . . . you understand? But do not waste time, get round there, because if you don't, she's as good as dead.

POLICEMAN'S VOICE: OK, we're on our way. Would you be good enough to give us the address?

JULIA: I don't know it.

POLICEMAN'S VOICE: You mean to tell me you don't know where your gassy friend lives.

JULIA: Well it's not like that. I only met her this evening, because of the magazine *Health*, you see they published my number instead of the Japanese analyst's.

POLICEMAN'S VOICE: Japanese analyst?

JULIA: Yes, but my crazy friend isn't the only one who got it wrong . . . just imagine there was a woman who asked if it was all right to put a warm brick on her bum even although the window wasn't blue . . .

POLICEMAN'S VOICE: Just take it easy, madam.

JULIA: I am taking it easy. I'd like to see you in my place. Here was I making my going away video, as calm as you like . . . because I was going to commit suicide with paraquat weedkiller, when those women started phoning. Hello, Doctor, you'd better be a psychiatrist, if not I'm coming round to burn down your house . . . and we'll have a shoot-out, like *High Noon*. BANG BANG . . . because I am so overwrought, and I have bitten off a testicle from one of my clients and it rolled like a little ball under the cupboard and I'm carrying it around in an ice bag and the people at the hospital will sew it on right away.

POLICEMAN'S VOICE: Let's get this straight, madam, did I hear you say that you bit off a ball belonging to one of your clients?

JULIA: No, not me, for goodness' sake. I'm a vegetarian. But you're getting me confused. We've got to find out where my friend lives!

POLICEMAN'S VOICE: Quite so. Could you at least tell us her name?

JULIA: Silly me. It's coming back to me now – she's called Katie.

POLICEMAN'S VOICE: Uh huh. Katie. Surname?

JULIA: I don't know. She didn't tell me. But she did say that she is a doctor.

POLICEMAN'S VOICE: That's a start. Now try hard to recall any other detail that may have emerged during the conversation.

JULIA: Yes, well, she said that she was following her jockey's diet and that she is trying to give up smoking.

POLICEMAN'S VOICE: Not a great deal of help, but carry on.

JULIA: She's another one who puts up terrorist posters on the wall.

POLICEMAN'S VOICE: Terrorist posters?

JULIA: That's right. She does mad things. She boils the chicken then doesn't eat it.

POLICEMAN'S VOICE: If she doesn't eat it, what does she do with it?

JULIA: She throws it out. No, no, as you were. It's me that throws it out. She puts it in the post, so that it is rotten and stinking when it gets to the landlady.

POLICEMAN'S VOICE: That is an interesting detail.

JULIA: Maybe I am going on a bit, but I assure you that the story is really tragic.

POLICEMAN'S VOICE: Madam, put yourself in my place. What would you think of somebody who phones you up to tell you that she is going to kill herself, but won't tell you where she lives?

JULIA: But she didn't tell me right away that she was going to kill herself. At the beginning, she just wanted a wee chat with another human being, not with a doctor.

POLICEMAN'S VOICE: And in the course of talking to you, she decided to gas herself.

JULIA: She had already made up her mind . . . same as me, so that's why, as I was just telling you, I was having a quiet chat with my husband, who's not here, because we don't live together any more . . . Maybe I still love him, even if I tell him I don't, so he doesn't go around preening himself like the cock of the north. Well then, she, this gassy friend of mine, needled me a bit, in fact she actually insulted me . . . 'What do you mean scorching your clients on the bum' says she 'and forcing them to make humming sounds AIUA OOO.' Do you follow?

POLICEMAN'S VOICE: Couldn't be clearer.

JULIA: So, says she . . . I start humming the notes and what happens? The firemen come rushing in, the cats start miaowing and the neighbours are at it through the wall. No, the bit about the neighbours was me.

POLICEMAN'S VOICE: You don't say.

JULIA: Listen, I have the distinct impression that you are taking the mickey.

POLICEMAN'S VOICE: God forbid!

JULIA: Do you not realise that time is short and that poor woman is dying? What's keeping you back? There's all this claptrap on the telly about your data banks that can track down your criminals in a flash, but when it comes to saving some poor unfortunate that is gassing herself . . .

POLICEMAN'S VOICE: Stay calm, very calm. By the way, what did you say your name was?

JULIA: What have I got to do with it? It's not me that needs to be saved . . .

POLICEMAN'S VOICE: I'm not so sure about that.

JULIA: Take my word for it, I am all right now . . . all because of her, this Katie . . . she was like a mirror for me . . . a huge mirror . . . that gave a grotesque reflection . . . and everything became clear. She was talking the same language as me . . . An absurd photocopy. It was like being hit by lightning. All of a sudden I caught a glimpse of myself, and I looked . . . funny . . . like nothing on earth. These are the right words, funny and like nothing on earth. I saw my own madness, do you understand me, as though finally projected in the right frame. Here you are, I said to myself, I am down a bit but why am I staring at my navel and dipping my fingers in with the tears? Let's just stop shouting . . . God bless the ocean! I am going to stop staying all by myself at home with these electronic gadgets and traps and diets . . . oh my God, the spaghetti! It'll be all stuck together. But who cares? Do you know, it has just occurred to me, all of a sudden, that in next to no time it's going to be spring. Hello, hello! Anybody there? He's hung up on me. Must be crazy or something. Maybe we were cut off. (*Starts* *ringing the number, hears a buzz from the intercom, goes to answer*) Hello, what's going on?

DOORKEEPER'S VOICE: There is an ambulance here with some nurses. They're wanting to know if it was you that was burgled.

JULIA: Yes, it was me, but what's the ambulance for? I'm not injured, just a wee bit dazed from the punches.

DOORKEEPER'S VOICE: Sorry, there's a doctor here and he wants to talk to you personally.

JULIA: What doctor?

DOCTOR'S VOICE: Good evening. Now don't get excited. We're coming up right away.

JULIA: Wait a minute. There's been some mistake. Are you a doctor?

DOCTOR'S VOICE: They phoned us from the police station. We're on our way up. Open the door will you? Can you walk by yourself?

JULIA: What do you mean?

DOCTOR'S VOICE: Just what I say. Can you walk unaided? If not, we'll bring the stretcher.

JULIA: The stretcher? Hold it right there!

DOCTOR'S VOICE: Another thing. Be a good girl, take the wire from the bell. Isolate it, would you. We are not going to press the bell, but you can't be too careful . . . and, open the windows wide, if you can manage.

JULIA: No . . . You've got it all mixed up . . . it was the other woman who was on the gas . . . I was the one with the paraquat . . .

DOCTOR'S VOICE: And the weedkiller. I know, I know. The lads at the station told us all about it . . . the chicken stinking to high heaven slipped in the post box, the balls bit off in ice, and the blue window. Don't worry about a thing, we're coming, just relax and do not put up any resistance.

JULIA: What resistance could I put up? What do you want to do to me? Do you think I'm mad? I'm not going to any asylum.

VOICE AT THE DOOR: Now, open up or we'll have to knock the door down.

JULIA: (*In despair*) No, not the asylum . . . I'm not going to any asylum, no, no, no asylum . . .

Lights go down slowly as the music comes up.

Methuen World Classics *and* Methuen Contemporary Dramatists

Aeschylus (two volumes)
Jean Anouilh
John Arden (two volumes)
Arden & D'Arcy
Aristophanes (two volumes)
Aristophanes & Menander
Peter Barnes (three volumes)
Sebastian Barry
Brendan Behan
Aphra Behn
Edward Bond (five volumes)
Bertolt Brecht (six volumes)
Howard Brenton (two volumes)
Büchner
Bulgakov
Calderón
Jim Cartwright
Anton Chekhov
Caryl Churchill (two volumes)
Noël Coward (five volumes)
Sarah Daniels (two volumes)
Eduardo De Filippo
David Edgar (three volumes)
Euripides (three volumes)
Dario Fo (two volumes)
Michael Frayn (two volumes)
Max Frisch
Gorky
Harley Granville Barker
   (two volumes)
Peter Handke
Henrik Ibsen (six volumes)
Terry Johnson
Bernard-Marie Koltès

Lorca (three volumes)
David Mamet (three volumes)
Marivaux
Mustapha Matura
David Mercer (two volumes)
Arthur Miller (five volumes)
Anthony Minghella (two volumes)
Molière
Tom Murphy (four volumes)
Musset
Peter Nichols (two volumes)
Clifford Odets
Joe Orton
Philip Osment
Louise Page
A. W. Pinero
Luigi Pirandello
Stephen Poliakoff (two volumes)
Terence Rattigan
Christina Reid
Willy Russell
Ntozake Shange
Sam Shepard (two volumes)
Sophocles (two volumes)
Wole Soyinka
David Storey (two volumes)
August Strindberg (three volumes)
J. M. Synge
Sue Townsend
Ramón del Valle-Inclán
Frank Wedekind
Michael Wilcox
Oscar Wilde

Methuen Modern Plays

include work by

Jean Anouilh
John Arden
Margaretta D'Arcy
Peter Barnes
Sebastian Barry
Brendan Behan
Edward Bond
Bertolt Brecht
Howard Brenton
Simon Burke
Jim Cartwright
Caryl Churchill
Noël Coward
Sarah Daniels
Nick Dear
Shelagh Delaney
David Edgar
Dario Fo
Michael Frayn
John Godber
Paul Godfrey
David Greig
John Guare
Peter Handke
Jonathan Harvey
Iain Heggie
Declan Hughes
Terry Johnson
Sara Kane
Charlotte Keatley
Barrie Keeffe
Robert Lepage
Stephen Lowe

Doug Lucie
Martin McDonagh
John McGrath
David Mamet
Patrick Marber
Arthur Miller
Mtwa, Ngema & Simon
Tom Murphy
Phyllis Nagy
Peter Nichols
Joseph O'Connor
Joe Orton
Louise Page
Joe Penhall
Luigi Pirandello
Stephen Poliakoff
Franca Rame
Mark Ravenhill
Philip Ridley
Reginald Rose
David Rudkin
Willy Russell
Jean-Paul Sartre
Sam Shepard
Wole Soyinka
C. P. Taylor
Theatre de Complicite
Theatre Workshop
Sue Townsend
Judy Upton
Timberlake Wertenbaker
Victoria Wood